Understanding Business Valuation Workbook

A Practical Guide to Valuing Small to Medium Sized Businesses

GARY TRUGMAN, CPA/ABV, MCBA, ASA, MVS

 AICPA

WILEY

Notice to Readers

Understanding Business Valuation Workbook: A Practical Guide to Valuing Small to Medium Sized Businesses does not represent an official position of the American Institute of Certified Public Accountants, and it is distributed with the understanding that the author and publisher are not rendering legal, accounting, or other professional services in the publication. If legal advice or other expert assistance is required, the services of a competent professional should be sought.

ISBN 978-194549-895-4 (paper)
ISBN 978-1-119-53375-7 (ePDF)
ISBN 978-194549-896-1 (ePUB)

V10014120_091919

Contents

Preface

The *Understanding Business Valuation Workbook* contains educational exercises that are intended to assist the student in enhancing the learning objectives of the chapters from the main textbook. The various exercises contained in this workbook should permit the student to test his or her knowledge based on the materials contained in each chapter.

There are also case studies included in this workbook that can be used to test the information learned and analytical skills of the student by applying theory from the textbook to a particular set of circumstances. And finally, there are exercises that are based on the student's research and analytical skills using many of the resources discussed in the textbook.

The importance of this workbook cannot be overemphasized. This is the best way to test your level of knowledge about the topics covered in *Understanding Business Valuation*. If you do not arrive at the suggested solution, work through the numbers again to see where you went wrong.

As much as I hate to do this, I have also included homework problems in each chapter that either your professor may want to assign to the class or that you may want to tackle on your own as an additional learning experience. You can never learn too much, so have at it!

To get the most out of this workbook, do not cheat by looking up the answers before you have completed the exercises. I know that it is tempting, but the only way that you can know that you learned something from reading all of my hard work is for you to be intellectually honest. Plus, if you have to pass an examination in school or the Accredited in Business Valuation (ABV) examination, do you really think that cheating is going to help you in the long run? I do not think so!

There is one more thing that I hate to do to you, but I have to state that I have provided suggested solutions to the questions and case studies but not to the homework problems. What that means is that there may be other ways to come up with a solution that may be different from those that I have suggested. If you learned nothing else from reading the textbook, you should be clear about the fact that business valuation is a highly subjective process. This means that we can reach different answers for the same question. Of course, mine will be right (only kidding). However, I am using this workbook to enhance your learning experience so I will avoid the more controversial stuff.

Finally, this workbook is divided into the same topical chapters as the main textbook. The last chapter (Chapter 28) in this workbook contains a major case study that will take the student from the start of the engagement through the reconciliation process in determining a conclusion of value. It is intended to allow your instructor to use this as he or she sees fit. There are various appendices that will have to be downloaded at the appropriate time, and your instructor has the suggested solutions.

Have fun with this.

CHAPTER 1

Overview of Business Valuation

The purpose of this chapter was to give you a very brief history of the valuation profession, explain why businesses are valued, provide some background about who values businesses, and familiarize you with professional valuation organizations.

1. In developing a buy-sell agreement provision for the withdrawal of an owner of a closely held business interest, the best basis for the buyout price is:

    a. A price provision designated in the agreement.
    b. A formula designated in the agreement.
    c. A valuation done by a qualified valuation analyst.
    d. A set of terms recommended by an attorney.

2. In which of the following valuation assignments is it not likely that valuations as of multiple dates would be performed?

    a. Divorce.
    b. Gift tax.
    c. Damages litigation.
    d. Employee stock ownership plans.

3. Which of the following statements is incorrect?

    a. Business valuations are performed for companies and interests of all sizes and types.
    b. The level of data available for the valuation of small and mid-size companies tends to be less than the amount of data available for larger companies.
    c. The conceptual valuation principles are different for companies of different sizes.
    d. Having less data creates a larger risk of not being able to interpret the existing data properly.

4. Which of the following is a disadvantage of a CPA who performs business valuations?

    a. Accountants are educated in financial concepts and terminology.
    b. Accountants are used to working with financial statements and concepts that are either GAAP-oriented or tax-oriented.
    c. Accountants are frequently exposed to revenue rulings and tax laws.
    d. Accountants are skilled in working with numbers.

5. Which organization promulgated the *Uniform Standards of Professional Appraisal Practice* (USPAP)?

   a. The American Institute of Certified Public Accountants (AICPA).
   b. The American Society of Appraisers.
   c. The Appraisal Foundation.
   d. The National Association of Certified Valuation Analysts.

6. Which of the following statements is incorrect?

   a. The purpose of the valuation will influence the standard of value, the methodologies used, the level of research performed, and possibly the date of valuation.
   b. Valuing smaller businesses can be extremely challenging because most of the empirical data that is regularly used by a valuation analyst applies to larger companies and only tangentially applies to smaller ones.
   c. The level of data available for the valuation of small and mid-sized companies tends to be greater than the amount of data available for larger companies.
   d. It is imperative that the valuation analyst understand the purpose of the assignment before the process can begin.

7. Which of the following is not a group that generally performs business valuation services?

   a. Attorneys.
   b. Accountants.
   c. College professors.
   d. Investment bankers.

8. To obtain the accreditation of ABV, a candidate must complete all of the following except:

   a. Be a member in good standing of the AICPA.
   b. Hold a valid and unrevoked CPA certificate or license.
   c. Pass a comprehensive business valuation examination.
   d. Pass two comprehensive business valuation case studies.

9. Which of the following is a disadvantage for a business broker that performs business valuations?

   a. They sell businesses.
   b. They are not accountants.
   c. They sometimes use rules of thumb to price businesses.
   d. They sometimes specialize in certain industries.

10. Which professional organization offers the ABV designation?

    a. The AICPA.
    b. The American Society of Appraisers.
    c. The Appraisal Foundation.
    d. The National Association of Certified Valuation Analysts.

11. Which of the following is the least likely reason for a business to be valued?

    a. Marital dissolution.
    b. Financing.
    c. Insurance claim.
    d. Marriage of the owner.

12. Which of the following assignments may require more than one valuation?

    a. Spin-off.
    b. Acquisition.
    c. Merger.
    d. Bankruptcy.

CHAPTER 2

Business Valuation Standards

This chapter was dedicated solely to business valuation standards. Therefore, it was designed to familiarize you with the business valuation and some standards of the AICPA as well as those of other valuation organizations.

1. Which business organization has not officially adopted the definitions in the International Glossary of Business Valuation Terms?
   a. American Institute of Certified Public Accountants (AICPA).
   b. National Association of Certified Valuation Analysts (NACVA).
   c. The Appraisal Standards Board of the Appraisal Foundation (ASB).
   d. The Canadian Institute of Chartered Business Valuators (CICBV).

2. All of the following are exceptions from the Statement on Standards for Valuation Services (SSVS) No. 1 except:
   a. Valuing publicly traded stock, including consideration of a blockage discount.
   b. Internal use assignments from employers to employee members not in public practice.
   c. Engagements that are exclusively for the purpose of determining economic damages.
   d. Mechanical computations when the member does not apply valuation approaches and methods.

3. In determining whether one can reasonably expect to complete the valuation engagement with professional competence, the valuation analyst should consider all of the following except:
   a. Subject interest.
   b. Valuation date.
   c. Capital structure.
   d. Scope of the engagement.

4. Nonfinancial information should be obtained to understand the nonfinancial components of the company, including all of the following except:
   a. Products or services.
   b. Financial structure.
   c. Industry markets.
   d. Management team.

5. For an intangible asset, the valuation analyst should consider which of the following?

   a. Terminal value.
   b. Capitalization rate.
   c. Capital structure.
   d. Remaining useful life.

6. The three common valuation approaches include all of the following except:

   a. Rule of thumb.
   b. Income approach.
   c. Market approach.
   d. Asset approach.

7. In performing a calculation engagement, the valuation analyst should consider all of the following except:

   a. Identity of the client.
   b. All applicable valuation methods.
   c. Valuation date.
   d. Purpose and intended use.

8. Which of the following is an example of a service that does not rise to the level of an engagement to estimate value?

   a. Determining the value of relatively small blocks of publicly traded stock with a per share price that is readily ascertainable.
   b. Valuing a block of publicly traded stock if the analysis includes consideration of a discount for blockage.
   c. Valuing stock that is not publicly traded.
   d. Computing the fair market value of assets in a charitable remainder trust if the engagement requires the application of valuation methods and professional judgment.

9. Which of the following is not one of the four general standards under the AICPA Code of Professional Conduct?

   a. Professional competence.
   b. Due professional care.
   c. Independence.
   d. Planning and supervision.

10. Which of the following is not one of the three frequently used market approach valuation methods for intangible assets?

   a. Guideline public company method.
   b. Comparable uncontrolled transactions method.
   c. Comparable profit margin method.
   d. Relief from royalty method.

11. The detailed report should include all of the following sections except:

   a. Financial statement analysis.
   b. Reconciliation of calculations of value.

c. Valuation adjustments.

d. Sources of information.

12. Which type of report provides an abridged content for a valuation engagement?

a. Detailed report.

b. Summary report.

c. Calculation report.

d. Oral report.

13. Which organization is the author of the SSVS No. 1?

a. Institute of Business Appraisers.

b. American Society of Appraisers.

c. AICPA.

d. National Association of Certified Valuation Analysts.

14. If valuation services are performed for a client for whom the valuation analyst's firm also performs attest services, the valuation analyst should consult with which AICPA Professional Standard to ensure compliance?

a. ET section 1.200.001—Independence Rule.

b. ET section 1.310.001—Standards Rule.

c. ET section 0.400.09—Confidential Client Information.

d. ET section 0.300.060—Due Care.

15. The understanding established between the valuation analyst and the client, whether in writing or oral, should include all of the following except:

a. Client responsibilities.

b. Applicable assumptions and limiting conditions.

c. Type of report to be issued.

d. Types of discounts to be applied.

16. Which of the following is not considered financial information that should be obtained?

a. Income tax returns.

b. Organizational structure.

c. Owner's compensation and perquisites.

d. Prospective financial statements.

17. When applying the capitalization of benefits, the valuation analyst should consider which of the following?

a. Discount rate.

b. Terminal value.

c. Nonrecurring revenue.

d. Relief from royalties.

18. Which of the following is true regarding subsequent events?

    a. The valuation should be updated to reflect subsequent events.
    b. Subsequent events should be disclosed in a report if they affect the value determined.
    c. Subsequent events are generally known or knowable at the date of valuation.
    d. Certain subsequent events may warrant disclosure as long as they are informational only.

19. Which type of report should be issued for a calculation engagement?

    a. Calculation report.
    b. Detailed report.
    c. Summary report.
    d. Any of the above.

20. The exemption for certain controversy proceedings applies to which provision of the SSVS?

    a. Developmental provisions.
    b. Reporting provisions.
    c. Overall engagement provisions.
    d. Documentation provisions.

21. Which of the following statements is true?

    a. Both the attorney and the valuation analyst act as advocates for the client.
    b. Neither the attorney nor the valuation analyst acts as an advocate for the client.
    c. The valuation analyst acts as an advocate for the client, and the attorney acts as an advocate for his or her opinion.
    d. The attorney acts as an advocate for the client and the valuation analyst acts as an advocate for his or her opinion.

22. A detailed report is appropriate for:

    a. Valuation engagements.
    b. Calculation engagements.
    c. Both valuation and calculation engagements.
    d. Neither valuation nor calculation engagements.

23. Which of the following statements relating to oral reports is true?

    a. Oral reports are prohibited by the SSVS.
    b. Oral reports are allowed only for valuation engagements.
    c. Oral reports are allowed only for calculation engagements.
    d. Oral reports are allowed for both valuation and calculation engagements.

24. A member's independence may be impaired in a valuation engagement for which of the following clients?

    a. Tax client.
    b. Attest client.
    c. Personal financial planning client.
    d. Litigation client.

CHAPTER 3

Getting Started

In this chapter, I explained what the valuation analyst needs to know to learn about the engagement, factors to consider in deciding whether to accept the engagement, how to define the engagement, writing engagement letters, and creating the initial document request.

1. Before accepting an assignment, considerations should include all of the following except:
   a. The standard of value.
   b. The purpose and function of the engagement.
   c. The amount of time required to do the job.
   d. The type of report to be issued.

2. In performing a business valuation for a marital dissolution, which of the following is correct?
   a. The valuation analyst can represent only the plaintiff or the defendant, never both.
   b. The valuation analyst can be mutually retained by both parties as long as both parties agree.
   c. The valuation analyst can represent the plaintiff, and the valuation analyst's partner in another office can represent the defendant.
   d. The valuation analyst can represent both the plaintiff and the defendant but can act as an advocate for only one.

3. Which of the following is not a reason why the intended use of a valuation is important?
   a. The intended use can affect the determination of appropriate methods.
   b. The intended use can determine the type of report to be issued.
   c. The intended use can help determine conflicts of interest.
   d. The intended use can affect the manner in which the job is performed.

4. Which of the following statements is correct about a valuation engagement?
   a. It is allowable for a valuation analyst to streamline the process to save the client money.
   b. If expert testimony is anticipated, the judge or jury will remember that the valuation analyst qualified his or her opinion and that is the reason for an incomplete report.

    c. If a client informs the valuation analyst that there will be severe scope limitations, the best solution may be to decline the assignment.

    d. The valuation analyst should accept all assignments, regardless of potential scope limitations.

5. A good engagement letter will include all of the following except:

    a. A detailed background of the company to be valued.

    b. The standard of value that will be used.

    c. The effective date of the valuation.

    d. The responsibilities of the client.

6. Which of the following statements is true?

    a. A valuation engagement should always be completed.

    b. The valuation analyst should never do less than a valuation engagement if the end result will be misleading or prone to error.

    c. Accountant valuation analysts do not need to include language in their engagement letter relating to financial statement opinions.

    d. Nonaccountants are subject to the American Institute of Certified Public Accountants (AICPA) standards and perform either valuation or calculation engagements.

7. An appraisal as defined by the Business Valuation Committee of the American Society of Appraisers has all of the following qualities except:

    a. It is expressed as a single dollar amount or as a range.

    b. It considers all relevant information as of the appraisal date.

    c. The appraiser conducts appropriate procedures to collect and analyze all information expected to be relevant.

    d. The valuation is based only upon the approach(es) selected by the appraiser.

8. A limited appraisal as defined by the Business Valuation Committee of the American Society of Appraisers has all of the following qualities except:

    a. It is expressed as a single dollar amount or as a range.

    b. It considers all relevant information as of the appraisal date.

    c. The appraiser conducts limited procedures to collect and analyze all information expected to be relevant.

    d. The valuation is based upon the approach(es) deemed by the appraiser to be appropriate.

9. If a client is unwilling to pay for a valuation engagement for litigation purposes, a good compromise may be to:

    a. Perform a valuation engagement and charge the fees for a calculation engagement.

    b. Refer the client to another appraiser who charges lower fees.

    c. Perform a valuation engagement with a summary report, and, in the event that the client is unable to settle, upgrade to a detailed report for trial.

    d. Perform a valuation engagement without compromising.

10. Which of the following is not a type of service as defined by the Business Valuation Committee of the American Society of Appraisers?

    a. Summary appraisal.
    b. Appraisal.
    c. Limited appraisal.
    d. Calculation.

11. Which of the following is a step necessary to ensure there is no conflict of interest?

    a. Check with all staff to make sure no conflict exists.
    b. Check with other partners and office locations to make sure no conflict exists.
    c. Complete a conflict of interest verification form.
    d. All of the above are necessary.

12. How often should valuation analysts prepare engagement letters?

    a. Never.
    b. For litigated assignments.
    c. For full valuation assignments.
    d. For every assignment.

13. Which of the following statements regarding effective date(s) is correct?

    a. Valuations are similar to balance sheets in that they are of a specific point in time.
    b. Valuations are similar to income statements in that they are of a specific period of time.
    c. The valuation date is of little importance to the valuation process.
    d. The most common valuation date is the current date.

14. Which of the following statements is incorrect regarding what may be valued?

    a. The entire company may be valued. This is referred to as the equity of the company.
    b. The entire capital structure may be valued. This is referred to as the invested capital of the company.
    c. A portion of the equity may be valued. This is a simple calculation taking the percentage of the total equity.
    d. The value of the company excluding certain assets may be valued.

15. Which of the following is not an acceptance consideration?

    a. Will an asset appraiser be needed?
    b. Are we aware of any potential fee collection problems?
    c. Is the staffing commitment required by the engagement beyond our capabilities?
    d. Is the professional competence necessary to perform the engagement beyond our capabilities?

16. Which of the following does not need to be included in the engagement letter?

    a. Detailed description of the documents requested.
    b. The standard of value that will be used.
    c. The responsibilities of the client.
    d. Payment terms.

17. In the first paragraph of the engagement letter, which name should appear as being engaged to determine the company value?

    a. The valuation analyst expected to sign the report.
    b. All valuation analysts expected to participate in preparation of the report.
    c. The firm name.
    d. The individual supervising the project.

18. In the detailed description of the valuation subject in the engagement letter, all of the following should be included except:

    a. The type of equity to be valued.
    b. The size of the interest to be valued.
    c. A brief history of the company to be valued.
    d. Which assets and liabilities are to be included in the value.

19. Which of the following statements regarding standardized checklists is true?

    a. The valuation analyst frequently knows a lot about the subject company, making modifying the standardized checklist easy.
    b. Sending out a standardized checklist may demonstrate a lack of interest by the valuation analyst if irrelevant items are included.
    c. This type of document should be used for every valuation, regardless of size.
    d. Setting up multiple checklists proves to be a time waster.

20. Which of the following items is typically included in a document checklist for a medical practice but is excluded from a general checklist?

    a. Accounts receivable aging as of the date of valuation.
    b. Copies of stockholder agreements.
    c. Reports of other professionals, including appraisals on specific assets.
    d. List of all specialties or subspecialties.

21. Which of the following criteria does not have to be addressed in a highest and best use analysis?

    a. Physically possible.
    b. Legally permissible.
    c. Financially feasible.
    d. Economically possible.

CHAPTER 4

Valuation Principles and Theory

In this chapter, I explained the principles of valuation, various standards of value, how the purpose of the valuation influences the standard of value, the concept of subsequent events (items that are known or knowable), and the influence of the Internal Revenue Service (IRS) on business valuations. The chapter also exposed you to many of the key revenue rulings.

1. In determining the investment value of a closely held company that your publicly traded client is considering acquiring, which of the following issues would generally be considered least important?

    a. Restating the target enterprise's cash-basis historical and projected financial statements to the accrual basis.
    b. Adjusting owner's compensation.
    c. Recognizing expected cost savings from combined operations.
    d. Understanding the target organization's cost of capital.

2. In a possible merger of two similar companies, the board of directors of one of the companies has asked the analyst to determine the likely combined profitability and value of the new company, including synergies. Which of the following standards of value is appropriate for this case?

    a. Intrinsic value.
    b. Investment value.
    c. Fair value.
    d. Economic value.

3. Which of the following is not one of the three main valuation principles that constitute the foundation of valuation theory?

    a. The principle of supply and demand.
    b. The principle of alternatives.
    c. The principle of substitution.
    d. The principle of future benefits.

4. Which valuation principle states, in essence, that nobody will pay more for something than he or she would pay for an equally desirable substitute?

    a. The principle of supply and demand.
    b. The principle of alternatives.
    c. The principle of substitution.
    d. The principle of future benefits.

5. Which of the following is not an application of the principle of substitution?

   a. The market approach estimates the value of the business being appraised from information derived from the market.

   b. The asset-based approach simulates the starting of an equivalent business from scratch.

   c. The income approach considers normalization adjustments to eliminate control adjustments.

   d. The income approach looks to financial equivalents to estimate value.

6. Which of the following is not a frequently used standard of value for business valuations?

   a. Fair market value.

   b. Book value.

   c. Fair value.

   d. Investment value.

7. "The amount at which property would change hands between a willing buyer and a willing seller, when the former is not under any compulsion to buy, and the latter is not under any compulsion to sell, both parties having reasonable knowledge of relevant facts" is a common definition of:

   a. Fair market value.

   b. Fair value.

   c. Investment value.

   d. Intrinsic value.

8. Which of the following is not one of the components included in the definition of fair market value?

   a. Cash or cash equivalent value.

   b. Value to a particular buyer.

   c. Exposure for sale on the open market

   d. Neither party under compulsion to act.

9. Which of the following statements regarding price and value is correct?

   a. Price and value are interchangeable and mean the same thing.

   b. Conditions in the real world often influence value without affecting price.

   c. Price and value are always equal in the valuation.

   d. Price is what you pay, and value is what you get.

10. Which of the following statements is correct?

   a. Fair value considers a willing buyer and a willing seller.

   b. Fair market value considers that the buyer is not always compelled but the seller is always under compulsion.

   c. Fair value assumes the buyer and seller have equal knowledge.

   d. Fair value considers the concept of fairness to the seller.

11. Which standard of value considers value to a particular buyer?

   a. Fair market value.

   b. Fair value.

c. Investment value.

d. Intrinsic value.

12. All of the following valuation purposes are prepared using fair market value except:

    a. Estate and gift taxes.
    b. Employee stock ownership plans.
    c. Financial reporting.
    d. Ad valorem taxes.

13. In most states, which standard of value is used to value stockholder disputes?

    a. Fair market value.
    b. Fair value.
    c. Investment value.
    d. Intrinsic value.

14. Which of the following valuation purposes uses investment value as the applicable standard of value?

    a. Financial acquisitions.
    b. Strategic acquisitions.
    c. Financial reporting.
    d. Estate and gift taxes.

15. Which of the following comments concerning Revenue Ruling 59-60 is incorrect?

    a. According to the author, it is probably the greatest treatise ever issued on valuation.
    b. The ruling covers what is known as the formula approach or excess earnings method.
    c. The ruling discusses the eight factors to consider, at a minimum, in valuing closely held businesses.
    d. The ruling outlines that valuation is a prophecy about the future.

16. Which Revenue Ruling discusses what is known as the formula approach or excess earnings method of valuation?

    a. Revenue Ruling 59-60.
    b. Revenue Ruling 68-609.
    c. Revenue Ruling 77-287.
    d. Revenue Ruling 93-12.

17. Which standard of value applies to all federal tax valuations?

    a. Fair market value.
    b. Fair value.
    c. Investment value.
    d. Intrinsic value.

18. Which standard of value is frequently used by financial analysts based on all of the facts and circumstances of the business or the investment, often ignoring the fluctuations of the stock market?

    a. Fair market value.
    b. Fair value.
    c. Investment value.
    d. Intrinsic value.

19. The concept that there are three economic reasons that investors will invest in certain stock—dividends, capital appreciation, or a combination of the two—is based on which principle?

    a. The principle of supply and demand.
    b. The principle of alternatives.
    c. The principle of substitution.
    d. The principle of future benefits.

20. Which of the following relates to the concept of highest and best use?

    a. Definitions of value.
    b. Premise of value.
    c. Standards of value.
    d. Principle of substitution.

21. Which of the following is an example of a premise of value?

    a. Intrinsic value.
    b. Fair market value.
    c. Going concern value.
    d. Minority interest value.

22. Assuming a discount rate of 10%, which of the following has the highest cash value?

    a. $85,000 cash purchase.
    b. $125,000 purchase financed over 5 years.
    c. $150,000 purchase financed over 7 years.
    d. $200,000 purchase financed over 10 years.

23. "The price that would be received to sell an asset or paid to transfer a liability in an orderly transaction between market participants at the measurement date" is the definition of which of the following?

    a. Fair market value.
    b. Fair value.
    c. Investment value.
    d. Intrinsic value.

24. Which of the following statements is true in regard to fair value?

    a. Willing buyer and willing seller.
    b. Hypothetical buyer and seller.
    c. Applicable to minority blocks.
    d. Assumes reasonable knowledge by both parties.

25. In most states, stockholder disputes have the same standard of value as which of the following?

    a. Financial reporting.
    b. Estate and gift tax.
    c. Strategic acquisitions.
    d. Employee stock ownership plans.

26. Which standard of value is applicable to strategic acquisitions?

    a. Fair market value.
    b. Fair value.
    c. Investment value.
    d. Intrinsic value.

27. Which Revenue Ruling modified 59-60 by making it applicable to income and other taxes, as well as to estate and gift taxes?

    a. Revenue Ruling 65-192.
    b. Revenue Ruling 68-609.
    c. Revenue Ruling 77-287.
    d. Revenue Ruling 93-12.

28. Which Revenue Ruling was intended "to provide information and guidance to taxpayers, IRS personnel, and others concerned with the valuation, for Federal tax purposes, of securities that cannot be immediately resold because they are restricted from resale pursuant to Federal security laws"?

    a. Revenue Ruling 59-60.
    b. Revenue Ruling 68-609.
    c. Revenue Ruling 77-287.
    d. Revenue Ruling 93-12.

29. Which Revenue Ruling allows appropriate minority discounts to be applied when minority interests of family members in a closely held corporation are valued?

    a. Revenue Ruling 59-60.
    b. Revenue Ruling 68-609.
    c. Revenue Ruling 77-287.
    d. Revenue Ruling 93-12.

30. Which of the following is not one of the eight factors outlined in Revenue Ruling 59-60 for determining fair market value?

    a. The book value of the stock and the financial condition of the business.
    b. Sales of the stock and the size of the block of stock to be valued.
    c. The earnings capacity of the company.
    d. The dividends paid by the company.

CHAPTER 5

Data Gathering

In this chapter, I explained which items have an impact on value, internal and external information sources used for gathering data, and types of data sources.

1. In valuing a commercial printer with sales of $4 million, which source of industry performance data would be most useful?
   a. Compustat.
   b. *Value Line Investment Survey.*
   c. Risk Management Association (RMA) *Annual Statement Studies.*
   d. Bizcomps.

2. Which of the following is not a source of industry data?
   a. Wall Street brokerage reports.
   b. *Federal Reserve Statistical Release.*
   c. *Value Line Investment Survey.*
   d. *Almanac of Business and Industrial Financial Ratios.*

3. A publication best known for current national economic data is:
   a. Standard & Poor's *Industry Surveys.*
   b. *Federal Reserve Bulletin.*
   c. *Stocks, Bonds, Bills, and Inflation Yearbook.*
   d. *U.S. Industry & Trade Outlook.*

4. All of the following is nonfinancial information that the valuation analyst should gather except?
   a. Markets and marketing information.
   b. Form of organization and ownership of the business.
   c. Forecasts or projections.
   d. Equipment information.

5. Which of the following is not financial information that the valuation analyst should gather?
   a. Financial statements.
   b. Forecasts or projections.
   c. Legal documents.
   d. Information supporting balance sheet adjustments.

6. Which of the following is not a key economic indicator?

   a. Gross domestic product.
   b. Industry growth.
   c. Consumer confidence.
   d. Unemployment.

7. Which of the following is not a source of economic data?

   a. *U.S. Industry & Trade Outlook.*
   b. *Wall Street Journal.*
   c. *Federal Reserve Bulletin.*
   d. *Economic Report of the President.*

8. Which of the following is generally the best source of industry data for small industries?

   a. U.S. Department of Commerce.
   b. Trade associations.
   c. Wall Street brokerage firms.
   d. Local chambers of commerce.

9. Which of the following statements is false?

   a. The form of organization is important due to the comparability of information received.
   b. The form of organization is important to determine the legal rights applicable to the interest being valued.
   c. The ownership of the organization is important to assess considerations such as control, minority, or swing vote issues.
   d. The ownership of the organization is important to determine what economic information must be obtained.

10. Which of the following is considered internal information?

    a. Personnel data.
    b. Industry data.
    c. Publicly traded guideline company data.
    d. Economic data.

11. Management forecasts include significant growth. Which of the following physical facilities factors is most important to consider in regard to these forecasts?

    a. The plant's size.
    b. Whether the plant is owned or rented.
    c. The current capacity of the plant.
    d. The location of the plant.

12. Which of the following is published by the Board of Governors of the Federal Reserve System?

    a. *Stocks, Bonds, Bill, and Inflation Yearbook.*
    b. *Federal Reserve Bulletin.*
    c. *Statistical Abstract of the United States.*
    d. *Economic Report of the President.*

13. Which of the following sources is an annual yearbook that contains historical data about returns in the capital markets since 1926 through the current year?

   a. *Valuation Handbook: U.S. Guide to Cost of Capital*.
   b. *Valuation Handbook: U.S. Industry Cost of Capital*.
   c. *Statistical Abstract of the United States*.
   d. *Standard & Poor's Industry Surveys*.

14. Which of the following is a source of international information?

   a. Bureau of Labor Statistics.
   b. Bureau of Economic Analysis.
   c. CIA.
   d. Federal Reserve Board.

15. Which of the following is not a source of national economic information?

   a. Bureau of Labor Statistics.
   b. Bureau of Economic Analysis.
   c. *Standard & Poor's Industry Surveys*.
   d. Federal Reserve Board.

16. Which of the following is a source used to determine beta?

   a. Standard & Poor's Compustat.
   b. EDGAR Online.
   c. Zack's *Earnings Forecaster*.
   d. Mergerstat.

17. All of the following are financial benchmarking data sources except?

   a. Microbilt's Integra *Business Profiler*.
   b. *Mergerstat Review*.
   c. RMA *Annual Statement Studies*.
   d. *Almanac of Business and Industrial Financial Ratios*.

18. Which of the following statements is true?

   a. Value can be determined by obtaining only the financial statements and tax returns.
   b. The financial information is considered more important than nonfinancial information.
   c. Nonfinancial information is not required to perform a business valuation.
   d. Nonfinancial information is considered to be as important as the financial information.

19. Nonfinancial information is obtained through which of the following?

   a. Document requests.
   b. Management interviews.
   c. Independent research.
   d. All of the above.

20. Which of the following sources provides state and local information?
    a. Bureau of Labor Statistics.
    b. U.S. Census Bureau.
    c. Bureau of Economic Analysis.
    d. Federal Reserve Board.

21. ABC, Inc. operates in the automobile industry. The industry has a business cycle of four years. How many years of financial statements should be obtained for this valuation?
    a. Four.
    b. Five.
    c. Six.
    d. Ten.

22. Which of the following will indicate lower risk?
    a. The company has a single supplier.
    b. The company's industry is highly competitive.
    c. The company has hundreds of small customers.
    d. The company is dependent on one product.

23. If an outcome of a lawsuit cannot be quantified, the lawsuit should:
    a. Be ignored.
    b. Be considered as an additional risk factor.
    c. Be discussed in the report but requires no adjustments.
    d. Be considered a factor in the discount for lack of control.

24. *The World Factbook* is produced by:
    a. Bureau of Economic Analysis.
    b. Central Intelligence Agency.
    c. Federal Reserve Board.
    d. International Trade Administration.

25. All of the following are sources for industry outlooks except:
    a. RMA *Annual Statement Studies*.
    b. Standard & Poor's *Industry Surveys*.
    c. *U.S. Industry & Trade Outlook*.
    d. Brokerage house industry studies.

26. Which of the following is not a source for finding public guideline company information?
    a. *Value Line Investment Survey*.
    b. *SEC Directory*.
    c. Pratt's Stats.
    d. Mergent.

27. Sources of forecast financial data include all of the following except:
    a. *Value Line Investment Survey.*
    b. *S&P Earnings Guide.*
    c. Zack's *Earnings Forecaster.*
    d. Brokerage houses.

28. Merger and acquisition data can be obtained from all of the following sources except:
    a. SunGard's Market Map.
    b. Bizcomps.
    c. *Mergerstat Review.*
    d. Done Deals.

29. All of the following individuals should be considered for the on-site interview except:
    a. The company's attorney.
    b. The company's accountant.
    c. The company's management.
    d. The company's entry-level employees.

CHAPTER 6

Data Analysis

In this chapter, I explained what to do with all the data that should have been collected in the previous chapter. This discussion included how to use the data, as well as what it means. Therefore, you should understand how to perform economic, industry, subject-company, and financial analysis. You should also understand when and how to make financial statement adjustments.

1. Which of the following is not a frequently asked industry question?

    a. What percentage of the market share does the company have?
    b. Is it a cyclical industry?
    c. What are the barriers to entry?
    d. What is the forecast for growth within the industry?

2. Which of the following is/are factors to consider in the subject-company analysis?

    a. Products and services offered.
    b. Customer base.
    c. Ownership structure.
    d. All of the above.

3. Which of the following is not an analytical tool used by valuation analysts for financial analysis?

    a. Comparative company analysis.
    b. Trend analysis.
    c. Income tax analysis.
    d. Financial ratio analysis.

4. Which analysis tool eliminates the size differentials between the subject company and its peer group for easier analysis?

    a. Trend analysis.
    b. Operational analysis.
    c. Gross profit analysis.
    d. Common size analysis.

The following information is to be used for questions 5–8. Included in the table are the income statement and balance sheet for ABC, Inc.

Revenue	1,400,000		Cash	250,000
Cost of Goods Sold	500,000		Accounts Receivable	400,000
Gross Profit	900,000		Inventory	200,000
Operating Expenses	700,000		Fixed Assets	900,000
Interest Expense	75,000		Total Assets	1,750,000
Net Income	125,000			
			Accounts Payable	200,000
			Long-Term Debt	750,000
			Equity	800,000
			Total Liabilities and Equity	1,750,000

5. What is ABC, Inc.'s current ratio?

   a. 0.89×.
   b. 3.25×.
   c. 4.25×.
   d. 8.75×.

6. What is ABC, Inc.'s debt-to-equity ratio?

   a. 0.25×.
   b. 0.94×.
   c. 1.19×.
   d. 2.19×.

7. What is ABC, Inc.'s average collection period if 100% of revenue is on credit?

   a. 52 days.
   b. 104 days.
   c. 208 days.
   d. 3,836 days.

8. What is ABC, Inc.'s average inventory holding period?

   a. 54 days.
   b. 86 days.
   c. 104 days.
   d. 146 days.

9. Which analysis measures profitability, turnover, and leverage all in one ratio?

   a. Common size analysis.
   b. DuPont analysis.
   c. Trend analysis.
   d. Bardahl analysis.

10. Which of the following is not a source of comparative industry data?

   a. Trade association surveys.
   b. U.S. Census Bureau.
   c. Integra information.
   d. Risk Management Association (RMA).

11. Which analysis is used to determine how much working capital is required in the subject company's operations?

 a. Common size analysis.
 b. DuPont analysis.
 c. Trend analysis.
 d. Bardahl analysis.

12. Which of the following is not considered a discretionary adjustment?

 a. Owner's perquisites.
 b. Switch from LIFO inventory to FIFO to match industry.
 c. Rent expenses.
 d. Entertainment expenses.

Use the following information for questions 13–18.

ABC, Inc.

	Year 1	Year 2	Year 3	Year 4	Industry Common Size
Revenue	1,325,154	1,478,531	1,375,564	1,754,253	100%
Cost of Sales	525,143	575,135	604,658	702,451	45%
Gross Profit	800,011	903,396	770,906	1,051,802	55%
Operating Expenses	725,124	725,468	795,453	845,245	45%
Operating Income	74,887	177,928	(24,547)	206,557	10%
Interest Expense	24,057	26,451	28,254	32,546	3%
Income Before Taxes	50,830	151,477	(52,801)	174,011	7%
Income Taxes	20,332	60,591	—	69,604	3%
Net Income	30,498	90,886	(52,801)	104,407	4%

	Year 1	Year 2	Year 3	Year 4
Cash	225,124	276,013	237,219	255,300
Accounts Receivable	111,245	125,465	132,546	145,246
Inventories	52,546	54,685	58,455	78,546
Other Current Assets	7,654	7,265	7,685	7,545
Fixed Assets	952,465	965,454	975,564	1,125,654
Total Assets	1,349,034	1,428,882	1,411,469	1,612,291
Accounts Payable	65,325	67,565	71,250	73,545
Long-Term Debt—Current	105,012	108,654	112,546	105,465
Long-Term Debt	742,565	725,645	753,456	854,657
Equity	436,132	527,018	474,217	578,624
Total Liabilities and Equity	1,349,034	1,428,882	1,411,469	1,612,291

13. The compound annual growth rate for ABC, Inc. from year 1 through year 4 is:

   a. 7.3%

   b. 8.1%

   c. 9.8%

   d. 10.8

14. On a common size basis, which year showed the highest gross profit?

   a. Year 1.

   b. Year 2.

   c. Year 3.

   d. Year 4.

15. On a common size basis, how many years had operating income higher than the industry average?

   a. One.

   b. Two.

   c. Three.

   d. Four.

16. What is the quick ratio at the end of year 3?

   a. 2.0.

   b. 2.3.

   c. 5.2.

   d. 6.0.

17. What is the EBIT-to-total-assets ratio for year 2, assuming that an average total assets for the year is used?

   a. 0.060×.

   b. 0.065×.

   c. 0.109×.

   d. 0.128×.

18. What year was the current ratio the highest?

   a. Year 1.

   b. Year 2.

   c. Year 3.

   d. Year 4.

19. The purpose of a trend analysis is to:

   a. Compare the subject company's operating performance with that of its peer group.

   b. Compare the subject company's performance over the past several years.

   c. Determine information regarding the quality and stability of the earnings or cash flows from the business.

   d. Determine information about the gross profit the company has been able to achieve.

20. Through normalization adjustments, the valuation analyst is trying to create what type of financial statements?

   a. GAAP-basis financial statements.

   b. Economic-basis financial statements.

    c. Tax-basis financial statements.

    d. Cash-basis financial statements.

21. Adjusting the inventory accounting method from LIFO to FIFO is an example of what type of adjustment?

    a. Control.

    b. Nonoperating.

    c. Discretionary.

    d. Comparability.

22. The DuPont analysis measures all of the following except:

    a. Profitability.

    b. Performance.

    c. Turnover.

    d. Leverage.

23. What is the formula for times interest earned?

    a. Net income/interest expense.

    b. EBIT/interest expense.

    c. EBITDA/interest expense.

    d. Interest expense/net income.

24. Which one of the following Z-scores indicates a significant risk of bankruptcy?

    a. 1.2.

    b. 1.7.

    c. 2.5.

    d. 3.4.

25. Which of the following statements is true?

    a. Value can be determined by obtaining only the financial statements and tax returns.

    b. The financial information is considered more important than nonfinancial information.

    c. Nonfinancial information is not required to perform a business valuation.

    d. Nonfinancial information is as important as, and in some instances more important than, financial information.

26. Nonfinancial information is obtained through which of the following?

    a. Document requests.

    b. Management interviews.

    c. Independent research.

    d. All of the above.

27. If all of the following economic data are relevant, which economic data should be considered first?

    a. Local economy.

    b. State economy.

    c. National economy.

    d. International economy.

28. Which of the following statements regarding equipment is true?
    a. Older equipment usually means lower maintenance costs and a higher level of productivity.
    b. Older equipment usually means lower maintenance costs and a lower level of productivity.
    c. Older equipment usually means higher maintenance costs and a higher level of productivity.
    d. Older equipment usually means higher maintenance costs and a lower level of productivity.

29. Which of the following is a reason why internal financial statements should be heavily scrutinized?
    a. They include adjustments that an outside accountant makes.
    b. They are closer to the date of valuation than any other information.
    c. The reporting may not be consistent with year-end financials.
    d. Supporting information is generally not available.

30. Why is understanding information about the products and services that the appraisal subject sells to its customers important?
    a. To assist in selecting guideline public companies.
    b. To understand the factors that affect these products and services.
    c. To understand what the alternative products are.
    d. All of the above.

31. Which of the following items is a concern to the valuation analyst?
    a. High employee turnover.
    b. Dependence on few suppliers.
    c. Dependence on few customers.
    d. All of the above.

32. Which of the following factors about equipment does a valuation analyst not need to consider?
    a. Type used.
    b. Age.
    c. Technical specifications.
    d. Availability of parts.

Use the following to answer questions 33–36.

A valuation analyst is valuing a business with $5 million in revenues. This business primarily fabricates prehung doors that are sold to large tract-home builders in a high-population-growth region of the country. The industry research is presented here. To identify the industry risks that apply to the subject company, the valuation analyst uses the methodology developed by Michael Porter.

INDUSTRY RESEARCH MEMO
The building materials supply business in the United States is highly fragmented, despite increased consolidation in metropolitan areas, including 50,000

companies with combined annual sales of $250 billion. The industry includes giants like Home Depot ($58 billion in sales) and Lowe's ($26 billion), about 250 companies with annual sales over $100 million, and 3,500 companies with annual sales over $10 million. Some independently owned stores belong to wholesale cooperatives like Ace Hardware and TruServ Corp. These operations buy materials in bulk, resell them to members, and allow members to use their trademarks.

Building materials are sold primarily through two distribution channels: (1) wholesale supply outlets and (2) retail outlets like home stores, hardware stores, and lumberyards. The two major types of customers are the do-it-yourself (DIY) and the small or mid-sized commercial contractor. The consumer home improvement market has been the main focus of the large companies like Home Depot that can offer low prices because of large economies of scale in buying. Smaller companies, often family-owned lumberyards that have expanded into a broader range of products, can compete effectively (1) by catering to contractors (for whom price is less important than other services) and (2) by providing convenient service locations.

Products can include everything involved in the making of a house: lumber, hardware, windows, doors, cabinets, paint, plumbing and electrical products, tools, floor coverings, wallpaper, and lawn and garden products. In addition to products, many companies sell installation services using their own or outside contractors.

The largest-volume items sold by most companies are lumber and plywood panels, which are commodity products with relatively low margins. While many companies concentrate on selling only lumber, most also carry a broad assortment of higher-margin goods. Big chains buy many products directly from large suppliers like Georgia-Pacific and Louisiana-Pacific, while smaller companies buy from a large number of regional distributors. Some home builders, like Centex and Pulte, are large enough to have their own supply operations and also sell to other builders.

Consumer-oriented merchants use typical retail marketing activities such as television, radio, and print advertising; direct mail campaigns; and special sales events. Contractor-oriented companies establish and maintain long-term relationships with local builders and contractors.

The typical gross margin for lumber companies selling commodity products primarily to contractors is 20%. Home Depot and Lowe's, which sell mainly to consumers, have gross margins close to 30%.

According to Mr. Jones, president of the Window & Door Manufacturers Association (WDMA), the window and door industry has been affected by the economy less than other industries: "There's still a healthy demand for windows and doors." Residential construction remains the main driver for the industry with remodeling accounting for a large share of the volume.

While the U.S. housing market was stronger than expected in 20X2 with an overall growth of 4.3% to 1.873 million units, 20X3 growth is anticipated to be down about 0.5% to 1.863 million starts. Single-family home starts are expected to remain the same, but multifamily and manufactured housing starts are anticipated to decrease 2% from 20X2. Housing starts are projected to reach 1.965 million units in 20X6, an annual growth of 1.8%.

In 20X3, WDMA projects 86.3 million residential doors and 12.1 nonresidential doors of all types will be sold. The number of residential doors sold is expected to steadily increase from 86.3 million to reach 90.6 million in 20X6, representing an annual growth rate of 1.6%.

33. Which of the following statements best assesses the "bargaining power of suppliers" industry factor as it relates to the subject company?

    a. The supplier group's products are differentiated.
    b. The supplier group is dominated by few companies.
    c. There are credible substitute products for sale to the industry.
    d. The supplier group poses a credible threat to forward integration.

34. Which of the following statements best assesses the "availability of substitute products" industry factor as it relates to the subject company?

    a. There is a high switching cost.
    b. There are few substitute products.
    c. The price trade-off of substitutes is significant.
    d. The performance trade-off of substitutes is significant.

35. Which of the following is not a strategy for a company seeking to obtain above-average earnings using the Porter analytical framework for competitive advantage?

    a. Focus.
    b. Differentiation.
    c. Cost leadership.
    d. Superior marketing.

36. Which of the following issues best assesses the "rivalry among existing competitors" industry factor as it relates to the subject company?

    a. High fixed costs.
    b. High barriers to exit.
    c. Slow industry growth.
    d. Numerous industry participants.

37. Which of the following statements regarding information obtained from RMA *Annual Statement Studies* is true?

    a. Information does not take size into account.
    b. Identified industries are too few to be meaningful.
    c. Debt-to-equity ratios are based on market values.
    d. Turnover ratios are derived from year-end financial statements.

38. Which of the following statements regarding industry analysis and external risk assessment is not true?

    a. Intense competition is associated with lower industry risk.
    b. High switching costs are associated with lower industry risk.
    c. Slow industry growth is associated with higher industry risk.
    d. High barriers to entry are associated with lower industry risk.

39. Which of the following statements regarding the compound annual growth rate (CAGR) is not true?

    a. CAGR utilizes only the first and last year of the range.
    b. CAGR is frequently used in the determination of a capitalization rate.
    c. CAGR is frequently used in the selection of the guideline companies.
    d. CAGR identifies the trend that occurred from year to year during the range.

40. Which comparative analysis is **least** helpful in assessing a company's similarity to publicly traded guideline companies?

    a. Compound growth rates.
    b. Common-size income statements.
    c. DuPont formula calculations.
    d. Accounting methods.

41. Which type of ratio measures management's use of company assets?

    a. Liquidity.
    b. Activity.
    c. Leverage.
    d. Coverage.

42. Which of the following statements is most accurate regarding adjustments to be made to financial data when using guideline public companies?

    a. Guideline company financial statements should be adjusted only for nonrecurring items.
    b. The subject-company financial statements should be adjusted to conform to each guideline company presentation.
    c. Guideline and subject-company financial statements should be adjusted for inconsistencies in accounting methods.
    d. The subject-company financial statements should be adjusted only for discretionary items.

43. Ratio analysis is helpful in each of these valuation considerations except:

    a. Selection and comparability of guideline companies.
    b. Assessment of company-specific risk.
    c. Determination of systematic risk.
    d. Identification of excess nonoperating assets.

44. Which of the following statements best describes the difference between a fragmented industry and a concentrated industry?

    a. A fragmented industry is one that is geographically dispersed, whereas a concentrated one is confined to a much smaller area.
    b. Industries that have few competitors are said to be fragmented, while industries that have many competitors are said to be concentrated.
    c. A fragmented industry is less apt to compete on the basis of price, whereas a concentrated one is more likely to use price as the primary basis of competition.
    d. Industries with many competitors are said to be fragmented, while industries where revenues are split between just a few competitors are said to be concentrated.

45. Barriers to entering an industry include all of the following except:

    a. Access to distribution channels.
    b. Economies of scale.
    c. Capital requirements.
    d. Rate of return requirements.

46. Which of the following statements is correct regarding an industry with low aggregate profitability?

  a. Low industry profitability typically implies low barriers to entry.
  b. Even with low industry profitability, some companies can generate superior returns.
  c. Individual companies will **not** be able to compete on a differentiation basis.
  d. Individual companies will have to compete on the basis of price.

47. Which of the following statements best describes industry structure?

  a. Industry structure is the most important consideration in a valuation.
  b. Debt to equity is relatively homogeneous.
  c. Industry structure is generally an irrelevant consideration in valuation.
  d. Industry structure is in a constant state of change.

48. In performing a guideline publicly traded company analysis, the valuation analyst determines that it is appropriate to capitalize a lease in which the subject company is the lessee. This would have the effect of

  a. Increasing return on total assets.
  b. Increasing the working capital ratio.
  c. Decreasing times interest earned.
  d. Decreasing the debt-to-equity ratio.

49. Under which of the following industry conditions would vertical integration be most appropriate?

  a. Critical supply sources.
  b. Low barriers to entry.
  c. High debt levels.
  d. Diversified customers.

50. Which of the following statements about ratios is correct?

  a. The higher the ratio calculated by dividing sales by trade receivables, the longer the time between a sale and the cash collection.
  b. The higher the ratio calculated by dividing the gross cash flow (net profit plus depreciation) by the current portion of long-term debt, the less likely it is that a company can service its long-term debt.
  c. The higher the ratio calculated by dividing earnings before interest and taxes (EBIT) by annual interest expense, the higher a company's capacity to take on additional debt.
  d. The higher the number calculated by dividing 365 by the ratio of sales to receivables, the lower the probability of delinquencies in accounts receivable.

51. Which of the following is the strongest indicator that a manufacturing business is highly vulnerable to business downturns?

  a. A low ratio of fixed assets to tangible net worth.
  b. A high ratio of sales to trade receivables.
  c. A low ratio of cost of goods sold to inventory.
  d. A high current ratio.

52. Which of the following statements is correct when comparing a subject company's inventory turnover ratio with industry composite information?

    a. If the company's ratio is higher than the industry norm, the company's inventory is older than that of its peers.
    b. If the company's ratio is higher than the industry norm, the company may be losing sales due to insufficient on-hand inventory.
    c. If the company's ratio is higher than the industry norm, the company's inventory may be obsolete.
    d. If the company's ratio is lower than the industry norm, the inventory-related component of cash flow will be better for the company than the same component is for the industry.

53. Which of the following uses of RMA *Annual Statement Studies* ratios would be the **least** appropriate in valuing a controlling interest?

    a. The debt/worth ratio to determine the typical capital structure of the industry.
    b. The current ratio to evaluate whether the subject company has excess working capital.
    c. The sales/working capital ratio to determine the subject company's incremental working capital needs.
    d. The sales/fixed asset ratio to determine normalized future capital expenditures.

54. Which of the following ratios measure(s) business risk?

    I. Percentage change in operating earnings/percentage change in sales.
    II. Percentage change in income to common equity/percentage change in EBIT.

    a. I only.
    b. II only.
    c. Both I and II.
    d. Neither I nor II.

55. A valuation analyst decides to value a company's manufacturing facility separately from its operations. Which of the following adjustments to the income statement is generally **not** appropriate?

    a. Add back depreciation on the facility.
    b. Subtract a market rent for the facility.
    c. Add back interest expense related to the facility's mortgage.
    d. Subtract taxes related to the appreciation in the facility's market value.

56. When considering ratio analysis, an ABV is typically **least** concerned with which of these findings?

    a. The trend of one ratio over the past five years.
    b. The calculation of a ratio before any adjustments are made to the balance sheet or income statement.
    c. Potentially different accounting policies between the subject company and the guideline companies.
    d. Potentially different accounting policies between the subject company and standard industry practice.

57. Which of the following adjustments is generally **not** made when valuing a minority interest?

    a. Gain or loss on sale of operating asset.
    b. Imputed interest on interest-free officer loan.
    c. Adequacy of management's allowances and reserves for inventory.
    d. Earnings from discontinued operations.

58. Which of the following resources would provide the most assistance when normalizing officers' compensation?

    a. IBA database.
    b. Proxy statements.
    c. Federal Reserve Bulletin.
    d. *Standard & Poor's Industry Surveys.*

59. Underutilized capacity is a consideration in determining the fair market value of the company in all of the following circumstances except:

    a. Most willing buyers would make an adjustment for this factor.
    b. The underutilized capacity can be used by potential buyers.
    c. The business is worth more to a specific buyer than it is in the hands of the current owner.
    d. The valuation is made under a different set of assumptions than how the business actually operates.

60. Which of the following analytical tools is **least** useful in determining the level of excess assets?

    a. Liquidity ratios.
    b. Common-sized financial statements.
    c. Trend analysis of guideline companies.
    d. Price/earnings multiples of publicly traded companies.

61. What does the DuPont formula measure?

    a. Liquidity and activity.
    b. Leverage and solvency.
    c. Profitability, liquidity, and market value.
    d. Profitability, activity, and leverage.

62. The company you are valuing has a higher level of pretax income to fixed assets than the industry median. Which of the following best explains this difference?

    a. The company uses the straight-line method of depreciation.
    b. The company has inefficient asset utilization.
    c. The company invests heavily in fixed assets on an ongoing basis.
    d. The company's plant and equipment are twice the industry average age.

63. Which of the following forecasts would be most valuable for purposes of financial analysis involving a company experiencing consistently higher growth in profitability than its industry?

    a. A one-year forecast of operating cash flow.
    b. A five-year earnings forecast.
    c. A forecast covering the period of abnormal growth.
    d. A five-year forecast of debt-free cash flow.

64. Which of the following statements is correct regarding a switch from the FIFO method to the LIFO method of inventory accounting for financial reporting purposes?

    a. A switch results in a lower current ratio during periods of rising prices.
    b. A switch results in a more accurate inventory valuation during periods of rising prices.
    c. A switch is required to be applied to all inventory classifications.
    d. A switch removes the opportunity to affect net income by varying purchasing policy.

65. Why is cash flow from operations an incomplete measure of performance?

    a. It does not include depreciation and amortization.
    b. It does not account for replacement of physical assets.
    c. It can be manipulated by issuing new stock.
    d. It does not take into account changes in working capital.

66. Which of the following statements regarding nonoperating assets is true?

    a. Buildings, copyrights, and patents are considered nonoperating assets.
    b. A nonperforming loan to an active owner/employee is an operating asset.
    c. Normalizing adjustments to the income statement related to the nonoperating assets are unnecessary.
    d. Normalizing adjustments related to nonoperating assets are often inappropriate when valuing minority interests.

67. In the valuation of a trucking company that delivers parts to automotive manufacturers, the following information was obtained from research of current trends in the U.S. economy. Which information would have the most significant effect on the valuation conclusions?

    a. Growth in the gross domestic product (GDP) is expected to be 2%.
    b. The trade deficit is expected to increase.
    c. Manufacturing inventories are at an all-time low.
    d. Interest rates are not expected to go up in the near term.

68. Which of the following circumstances does not tend to intensify rivalry among competitors?

    a. Switching costs are high.
    b. Industry growth is slowing.
    c. Rivals have similar market shares.
    d. Capacity is added in large increments.

69. Common-size balance sheets are generally used to make which of the following assessments for the subject company?

    a. Debt-to-total capital ratio to be used in the weighted average cost of capital.
    b. Analysis of business trends.
    c. Amount of working capital at the valuation date.
    d. Analysis of turnover ratios.

70. Which of the following measures provides the best way to analyze a company's return on equity performance?

    a. Vertical analysis.
    b. DuPont analysis.

    c. Technical analysis.
    d. Trend analysis.

71. When valuing a minority interest, which of the following would be an appropriate reason for adjusting net income, based on a review of officers' compensation?

    a. Officers' compensation includes a position normally classified as cost of sales.
    b. Officers' compensation includes a family member who is overcompensated.
    c. Officers' compensation includes a bonus related to the sale of a division.
    d. Officers' compensation includes commissions for obtaining new business.

72. When performing an analysis of industry structure and conduct, which of the following is not evaluated?

    a. Competitor response.
    b. Substitute products.
    c. Staffing.
    d. Suppliers.

73. Which of the following sources of information about the automotive industry should be viewed as the most reliable for an industry analysis?

    a. A Daimler-Chrysler study on owners' satisfaction.
    b. Information from General Motors' annual proxy statement.
    c. Crash test statistics published by *Consumer Reports*.
    d. Wall Street analysts' reports on publicly traded automotive companies.

74. A company can maintain above-average profitability by using all of the following means except:

    a. Cost advantages.
    b. Product differentiation.
    c. Legal barriers such as patents.
    d. Optimal financing mix for new investments.

75. The U.S. Census Bureau four firm concentration ratio of 93 (meaning only four firms comprise 93% of industry's sales) would indicate an industry structure best described as:

    a. Pure competition.
    b. Monopolistic competition.
    c. Oligopoly.
    d. Monopoly.

76. All of the following are types of normalization adjustments made in directly valuing a minority interest except:

    a. Litigation settlement.
    b. Discontinued operations.
    c. Nonoperating assets.
    d. Change in accounting principles.

77. To sustain a competitive advantage, a company may not rely on which of the following?

    a. Entry barriers.
    b. Barriers to imitation.

c. Buyer switching costs.

d. First-to-market advantage.

78. A company that is targeting baby boomers for the launch of a new product line would be most concerned about which of the following types of risk?

    a. Global.
    b. Sociocultural.
    c. Demographic.
    d. Technological.

79. Which of the following normalizing adjustments would be most appropriate only under the standard of investment value?

    a. Eliminate acquisition costs for a new subsidiary.
    b. Eliminate leaseholds written off upon termination of a lease.
    c. Eliminate labor costs to be saved by acquiring a competitor's technology.
    d. Eliminate above-market portion of compensation paid to the CEO/shareholder.

80. Which of the following statements regarding accounts receivable turnover is incorrect?

    a. A low accounts receivable turnover can indicate excessive bad debt losses.
    b. A low accounts receivable turnover can indicate an overly restrictive credit policy limiting sales.
    c. Accounts receivable turnover can be expressed as the number of times per year the accounts turn over on average.
    d. Accounts receivable turnover can be expressed as the number of days, on average, required for collecting accounts.

81. Which of the following statements is not true regarding ratio analysis?

    a. Ratio analysis ignores company size.
    b. Ratios involve a process of standardization.
    c. Ratios measure a company's relationships by relating costs to benefits.
    d. Ratios have a nonlinear relationship between numerator and denominator.

82. Which of the following parts of a valuation engagement is dependent on the economic analysis?

    a. Forecasting future performance.
    b. SWOT analysis.
    c. Determining pricing multiples.
    d. Both a and c.

83. Which of the following types of businesses would be countercyclical to the economy?

    a. Medical practice.
    b. Tractor-trailer driving school.
    c. Electronics manufacturer.
    d. High-end luxury retailer.

84. Which of the following is not one of Porter's Five Forces?

    a. Threat of existing firms.
    b. Threat of new entrants.
    c. Bargaining power of suppliers.
    d. Rivalry of existing firms.

85. Which of the following is not a barrier to entry according to Porter?

    a. Capital requirements.
    b. Government.
    c. Asset specificity.
    d. Trademarks.

86. Which of the following is not an example of an entry barrier?

    a. Proprietary know-how.
    b. Interrelated businesses.
    c. High scale threshold.
    d. Access to distribution channels.

87. In Porter's model, the term *substitute products* often refers to which of the following?

    a. The principle of substitution.
    b. Products in the same industry.
    c. Products in other industries.
    d. Products that have complementary features.

88. Suppliers have strong bargaining power when:

    a. There are few suppliers among which customers may choose.
    b. There are few or no substitute products available.
    c. The supplier's product is necessary to customers.
    d. There are many competitive suppliers and substitute products.

CHAPTER 7

Statistics for Valuation and Economic Damages

This chapter was intended to be a basic primer on statistics as used in valuation and economic damages. I covered the following topics: population and samples, discrete and continuous variables, frequency distributions, measures of central tendency, measures of variation, probability, correlation, and drinking the statistics Kool-Aid.

1. In using regression analysis, a high coefficient of determination, or R^2 (R-squared), indicates:
   a. A high standard error of estimate.
   b. A low coefficient of correlation.
   c. A high variance between the variables.
   d. A high correlation between the variables.

2. Which of the following best describes the term *coefficient of determination*?
   a. The measure of variability.
   b. The linear association between two variables.
   c. How large the standard deviation is compared to the mean.
   d. The goodness of fit for the estimated regression equation.

3. The mean monthly return on an investment is 1.25%, with a standard deviation of 4.0% and a variance of 16.0%. What is the coefficient of variation for this investment?
   a. 0.31.
   b. 3.20.
   c. 4.00.
   d. 12.80.

4. Simple linear regression allows the analyst to do all of the following except:
   a. Use one variable to make predictions about another.
   b. Test hypotheses about the relationship between two variables.
   c. Quantify the strength of the relationship between two variables.
   d. Identify causal relationships between two variables.

5. Which of the following is not a measure of dispersion?
   a. R-squared.
   b. Range.

   c. Standard deviation.
   d. Variance.

6. Which of the following represents the smallest group?

   a. A universe.
   b. A population.
   c. A sample.
   d. A range.

7. Which of the following terms describes a variable that can assume one value?

   a. Inferential.
   b. Constant.
   c. Continuous.
   d. Range.

8. Which of the following is not a measure of central tendency?

   a. Mean.
   b. Median.
   c. Range.
   d. Mode.

9. The harmonic mean is:

   a. The standard deviation of the arithmetic mean.
   b. The reciprocal of the arithmetic mean.
   c. The same as the geometric mean.
   d. A musical instrument.

Use the following information for questions 10–13.

Pricing Multiples

Company 1	23.4
Company 2	38.4
Company 3	30.2
Company 4	28.4
Company 5	29.4

10. The mean pricing multiple is:

   a. 28.3.
   b. 29.6.
   c. 30.0.
   d. 38.4.

11. The median pricing multiple is:

   a. 28.4.
   b. 29.4.
   c. 30.2.
   d. 30.3.

12. The standard deviation of the pricing multiples is:
    a. 4.5.
    b. 5.4.
    c. 5.8.
    d. 6.5.

13. The harmonic mean of the pricing multiples is:
    a. 29.2.
    b. 30.4.
    c. 32.3.
    d. 36.8.

14. If an item is 1 standard deviation from the mean, what percentage of the data falls within that area?
    a. 68.27%.
    b. 82.43%.
    c. 95.45%.
    d. 99.73%.

15. Which of the following statements is false regarding the standard deviation?
    a. The standard deviation is a useful measure of dispersion if the data are skewed.
    b. The standard deviation tells us how far the data are located from the mean.
    c. Fully 95% of the population will be within 2 standard deviations plus or minus.
    d. The standard deviation should be used only if the data are normally distributed.

16. Which of the following statements is true about a probability?
    a. A probability measures the likelihood that a particular event will occur.
    b. A probability assumes a value between 0 and 1.
    c. Both a and b
    d. None of the above.

17. A correlation coefficient of −1.0 indicates which of the following?
    a. A perfect linear relationship with a positive slope between two variables.
    b. No linear relationship between the two variables.
    c. A perfect linear relationship with a negative slope between two variables.
    d. A moderate linear relationship with a negative slope between two variables.

18. A correlation coefficient:
    a. Measures the degree to which variations in two variables are linearly related.
    b. Assumes a value between 0 and + 1.
    c. Measures how the changes in one variable causes the change another variable.
    d. All of the above.

19 . When using statistics in a business valuation, which of the following statements is/are true?

   a. Valuation analysts should always use all of the data points that are made available to ensure that the sample size is sufficient.
   b. Outliers should always be removed from the data set in order to perform a proper analysis.
   c. The data analyzed must be sufficient in terms of quantity to make the statistical analysis meaningful.
   d. All of the above.

CHAPTER 8

Developing Forecasts for Business Valuations and Economic Damages

In this chapter, I explained the difference between a forecast and a projection, the factors to look for when evaluating a forecast provided by management, the steps to take in preparing a forecast, sales forecasting techniques, forecasting various items on the income statement and balance sheet, applicable standards CPAs must follow when preparing a forecast for these types of engagements, and the acceptance of forecasts in various courts.

1. Which of the following is not a possible solution if the valuation analyst does not agree with management's forecast?

   a. Insist on using the consultant's forecast, perhaps with footnotes about management's disagreements with the forecasts.

   b. Use two or more scenarios for the forecasts, resulting in a range of estimated values.

   c. Rely on the forecast regardless.

   d. Use management's forecasts and adjust the discount rate. This is usually accomplished through the specific company risk adjustment.

2. Factors to consider when evaluating management's forecast include all of the following except:

   a. Company-specific factors.

   b. Industry trends.

   c. Economic trends.

   d. Guideline company trends.

3. Common adjustments to the financial statements include all of the following except:

   a. Depreciation may be adjusted to reflect current economic write-offs more accurately, based on the value determined by the machinery and equipment appraisers or real estate appraisers.

   b. Inventory accounting may be changed from FIFO to LIFO.

   c. Nonrecurring items should be removed.

   d. Nonoperating income or expense items may be eliminated, if appropriate.

4. When preparing a forecast, which of the following financial statement adjustments is/are common?

   a. Depreciation.
   b. Nonrecurring items.
   c. Related party adjustments.
   d. All of the above.

5. Which of the following factors is not included in deriving net cash flow to invested capital when preparing a forecast?

   a. Normalized noncash charges.
   b. Working capital.
   c. Debt.
   d. Capital expenditures.

6. When preparing prospective financial information for a valuation, if the engagement has not been engaged to perform accounting services to that information, which of the following standards provides that a report does not have to be issued on the prospective information?

   a. Statement on Standards for Valuation Services.
   b. Statements on Auditing Standards.
   c. Statements on Standards for Accounting and Review Services.
   d. Statement on Standards for Attestation Engagements.

7. What is the difference between a forecast and a projection?

   a. There is no difference; both are forward looking.
   b. A forecast is based on company expectations, whereas a projection uses hypothetical assumptions.
   c. A forecast is obtained by management, whereas a projection always uses a linear regression to predict the future.
   d. A forecast is obtained by management, whereas a projection is prepared by the valuation analyst.

8. What factor is not relevant when preparing a forecast?

   a. Goals of the client with respect to the valuation.
   b. Historical financial performance.
   c. Expected economic and industry trends.
   d. Common sense.

CHAPTER 9

The Market Approach—Part I

In this chapter, I started to explain the market approach. There was a lot of important information in this chapter. After an introduction to the market approach, I covered the guideline public company method, including a discussion about the methodology, selecting potential guideline companies, analyzing guideline companies, using valuation multiples, and advantages and disadvantages of the guideline public company method, concluding with an illustration of the guideline company method.

1. Under the market approach, which of the following conclusions from your ratio analyses would typically indicate a valuation multiple at the higher end of the range?

   a. High current ratio and high receivable days outstanding.
   b. Low receivable days outstanding and high days inventory.
   c. High ratio of sales to fixed assets and high ratio of debt to equity.
   d. High times interest earned and high fixed charges coverage.

2. Which of the following risks are not embedded in valuation multiples of publicly traded guideline companies?

   a. Macroenvironmental.
   b. Diversifiable.
   c. Industry.
   d. Economic.

3. Which of the following is an example of a benefit stream applicable to the estimation of market value of invested capital (MVIC)?

   a. Revenue.
   b. Net income.
   c. Pretax income.
   d. Book value of equity.

4. The following information relates to XYZ Co., Inc., a public company: market value of common stock $10,000,000, market value of interest-bearing debt $12,000,000, pretax income $8,000,000, interest expense $1,000,000, income tax expense $3,200,000. XYZ's market value of invested capital to earnings before interest and taxes (MVIC/EBIT) multiple is used to value 100% of the equity of closely held Smith Manufacturing, Inc. Relevant information for Smith Manufacturing, Inc. is as follows: book value of equity $1,000,000, market value of interest-bearing debt $300,000, pretax income $350,000, interest

expense $40,000, and income tax expense $105,000. What is the fair market value of the Smith Manufacturing, Inc.'s equity?

a. $554,000.
b. $652,000.
c. $663,500.
d. $952,000.

5. When should a valuation analyst consider using the market approach to estimate the fair market value of an ownership interest in a closely held business?

a. If valuing a controlling interest.
b. If time and fees allow using the approach.
c. If estimating fair market value of a closely held business.
d. If the size of the subject company is large enough to be of similar size to the guideline public companies.

6. In the market approach to valuing a noncontrolling ownership interest, which of the following statements is/are correct when using publicly traded guideline companies?

I. No minority interest discount is typically taken.
II. A lack of marketability discount is usually taken from the indicated publicly traded value.
III. No adjustment should be made to the financial data of the selected publicly traded guideline companies.

a. I only.
b. I and II only.
c. II and III only.
d. I, II, and III.

7. When utilizing publicly traded guideline company pricing multiples, in which of the following circumstances would you typically consider using an invested capital method?

a. The subject company is asset-intensive and unable to service its debt.
b. The ownership interest at issue is noncontrolling.
c. The capital structures of the guideline and subject companies are materially different.
d. The earnings growth rates of the guideline and subject companies are materially different.

8. Which of the following statements is true of the market approach?

a. It is not a forward-looking approach.
b. Most of the important assumptions are explicitly stated.
c. The value derived includes all of the business's operating assets.
d. It is the most flexible approach for considering unique operating characteristics.

9. Which of the following is not true with regard to the identification of guideline public companies?

a. Management of the subject company is a good source of information on guideline public companies.
b. Companies should be comparable to the subject based on size, growth, and profitability.

c. The selection process should identify guideline public companies with similar risks and opportunities.

d. Examining detailed business descriptions is an essential step in the identification process.

10. When the capital structures of the guideline companies and the subject company are considerably different, which of the following is the best way to analyze the capital structures?

a. Book value of debt to book value of equity.

b. Market value of debt to market value of invested capital.

c. Book value of debt to market value of invested capital.

d. Fair value of debt to fair value of equity.

11. Which of the following benefit streams should be used when developing pricing multiples with MVIC in the numerator?

a. Book value of equity.

b. Pretax income.

c. Net income.

d. Net revenue.

12. Which of the following guideline company financial data should not be considered when using the market approach for a valuation date of December 31, 2017?

a. Latest quarter ended September 30, 2017.

b. Estimated year ended December 31, 2017.

c. Restated year ended December 31, 2017.

d. Projected year ending December 31, 2018.

The following information should assist you in answering questions 13–18. Electech is a privately held company that produces circuit boards. The sole shareholder has asked you to estimate the fair market value of the equity of Electech for gift tax reporting purposes. The date of the gift was December 31, 20X1.

In your analysis of the circuit board industry, you discover that four of Electech's close competitors are publicly traded. The four companies are XYZ, ABC, PDF, and ITECH. You consider using the market approach in your analysis.

Electech
Balance Sheet for the Year Ended December 31, 20X1

	Book Value	Restated to Fair Market Value
Assets		
Cash	500,000	500,000
Receivables	1,600,000	1,300,000
Inventory	3,000,000	2,500,000
Fixed Assets	3,000,000	5,000,000
Intangible Assets/Goodwill	0	4,000,000
Total Assets	8,100,000	13,300,000

Electech
Balance Sheet for the Year Ended December 31, 20X1 *(continued)*

	Book Value	Restated to Fair Market Value
Liabilities		
Accounts Payable	1,600,000	1,600,000
Short-Term Debt	1,000,000	1,000,000
Long-Term Debt	1,500,000	1,500,000
Shareholder's Equity	4,000,000	9,200,000
Total Liabilities and Shareholder's Equity	8,100,000	13,300,000

Electech
Income Statement for the Year Ending December 31, 20X1

Net Sales	10,000,000
Cost of Goods Sold	5,000,000
Gross Profit	5,000,000
Selling, General, Administrative	2,500,000
Depreciation	750,000
Interest Expense	350,000
Pretax Income	1,400,000
Income Tax at 35%	490,000
Net Income	910,000

Guideline Companies
Selected Financial Data for the Year Ended December 31, 20X1

	XYZ	ABC	PDF	ITECH	Subject
Revenue	$38 million	$12 million	$18 million	$5 million	$10 million
MVIC	$92 million	$16 million	$18 million	$6 million	Unknown
Liquidity					
Current Ratio	3.0	2.2	2.2	1.9	1.7
Quick Ratio	2.2	1.3	1.5	0.2	0.7
Activity					
Working Capital Turnover	4.3	3.0	1.8	1.5	0
Asset Turnover	2.5	1.5	1.0	1.2	1.2

Leverage					
Total Liabilities/Total Assets	0.47	0.25	0.73	0.67	0.75
Interest Coverage	14×	9×	4×	6×	5×
Profitability					
EBIT Margin	16%	18%	13%	10%	17.5%
EBIT Margin Growth	29%	23%	18%	17%	0%
Growth					
Revenues	12%	8%	3%	5%	7%

All ratios calculated using fair market value (FMV).

Electech
Market Guideline Analysis

	XYZ	ABC	PDF	ITECH
MVIC/EBITDA	7	6	6	6
Price/Earnings	12	10	9	11

13. Which guideline company is most comparable to Electech in terms of capital structure?

   a. XYZ.
   b. PDF.
   c. ABC.
   d. ITECH.

14. Which guideline company is most comparable to Electech in terms of both growth and profitability?

   a. ABC.
   b. PDF.
   c. XYZ.
   d. ITECH.

15. What is Electech's working capital turnover (FMV basis)?

   a. 3.0×.
   b. 3.7×.
   c. 5.9×.
   d. 50.0×.

16. What is Electech's earnings before interest, taxes, depreciation, and amortization (EBITDA) margin?

   a. 20.1%.
   b. 21.5%.

    c. 17.5%.

    d. 25.0%.

17. Assuming you decide that ABC's MVIC/EBITDA and price-to-earnings (P/E) multiples are the most appropriate to apply to Electech, what is the indicated value of the equity of Electech using a P/E multiple? (Ignore any additional discounts or premiums.)

    a. $5,460,000.

    b. $9,100,000.

    c. $4,325,000.

    d. $12,600,000.

18. Assuming you decide that ABC's MVIC/EBITDA and P/E multiples are the most appropriate to apply to Electech, what is the indicated value of the equity of Electech using the MVIC/EBITDA multiple? (Ignore any additional discounts or premiums.)

    a. $5,460,000.

    b. $9,100,000.

    c. $12,500,000.

    d. $12,600,000.

19. Which of the following guideline companies would most likely be used?

    a. A stock trading at high volume with a price of $0.42.

    b. A stock that is actively traded; however, most of the participants are company insiders.

    c. A stock with high price volatility caused by a declining economy.

    d. A stock that is thinly traded.

20. In which of the following cases is the P/E multiple most appropriate?

    a. When the company has abnormal tax rates.

    b. When depreciation represents actual or economic physical wear and tear.

    c. When the company has low levels of income compared to its depreciation and amortization.

    d. When cash businesses are valued.

21. Which of the following risks should be considered in adjusting the valuation multiples that are determined from guideline companies?

    a. Business risk.

    b. Operating risk.

    c. Product risk.

    d. All of the above.

22. If you are valuing the equity of a company, the guideline public company essentially values:

    a. All assets and liabilities of the company.

    b. All assets of the company.

    c. All operating assets and liabilities of the company.

    d. All operating assets of the company.

23. The market approach is useful when:
    a. The guideline companies are thinly traded.
    b. The subject company is a professional practice.
    c. Sufficient financial information is not available to complete the steps involved in the approach.
    d. The public company is in the same industry, although larger than the subject company.

24. If the subject company is highly leveraged compared to the guideline companies, which valuation multiple would be least beneficial to use?
    a. Invested capital to EBITDA.
    b. Price to revenue.
    c. Price to earnings.
    d. Invested capital to EBIT.

25. For a guideline company to be considered, it must:
    a. Have revenue within 5% of the subject company's revenue.
    b. Be identical to the subject company.
    c. Have the same SIC code as the subject company.
    d. Be comparable to the subject company.

26. Which of the following normalization adjustments would generally not be made to the public companies?
    a. Officers' compensation.
    b. Standardization of accounting methods.
    c. Removal of extraordinary items.
    d. Adjustment to income taxes.

27. Which of the following is the definition of financial risk?
    a. The risk associated with the amount of leverage the company uses and the company's ability to cover its debt payments.
    b. The risk associated with the fixed versus variable cost structure.
    c. The risk associated with factors such as sales volatility and the volatility of the company's growth.
    d. The risk associated with the age of the company's assets.

28. What guideline public company price should be used in calculating multiples?
    a. The stock closing price on the date of valuation.
    b. The average of the high and low prices on the date of valuation.
    c. The average of the high and low prices for the six months before the date of valuation.
    d. The average of the company's high and low prices over the analysis period selected.

29. If no discretionary control adjustments are made for the subject company, the guideline company method results in a value that is:
    a. A minority marketable value.
    b. A minority nonmarketable value.
    c. A control marketable value.
    d. A control nonmarketable value.

The following information is used for questions 30 and 31. Public Company, Inc. (PCI) trades at a price of $40 per share. PCI currently has 500,000 shares outstanding and has interest-bearing debt of $12,000,000. PCI's earnings per share are $3.50 and their interest expense was $900,000 in the prior year. PCI's tax rate is 40%.

30. The price to earnings multiple on an equity basis is approximately:
    a. 7.5×.
    b. 11.4×.
    c. 12.1×.
    d. 14.0×.

31. The P/E multiple on a market value of investment capital basis is approximately:
    a. 11.4×.
    b. 8.7×.
    c. 18.2×.
    d. 14.0×.

32. In valuing ABC, Inc., we calculate an MVIC/EBIT multiple of 20×. ABC, Inc. has interest-bearing debt of $8,000,000 and has EBIT of $1 per share with 1,000,000 shares outstanding. ABC, Inc.'s interest expense per share is $0.25 and their income tax rate is 40%. What is the value of ABC, Inc.'s equity?
    a. $8,000,000.
    b. $12,000,000.
    c. $17,000,000.
    d. $20,000,000.

Use the following information for questions 33–38.

Black Company, Inc. is the subject of a business valuation assignment. While performing the valuation, you have selected what you believe to be three "good" guideline companies to be used in the guideline public company method (GPCM). Select financial data has been summarized in the following schedules.

Black Company, Inc.
Schedule 1
Normalized Balance Sheet
December 31,

	20X4	20X5	20X6
Current Assets			
Cash	4,330,952	11,384,878	26,231,047
Marketable Securities	13,281,325	9,576,522	7,783,266
Accounts Receivable	17,149,153	18,461,748	22,169,526
Allowance for Doubtful Accounts	−215,000	−245,000	−280,000
Due from Employees	43,904	29,955	19,866
Deferred Tax Assets	146,700	116,800	357,600
Other Current Assets	689,225	1,566,417	793,852
Total Current Assets	35,426,259	40,891,320	57,075,157

Fixed Assets

Gross Fixed Assets	5,177,150	5,894,486	6,348,894
Accum. Depreciation	2,990,394	3,663,926	4,254,910
Net Fixed Assets	2,186,756	2,230,560	2,093,984

Other Assets

Intangible Assets (Net)	4,787,633	4,322,360	6,456,810
Other Assets	708,831	278,054	625,040
Total Other Assets	5,496,464	4,600,414	7,081,850
Total Assets	43,109,479	47,722,294	66,250,991

Current Liabilities

Accounts Payable	33,170,617	39,103,462	51,050,068
Long-Term Debt (Current)	1,620,913	1,643,208	1,598,766
Accrued Expenses Payable	4,751,321	5,125,559	7,128,329
Other Current Liabilities	128,983	38,100	33,595
Total Current Liabilities	39,671,834	45,910,329	59,810,758

Long-Term Liabilities

Long-Term Debt	2,616,021	943,785	1,350,030
Deferred Taxes	336,700	251,800	232,600
Total Long-Term Liabilities	2,952,721	1,195,585	1,582,630
Total Liabilities	42,624,555	47,105,914	61,393,388

Stockholders' Equity

Common Stock	3,077	3,077	3,077
Retained Earnings	481,847	613,303	4,854,526
Total Stockholders' Equity	484,924	616,380	4,857,603
Total Liabilities and Stockholders' Equity	43,109,479	47,722,294	66,250,991

Black Company, Inc.
Schedule 2
Normalized Income Statement
for the Year Ended December 31,

	20X4	20X5	20X6
Total Revenues	23,266,768	29,236,739	38,913,153
Total Operating Expenses	21,783,770	26,587,507	29,749,932
Operating Income	1,482,998	2,649,232	9,163,221
Interest Expense	174,212	171,193	103,710
Total Other Income	1,147,441	1,296,567	654,388

Black Company, Inc.
Schedule 2
Normalized Income Statement
for the Year Ended December 31,

	20X4	20X5	20X6
Income Before Taxes	2,456,227	3,774,606	9,713,899
Income Taxes	924,278	1,420,384	3,655,340
Net Income	1,531,949	2,354,222	6,058,559
Additional Information			
Depreciation and Amortization in Operating Expenses	914,540	1,645,601	1,591,268

Guideline Company No. 1
Schedule 3
Balance Sheet as of December 31,

	20X4	20X5	20X6
	In Thousands of Dollars		
Revenues	800,580	922,988	1,101,222
Operating Expenses	666,841	774,125	915,880
Operating Income	133,739	148,863	185,342
Provision for Income Taxes	40,784	16,597	55,603
Net Income Available to Common	92,955	132,266	129,739
Earnings per Share	$1.11	$1.48	$1.49

Guideline Company No. 1
Schedule 4
Balance Sheet as of December 31,

	20X5	20X6
Current Assets	In Thousands of Dollars	
Cash and Equivalents	308,039	408,859
Marketable Securities	52,588	70,556
Accounts Receivable	1,117,238	1,183,737
Other Current Assets	85,142	110,458
Total Current Assets	1,563,007	1,773,610
Net Fixed Assets	183,245	250,995
Intangible Assets (Net)	65,341	135,062
Deposits and Other Assets	333,749	303,907
Total Assets	2,145,342	2,463,574

Current Liabilities

Current Portion of Long-Term Debt	41,704	47,782
Accounts Payable	1,366,516	1,488,222
Other Current Liabilities	229,736	213,600
Total Current Liabilities	1,637,956	1,749,604

Long-Term Liabilities

Long-Term Interest-Bearing Debt	96,698	128,349
Other Long-Term Liabilities	39,075	57,466
Total Long-Term Liabilities	135,773	185,815
Total Liabilities	1,773,729	1,935,419
Total Stockholders' Equity	371,613	528,155
Total Liabilities and Stockholders' Equity	2,145,342	2,463,574
Common Shares at End of Year (000)	89,369	87,073

Guideline Company No. 2
Schedule 5
Income Statement
for the Years Ended December 31,

	20X4	20X5	20X6
	In Thousands of Dollars		
Revenues	265,405	365,029	455,742
Operating Expenses	210,075	268,848	316,419
Operating Income	55,330	96,181	139,323
Interest Expense	1,266	5,703	4,659
Income Before Income Taxes	54,064	90,478	134,664
Provision for Income Taxes	20,146	34,834	49,271
Net Income Available to Common	33,918	55,644	85,393
Earnings per Share	$0.55	$0.89	$1.27

Guideline Company No. 2
Schedule 6
Balance Sheet as of December 31,

	20X5	20X6
Current Assets	**In Thousands of Dollars**	
Cash and Equivalents	66,376	171,043
Marketable Securities	451	446
Accounts Receivable	101,449	144,244
Other Current Assets	8,230	16,527
Total Current Assets	176,506	332,260
Net Fixed Assets	25,544	24,730
Intangible Assets (Net)	68,311	380,253
Deposits and Other Assets	18,376	17,106
Total Assets	488,737	754,349
Current Liabilities		
Current Portion of Long-Term Debt	20,855	24,730
Accounts Payable	151,649	191,682
Other Current Liabilities	54,093	78,702
Total Current Liabilities	226,597	297,718
Long-Term Liabilities		
Long-Term Interest-Bearing Debt	78,195	57,585
Other Long-Term Liabilities	6,308	5,604
Total Long-Term Liabilities	84,503	63,189
Total Liabilities	311,100	360,907
Minority Interest	2,352	1,852
Total Stockholders' Equity	175,285	391,590
Total Liabilities and Stockholders' Equity	488,737	754,349
Common Shares at End of Year (000)	66,690	67,034

Guideline Company No. 3
Schedule 7
Income Statement
for the Years Ended December 31,

	20X4	20X5	20X6
	In Thousands of Dollars		
Revenues	262,119	330,267	452,726
Operating Expenses	214,203	264,476	338,804
Operating Income	47,916	65,791	113,922
Interest Expense	8,179	9,061	10,665
Income Before Income Taxes	39,737	56,730	103,257
Provision for Income Taxes	17,610	24,381	42,082
Net Income Available to Common	22,127	32,349	61,175
Earnings per Share	$0.85	$1.18	$1.96

Guideline Company No. 3
Schedule 8
Balance Sheet as of December 31,

	20X5	20X6
Current Assets	In Thousands of Dollars	
Cash and Equivalents	51,580	134,692
Marketable Securities	3,500	1,334
Accounts Receivable	116,219	175,948
Other Current Assets	25,480	45,591
Total Current Assets	196,779	357,565
Net Fixed Assets	19,485	20,386
Intangible Assets (Net)	266,083	441,973
Deposits and Other Assets	11,729	13,100
Total Assets	494,076	833,024
Current Liabilities		
Current Portion of Long-Term Debt	6,966	5,733
Accounts Payable	169,502	235,057
Other Current Liabilities	48,547	83,255
Total Current Liabilities	225,045	324,045

Guideline Company No. 3
Schedule 8
Balance Sheet as of December 31, *(continued)*

	20X5	20X6
Long-Term Liabilities		
Long-Term Interest-Bearing Debt	114,443	177,151
Other Long-Term Liabilities	11,786	21,180
Total Long-Term Liabilities	126,229	198,331
Total Liabilities	351,274	522,376
Total Stockholders' Equity	142,802	310,648
Total Liabilities and Stockholders' Equity	494,076	833,024
Common Shares at End of Year (000)	27,414	31,157

At the valuation date, the prices of the common stock of the guideline companies were as follows:

	Guideline Company No.	
1	2	3
$27.655	$32.790	$41.100

Information about the multiples calculated by the valuation analyst is as follows:

Company	Market Multiples		
	MVE to Operating Cash Flow	MVE to EBT	MVE to Net Income
Guideline Company 1	11.06	12.99	18.56
Guideline Company 2	14.09	16.32	25.74
Guideline Company 3	11.01	12.40	20.93
Statistical Analysis			
Mean	12.05	13.91	21.74
Median	11.06	12.99	20.93
Standard Deviation	1.77	2.11	3.66
Coefficient of Variation	0.15	0.15	0.17
Linear Regression			
Slope	10.44	12.82	15.00
Intercept	256,803.14	152,772.91	580,408.57
R^2	0.79	0.78	0.76

MVE = market value of equity.

33. The coefficient of variation for the data indicates
    a. The guideline company multiples are a poor statistical choice to be used by the appraiser.
    b. The guideline company multiples are a good statistical choice to be used by the appraiser.
    c. The MVE-to-net-income multiple should be discarded because the coefficient of variation is different from the other two multiples.
    d. The MVE-to-net-income multiple is the best multiple to be used because the coefficient of variation is greater than the other two multiples.

34. Based solely on the data, which of the following statements is true?
    a. Guideline Company No. 2 should be eliminated because its multiples are outliers compared to those of the other companies.
    b. Having an R^2 that is below 1.0 makes all of these multiples poor choices to use.
    c. The standard deviation for the MVE to net income multiple invalidates that multiple from being used.
    d. The coefficient of variation, taken in conjunction with the R^2, indicates that all three multiples are statistically valid.

35. The MVE at December 31, 2006, for Guideline Company No. 2 is equal to:
    a. $2.2 million.
    b. $2.1 billion.
    c. $2.2 billion.
    d. $2.3 billion.

36. The MVIC-to-EBITDA multiple for Guideline Company No. 3 is:
    a. 10.91.
    b. 11.48.
    c. 11.52.
    d. 12.85.

37. Additional information determined by the valuation analyst was as follows:

Control premium	20%
Discount for lack of marketability	30%

   Assuming that the appropriate multiple for operating cash flow to be used for Black Company is 6.6, what is the minority, nonmarketable value?
    a. $42,300,000.
    b. $49,700,000.
    c. $59,600,000.
    d. $71,000,000.

38. After applying income and market approaches, using the GPCM and 12 actual transactions made by Black Company during the last 3 years, you reached the following indications of value for Black Company on a minority, nonmarketable basis:

Income Approach

Discounted Cash Flow	$21,800,000

Market Approach—GPCM

MVE to EBTDA	$48,900,000
MVE to EBT	$53,000,000
MVE to Net Income	$53,400,000

Market Approach—Black Company Transactions

Price to Revenue	$25,700,000
Price to Operating Income	$23,300,000
Price to Net Income	$21,600,000
Price to EBITDA	$25,100,000

Which of the following would be the most reasonable statement regarding the reconciliation process?

a. The indications of value from the GPCM should be given primary weight in this appraisal since they came from the public market and the statistics calculated were favorable.

b. The indications of value from the GPCM should be given little, if any, weight since there were only three guideline companies.

c. The fact that the transactions made by Black Company result in indications of the value that are similar to the value determined under the income approach supports the value of Black to the exclusion of the GPCM.

d. The fact that Black Company made these acquisitions of other companies should cause these transactions to not be used as an indication of the value because of the bias in the data given that Black Company was the willing buyer.

CHAPTER 10

The Market Approach—Part II

In this chapter, I finished explaining the market approach. The chapter included a discussion about the mergers and acquisitions (transaction) method, highlights of different private transaction databases, the practical application of the mergers and acquisitions method, internal transactions, and rules of thumb.

1. Which of the following is the best transactional-data source for a price-to-net income multiple?

   a. Bizcomps.
   b. Pratt's Stats.
   c. *Value Line Investment Survey.*
   d. Institute of Business Appraisers (IBA) market database.

2. Which of the following presents the most compelling reason for relying on internal transactions to determine the fair market value of an interest in a professional practice?

   a. The method is suggested by Revenue Ruling 59-60.
   b. There have been many transactions over the last five years.
   c. The buy-sell agreement requires the capital account to be used for all transactions.
   d. The transaction prices were based on death benefits that were provided by life insurance.

3. In which of the following circumstances is the guideline merged and acquired company method usually considered to be a better method to determine fair market value than the guideline publicly traded company method?

   a. Valuing a minority interest in a large company.
   b. Valuing a controlling interest in a small company.
   c. Valuing a minority interest when the guideline transactions involve financial buyers.
   d. Valuing a controlling interest when the guideline transactions involve strategic buyers.

4. If private companies are selected for use in the mergers and acquisitions method, the resulting value is on a _____ and _____ basis.

   a. control; marketable
   b. control; nonmarketable
   c. minority; marketable
   d. minority; nonmarketable

5. Which business transaction source has the database that is the largest known source of market transactions of small closely held businesses?

   a. IBA market database.
   b. Bizcomps.
   c. Pratt's Stats.
   d. Mergerstat.

6. Which of the following is included in a sale price listed with Bizcomps?

   a. Cash.
   b. Accounts receivable.
   c. Real estate.
   d. Fixtures and equipment.

7. Which of the following transactions listed in Bizcomps has the lowest cash-equivalent price?

   a. Purchase price of $125,000 paid for in cash.
   b. Purchase price of $125,000 paid for with a 25% down payment and a three-year note payable of $93,750 with a market rate of interest.
   c. Purchase price of $125,000 paid for with a 25% down payment and a three-year note payable of $93,750 with an interest rate below the market rate of interest.
   d. Purchase price of $125,000 paid for with a 25% down payment and a three-year note payable of $93,750 with an interest rate above the market rate of interest.

8. An advantage of Pratt's Stats over both Bizcomps and IBA is:

   a. The database contains more transactions.
   b. The database contains smaller transactions.
   c. The database contains more data points for each transaction.
   d. The database contains only asset sales.

9. Which of the following statements is true?

   a. Pratt's Stats reports larger transactions than Done Deals.
   b. Done Deals contains midmarket transaction data, with all of its transactions being publicly owned companies.
   c. Public Stats is a database of public transactions where 100% of the company is sold.
   d. Public Stats includes only national transactions.

10. Which of the following is not an advantage of the mergers and acquisitions method?

   a. It is easy to find comparable companies that have been acquired.
   b. Transactions are considered to be objective, because they come from the market.
   c. Transactions are assumed to be between informed buyers and sellers and are a good representation of fair market value.
   d. Transactions involve entire companies that have changed hands making it a logical application of the market approach.

11. Which of the following is not a source of business transactions?

    a. The Institute of Business Appraisers.
    b. The National Association of Certified Valuation Analysts.
    c. Bizcomps.
    d. Thomson Reuters Mergers & Acquisitions.

12. The information from the IBA market database includes all of the following except:

    a. Principal line of business.
    b. Year and month the transaction was consummated.
    c. Reported owner's compensation.
    d. Detailed entity description.

13. The Bizomps database lists a transaction with a sale price of $200,000, fixed assets of $50,000, and inventory of $25,000. The intangible assets value included in the purchase price was:

    a. $125,000.
    b. $150,000.
    c. $175,000.
    d. $200,000.

14. Which of the following is not an advantage of Pratt's Stats?

    a. The ability to consider both asset and stock sales.
    b. The ability to calculate multiples for S corporations versus C corporations.
    c. The ability to analyze both private and public companies.
    d. The ability to analyze up to eight different valuation multiples.

15. Which of the following is an advantage of the industry rule of thumb method?

    a. This method generally provides a sanity check on other valuation methods.
    b. Different sources of information may provide different rules of thumb.
    c. This method considers the economic reality of the situation.
    d. Information about the companies that made up the rule of thumb transactions is easily accessible.

16. Which of the following does Bizcomps report as a measure of earnings?

    a. Net cash flow.
    b. Gross cash flow.
    c. Seller's discretionary cash flow.
    d. EBITDA.

17. Which of the following databases would the analyst use to identify larger transactions?

    a. ADAM.
    b. Bizcomps.
    c. Pratt's Stats.
    d. Thomson Reuters Mergers & Acquisitions.

18. Which of the following is not a disadvantage of the mergers and acquisitions method?

    a. The information is less than perfect.
    b. There is a lack of information available about the transactions.
    c. It is easily understood by laypeople.
    d. Financial terms of the transaction are often not disclosed.

19. Which of the following are disadvantages of the industry method?

    a. Different sources may provide different rules of thumb for the same industry.
    b. The application of an uninformed rule of thumb may result in an incorrect estimate of value.
    c. While they are simplistic in their applications, rules of thumb may ignore the economic reality of the situation.
    d. All of the above.

CHAPTER 11

The Asset-Based Approach

In this chapter, I explained when to use the asset-based approach, the advantages and disadvantages of the asset-based approach, the adjusted book value method, how to communicate with other appraisers, economic obsolescence, how to find other appraisers, the liquidation value method, and the cost to create method.

1. In which situation is a tangible asset appraisal generally advisable?
   a. Valuation for a purchase price allocation.
   b. Valuation for a preferred stock interest with liquidation preferences.
   c. Valuation using a price-to-net-asset-value multiple.
   d. Valuation of an operating company as a going concern.

2. Which of the following statements is true about forced and orderly liquidations?
   a. Forced liquidation value is a premise of value used in bankruptcy proceedings.
   b. Orderly liquidation value is usually higher than forced liquidation value.
   c. Orderly liquidation value cannot be equal to forced liquidation value.
   d. Forced liquidation value is frequently used by business appraisers when valuing a company for a bank loan.

3. Which of the following is not a correct statement regarding the asset-based approach?
   a. The adjusted book value method and the asset accumulation method are two primary methods.
   b. The adjusted book value method assumes a realization of the appraised value of the company's assets as part of a going concern.
   c. If a partial interest is to be valued, the ability of that interest to cause the sale of the company's assets is not relevant.
   d. The adjusted book value method is best suited to a company that has no significant intangible assets.

4. In which circumstance is valuing a minority interest using an asset-based approach appropriate?
   a. An asset-based approach for a minority interest is always appropriate.
   b. An asset-based approach should never be used to value a minority interest.
   c. The controlling shareholder plans to liquidate the company.
   d. The controlling shareholder has no plans to liquidate the company.

5. An advantage of an asset-based approach is:
   a. Net tangible assets can be valued reliably under this approach.
   b. This approach is applicable only for tangible assets, liabilities, and identifiable intangible assets.
   c. This approach provides the valuation analyst with the cost of duplicating the business.
   d. This approach often is time consuming because the market data about the assets and liabilities may not be readily available.

6. Which of the following methods is not solely considered an asset-based method?
   a. Adjusted book value method.
   b. Cost to create method.
   c. Excess earnings method.
   d. Liquidation value method.

Refer to the following for questions 7–11. XYZ Company, a cash-basis taxpayer, is being valued using the adjusted book value method as of December 31, 20X1. The balance sheet at that date reflected the following:

Cash	$102,000	Notes Payable (Current)	51,000
Dell Stock (1,000 shares)	22,000	Notes Payable (LT)	1,240,000
Inventory (FIFO)	45,000	Stockholder Loans	410,000
Land and Building	1,500,000	Retained Earnings	233,000
Machinery	265,000		
Total Assets	1,934,000	Total Liabilities and RE	1,934,000

7. On December 31, 20X1, Dell stock traded for a low of $33.51 and a high of $34.02. The value of this asset used in the adjusted book value method would be:
   a. $22,000.
   b. $33,765.
   c. $33,510.
   d. $34,020.

8. XYZ Company had accounts receivable of $985,000 on December 31, 20X1. The company believes 85% of its receivables are collectible. The required accounts receivable adjustment would be:
   a. $0.
   b. $147,750.
   c. $837,250.
   d. $985,000.

9. XYZ Company provides detailed summaries of its inventory. On the LIFO basis, the value of the inventory is $12,000. The company believes $5,000 of its inventory is obsolete. The value of this asset used in the adjusted book value method would be:

   a. $7,000.
   b. $12,000.
   c. $40,000.
   d. $45,000.

10. At the valuation analyst's request, XYZ Company had valuations performed of its real estate and machinery. ABC Appraisals valued the subject company's land and building at $2,200,000 and the machinery at $142,000 due to inoperable machinery. The total value of the land and building and machinery used in the adjusted book value method would be:

    a. Machinery $142,000; Land and building $2,200,000.
    b. Machinery $142,000; Land and building $1,500,000.
    c. Machinery $265,000; Land and building $2,200,000.
    d. Machinery $265,000; Land and building $1,500,000.

11. XYZ Company's stockholder loan has been on the books at $410,000 since 20X1 when the company needed additional capital to purchase its current office. The company has paid no interest to the owner and has accrued no interest on the loan. According to management, the company has made no payments and will not be making payments in the near future. The value of this liability in the adjusted book value method would be:

    a. $0.
    b. $205,000.
    c. $410,000.
    d. $410,000 plus accrued interest.

12. Which of the following entities is most likely to be valued using an asset-based approach?

    a. Retail company.
    b. Accounting firm.
    c. Manufacturing company.
    d. Doctor practice.

13. Which of the following is a disadvantage of the asset-based approach?

    a. Net tangible assets can be valued more reliably under this approach than under the other two approaches.
    b. This approach is readily applicable to tangible assets.
    c. This approach creates a better reflection of the economic balance sheet of the appraisal subject.
    d. Net tangible assets can generally be seen and felt, giving the user of the appraisal a warmer feeling about the value.

14. Which term assumes that the asset will be sold?

   a. Replacement cost new.
   b. Reproduction cost new.
   c. Fair market value in place in use.
   d. Fair market value in exchange.

15. Which of the following is not a cost of liquidation?

   a. Commissions.
   b. Property taxes.
   c. Legal and accounting costs.
   d. Administrative costs and losses that many continue during liquidation.

16. Which method is useful for valuing intangibles such as customer lists, engineering drawings, and music libraries?

   a. The adjusted book value method.
   b. The liquidation value method.
   c. The cost to create method.
   d. All of the above.

17. In which situation is an asset-based approach generally advisable?

   a. Valuation of a not-for-profit organization.
   b. Valuation of a service industry company.
   c. Valuation of equity on a minority basis.
   d. Valuation of an operating company with intangible value.

18. Which of the following statements is true about forced and orderly liquidation?

   a. Forced liquidation value is usually higher than orderly liquidation value.
   b. Orderly liquidation value is usually higher than forced liquidation value.
   c. Orderly liquidation implies fire sale conditions.
   d. Forced liquidation value is always the same as orderly liquidation value.

19. Under the asset-based approach to valuing a company, which of the following statements is an argument for not tax-affecting the write-up of assets to fair market value?

   a. Buyers often pay less for stock than assets because of the trapped-in capital gain and because they cannot get a stepped-up basis.
   b. Because of the repeal of the general utilities doctrine, the assets cannot be transferred out of the corporation without incurring the tax.
   c. Tax can be permanently deferred, or deferred for a long time.
   d. A corporation will incur a tax when the assets are sold.

20. When going from cash basis of accounting to accrual basis, when should accounts receivable be tax affected?

   a. Accounts receivable should never be tax affected.
   b. Accounts receivable should always be tax affected.
   c. Accounts receivable should be tax affected if there is a likelihood that taxes would be paid by the entity on this adjustment.
   d. Accounts receivable are approximately the same at the beginning and end of each period.

21. An example of an identifiable intangible asset that should be included on the balance sheet of an asset-based method would be:
    a. Computer software.
    b. Assembled workforce.
    c. Architectural drawings.
    d. All of the above are identifiable intangible assets.

22. XYZ Manufacturing currently has a 5-year transferrable lease at a rate of $15 per square foot. The company has rented the facility for more than 30 years, and, for doing so, the lessor has discounted the required rental payments. Fair market rent for similar properties is $18 per square foot. How should this leasehold interest be treated for an asset-based approach?
    a. This contract should be treated as an asset at the present value of future benefits to the lessee.
    b. This contract should be treated as a liability at the present value of future liabilities to the lessee.
    c. This contract would affect only profitability; therefore, there is no balance sheet adjustment.
    d. This contract has value only if it can be extended longer than the current 5-year period.

23. The theoretical basis for the adjusted book value method is:
    a. The principle of supply and demand.
    b. The principle of alternatives.
    c. The principle of substitution.
    d. The principle of future benefits.

24. Which of the following has the highest designation of members who are experienced in the valuation and analysis of commercial, industrial, residential, and other types of properties and are qualified to advise clients on real estate investment decisions?
    a. SRPA.
    b. SRA.
    c. MAI.
    d. IFA.

25. Which of the following is generally not adjusted in performing a valuation by the adjusted net asset method?
    a. Cash.
    b. Accounts receivable.
    c. Inventory.
    d. Fixed assets.

26. What type of value is typically developed utilizing the asset-based method?
    a. Minority, marketable.
    b. Controlling, marketable.
    c. Minority, nonmarketable.
    d. Controlling, nonmarketable.

27. Which court case discusses giving primary consideration to the earnings of the company regardless of the assets in valuing a minority interest?
    a. *Estate of Joyce C. Hall v. Commissioner.*
    b. *Charles S. Foltz v. U.S. News & World Report, Inc.*
    c. *Estate of Samuel I. Newhouse v. Commissioner.*
    d. *Bernard Mandelbaum, et al. v. IRS Commissioner.*

28. Which of the following statements is true?
    a. The liquidation method should never be considered if the business is not contemplating liquidation.
    b. The liquidation method can be used regardless of whether the ownership being valued has the ability to liquidate.
    c. The liquidation method should be considered when the highest and best use of the property is to liquidate.
    d. The forced liquidation method allows three to six months to sell.

CHAPTER 12

The Income Approach

In this chapter, I explained when to use the income approach, advantages and disadvantages of using the income approach, using pretax or after-tax information, valuing invested capital instead of equity, the capitalization of benefits method, the discounted future benefits method, and the excess earnings method.

1. What is the formula used for the capitalization method?
   a. Year 0 benefit stream × (1 + Growth Rate)/(Discount Rate – Growth Rate).
   b. Year 0 benefit stream × [1/(Discount Rate – Growth Rate)].
   c. Year 0 benefit stream × (1 – Growth Rate)/(Discount Rate – Growth Rate).
   d. Year 0 benefit stream × [1 /(Discount Rate + Growth Rate)].

2. Why is cash flow from operations an incomplete measure of performance?
   a. It does not include depreciation and amortization.
   b. It does not account for replacement of physical assets.
   c. It can be manipulated by issuing new stock.
   d. It does not take into account changes in working capital.

3. Which statement best describes the basic premise of the income approach?
   a. An investor will demand a market rate of return.
   b. The investment amount is determined based on the cash flows.
   c. The fair market value of an asset is the present value of its expected cash flows.
   d. The fair market value of an asset is based on the investors other portfolio holdings.

4. Which of the following is not one of the commonly used methods within the income approach?
   a. Discounted future benefits model.
   b. Capital asset pricing model.
   c. Single-period capitalization model.
   d. Gordon growth model.

5. Using the following assumptions, what is the market value of equity using the capitalized net cash flow method?
   Assumptions:

   Earnings before interest and taxes—$1,500,000

   Annual working capital requirements—$200,000

Annual depreciation—$250,000

Annual capital expenditures—$350,000

Interest-bearing debt—$2,000,000

Cost of debt—8.0%

Weighted average cost of capital (WACC)—20%

Tax rate—40%

Long-term growth rate—3%

a. $1.6 million.
b. $2.8 million.
c. $3.6 million.
d. $5.3 million.

6. Which of the following statements regarding the excess earnings method is not true?

a. Most analysts agree that the required return on tangible assets is dependent upon the asset mix.

b. Intangible assets should be removed prior to performing the excess earnings analysis.

c. This method is more appropriate for a business with a material investment in tangible assets than a business with only minor tangible assets.

d. The direct capitalization rate applicable to excess earnings normally would have to be lower than the company's required equity rate.

7. For purposes of the following equation:

NCF^5 = Net cash flow expected in the fifth year of the projection period

k = Discount rate

g = Expected long-term sustainable growth rate, beginning with the last year of the projection as the base year

Which of the following is a correct equation to calculate the terminal value using a midyear discounting convention in a five-year discounted cash flow (DCF) model?

a. $\dfrac{NCF^5 (1+g)}{(k-g)(1+k)^5}$

b. $\dfrac{NCF^5 (1+g)}{(k-g)(1+k)^{4.5}}$

c. $\dfrac{NCF^5 (1+g)^{0.5}}{(k-g)(1+k)^5}$

d. $\dfrac{NCF^5 (1+g)(1+k)^{0.5}}{(k-g)(1+k)^{4.5}}$

8. What is the market value of invested capital on a controlling interest basis using the capitalized cash flow method assuming the following?

Assumptions:

Reported minority interest net cash flow—$1,000,000

Excess compensation—$500,000

Tax rate—40%

WACC—15%

Long-term growth rate—5%

   a. $9,100,000.
   b. $10,000,000.
   c. $13,650,000.
   d. $15,750,000.

9. Which of the following is not a primary growth consideration when using the discounted cash flow method?

   a. Inflation must be accounted for separately.
   b. Growth rates in the subject company's industry.
   c. An analysis of the subject company's historical growth.
   d. The analyst needs to estimate sustainable growth into perpetuity.

10. In the application of the capitalization of excess earnings method for the purpose of valuing equity, which of the following statements is most appropriate?

   a. Nonoperating assets should be excluded from the determination of value.
   b. When valuing a minority interest, nonoperating assets should be included in calculating the return on tangible assets.
   c. Nonoperating assets (and the related income) should generally be excluded from the calculation of the return on tangible assets.
   d. The cost basis of the net tangible assets is utilized in calculating the expected return on tangible assets.

11. Which of the following formulas correctly calculates the present value of net cash flows based on an August 31 valuation date using an end-of-year convention? The initial forecast period runs from September 30 to December 31 and the following periods are calendar years.

   a. $PV = NCF1/(1+k)^{.333} + NCF2/(1+k)^{1.333} + NCF3/(1+k)^{2.333} + ...$
   b. $PV = NCF1/(1+k)^{.666} + NCF2/(1+k)^{1.666} + NCF3/(1+k)^{2.666} + ...$
   c. $PV = NCF1/(1+k)^{.333} + NCF2/(1+k)^{1.0} + NCF3/(1+k)^{2.0} + ...$
   d. $PV = NCF1/(1+k)^{.666} + NCF2/(1+k)^{1.332} + NCF3/(1+k)^{1.998} + ...$

12. Which of the following statements is true regarding the level of value arrived at through the use of the discounted cash flow method?

   a. Most of the difference between minority and control results from differences in the projected cash flows.
   b. Add-backs for excess compensation paid to the controlling shareholder are necessary to arrive at a minority interest conclusion.
   c. The discounted cash flow method results in a minority interest value because the discount rate is derived from minority trades in publicly traded stocks.

    d. The discounted cash flow method results in a controlling interest conclusion because the controlling shareholder has control over the selected capital structure.

13. Determine the market value of invested capital of a company with the following net cash flow earned ratably throughout each of the noted years using the assumed discount rate and terminal growth rate.

    Net Cash Flow to Invested Capital:

Year 1	Year 2	Year 3	Year 4	Year 5
$2,500	$2,700	$3,025	$3,328	$3,600

    Assumptions:

    WACC—15%

    Terminal growth rate—3%

    a. $23.2 million.
    b. $23.5 million.
    c. $24.8 million.
    d. $25.3 million.

14. Which of the following statements is most correct regarding the excess earnings method?

    a. Pretax benefit streams are used in the excess earnings method when the cap rate is built up from Duff & Phelps data.
    b. The excess earnings method is most often applied to the owner's discretionary cash flow; thus all officer compensation should be excluded from the benefit stream capitalized.
    c. For cash-basis businesses, it is incorrect to tax-affect the accounts receivable and inventory.
    d. Poor performance can give rise to "negative goodwill," and thus the total value of the company's tangible assets may have to be reduced.

15. Under which circumstance would it be most appropriate to use the capitalization of earnings method?

    a. Predictable but uneven expected future earnings.
    b. Intermediate-term abnormal growth in earnings.
    c. Stable growth in earnings.
    d. Erratic and unpredictable changes in expected earnings.

16. All of the following are advantages of the income approach except:

    a. It requires a simple mathematical application that is frequently performed more quickly relative to the other approaches.
    b. Minimal judgment is needed in choosing the correct capitalization or discount rates.
    c. It values an enterprise based on its ability to generate earnings or cash flow.
    d. Financial markets frequently use the income approach in the decision-making process.

17. When creating or using forecasts, how far into the future should forecasts go?

    a. Until they represent sustainable future levels of income for the company.
    b. Two years.
    c. Five years.
    d. Ten years.

18. If forecasts prepared by the client seem to be flat, the appraiser should:

    a. Not use the forecasts, because they are unreliable.
    b. Use the forecasts and add a limiting condition to the report.
    c. Use a single-period model.
    d. Automatically eliminate this method with no further work.

19. Which value is the highest—a benefit stream of $25,000 with a cap rate of 20%, a benefit stream of $37,500 with a cap rate of 30%, or a benefit stream of $31,250 with a cap rate of 25%.

    a. Benefit stream of $25,000.
    b. Benefit stream of $31,250.
    c. Benefit stream of $37,500.
    d. They are all the same.

20. When using a discounted cash flow (DCF) model, the terminal-year capitalized value is often:

    a. The most significant component of the total value.
    b. Calculated as asset liquidation value.
    c. Calculated by using exit multiples, which make it a pure income approach.
    d. Of little significance since it is so far out into the future.

21. Which of the following statements about the excess earnings method is true?

    a. It is often preferred due to the many industry sources of information on required rates of return.
    b. Revenue Ruling 68-609 specifically stated that a return of 8% to 10% on tangible assets must be utilized.
    c. This method implies a control valuation.
    d. Nonoperating income and expenses should be included in the income stream.

22. The traditional discounted cash flow method includes all of the following except:

    a. Discount rate.
    b. A single period of expected cash flows.
    c. Prospective cash flows.
    d. Terminal value.

23. In which circumstance is using a simple average of historical earnings/cash flow in the capitalization of cash flow method appropriate?

    a. Cash flow is cyclical in nature and erratic.
    b. Cash flow is increasing steadily.
    c. Cash flow is declining steadily.
    d. The simple average should never be used; instead a weighted average should be used.

24. The discounted cash flow method is most often used when:
    a. Valuing very small companies.
    b. The company's performance is not currently at a normalized level.
    c. The company's future performance is expected to follow the past.
    d. Creating value in a company that is not currently earning income.

25. Capitalization is defined as:
    a. A single-period valuation model that converts a benefits stream into value by dividing the benefits stream by a rate of return that is adjusted for growth.
    b. A single-period valuation model that converts a benefits stream into value by dividing the benefits stream by a rate of return that does not consider growth.
    c. A multiperiod valuation model that converts revenue into value by dividing the revenue stream by a rate of return.
    d. A multiperiod valuation model that converts a future series of benefit streams into value by discounting them to present value.

26. Net cash flow for invested capital includes the returns available to all of the following classes of investor except:
    a. Common stockholders.
    b. Debt holders.
    c. Preferred stockholders.
    d. Trade creditors.

27. Revenue Ruling 68-609 was issued to correct which of the following?
    a. Revenue Ruling 59-60.
    b. Misinterpretations regarding the use of the excess earnings method.
    c. The manner in which to value small businesses.
    d. The income approach.

28. When selecting a benefit stream, special attention should be paid to which of the following?
    a. The nature of the business and its capital structure.
    b. The purpose and function of the appraisal.
    c. The particular subject of the valuation.
    d. All of the above.

29. The terminal value represents:
    a. The value at the point in time in which growth stops.
    b. The value at the point in time in which the business is in a stabilized and sustainable condition.
    c. The value at the point in time prior to accelerated growth.
    d. The value obtained using the discounted future benefits method.

30. The excess earnings method is:
    a. An income approach.
    b. An asset approach.
    c. A market approach.
    d. A hybrid of the income and asset approaches.

31. Which of the following is the best situation for using Revenue Ruling 68-609 as a primary value indicator?

    a. Valuing goodwill for most closely held entities.
    b. Primarily when no better methods are indicated.
    c. Primarily when valuing professional practices.
    d. Mostly for valuing smaller, less profitable entities.

32. The value derived under the income approach represents the value of:

    a. The operating assets of the company.
    b. The operating assets less liabilities of the company.
    c. The total assets of the company.
    d. The total assets less total liabilities of the company.

33. Which represents the highest value?

    a. Benefit stream of $100,000 and a capitalization rate of 15%.
    b. Benefit stream of $100,000 and a capitalization rate of 25%.
    c. Benefit stream of $200,000 and a capitalization rate of 25%.
    d. Benefit stream of $200,000 and a capitalization rate of 35%.

34. ABC, Inc. has net tangible assets of $1,000,000. The company expects a return of 12% on these assets. ABC's estimated future income is $1,200,000 and the valuation analyst has determined an appropriate capitalization rate of 30%. What is the total entity value using the excess earnings method?

    a. $3,333,333.
    b. $3,600,000.
    c. $4,000,000.
    d. $4,600,000.

35. Discounting is defined as follows:

    a. A single-period valuation model that converts a benefits stream into value by dividing the benefits stream by a rate of return that is adjusted for growth.
    b. A single-period valuation model that converts a benefits stream into value by dividing the benefits stream by a rate of return that does not consider growth.
    c. A multiperiod valuation model that converts revenue into value by discounting the revenue stream by a rate of return.
    d. A multiperiod valuation model that converts a future series of benefit streams into value by discounting them to present value.

36. Which of the following is the main difference between basic cash flow and cash flow for invested capital?

    a. Invested capital cash flow adds or subtracts debt borrowings or repayments, which are not considered for basic cash flow.
    b. Basic cash flow subtracts anticipated capital expenditures, which are not considered for invested capital cash flow.
    c. Invested capital cash flow adds back interest expense, which is not considered for basic cash flow.
    d. Basic cash flow subtracts preferred stock dividends, which are not considered for invested capital cash flow.

37. In which of the following valuations is using forecasted benefit streams most likely?

    a. A business that is growing at 4% and expects to continue at this rate in the future.

    b. A business that has erratic income streams.

    c. A business that has flat income streams.

    d. A business that is growing at an exceptionally high rate.

Use the following information for questions 38 and 39.

ABC, LLC's most recent financial statements reflect the following information:

Revenue—$1,000,000

Increase in Revenue—$50,000

Normalized Net Income—$85,000

Depreciation Expense—$94,000

Interest Expense—$30,000

Capital Expenditures—$110,000

New Debt Borrowings—$50,000

Principal Repayment—$40,000

Working Capital Requirements—$20,000

Tax Rate—40%

38. What is the net cash flow to common equity?

    a. $59,000.

    b. $67,000.

    c. $69,000.

    d. $79,000.

39. What is the net cash flow to invested capital?

    a. $59,000.

    b. $67,000.

    c. $69,000.

    d. $79,000.

40. When using forecasts of cash flow in a DCF model, the value obtained is:

    a. Control because it is the entire expected cash flow of the company.

    b. Minority because the discount rate is based on minority data.

    c. Control if adjustments are made to the cash flow for control perks.

    d. Control if a WACC is used at the optimal capital structure.

41. When using the DCF model in valuing a company that is expected to grow revenue and income, it is important to:

    a. Match the revenue and earnings growth with the capital needed to fuel that growth.

    b. Calculate a different WACC each year to reflect the change in capital structure.

    c. Subtract growth from the discount rate each year before discounting interim cash flows.

    d. Use only book depreciation to calculate cash flow since it is based on more realistic economic lives than depreciation based on tax depreciation.

Use the following case study to answer questions 42–44.

Case Study: ABC Dental Care, Inc.
Historical Income Statements
for the Years Ended December 31,

	20X1	20X2	20X3	20X4
Revenues	1,683,561	1,832,504	1,900,917	1,911,743
Operating Expenses				
Direct Costs	355,647	352,999	331,146	416,615
Officers' Compensation	125,467	78,436	51,820	33,328
Salaries and Wages	670,554	733,293	766,812	796,004
Depreciation	14,986	16,691	31,736	32,889
Other Operating Expenses	292,146	296,080	320,345	277,062
Total Operating Expenses	1,458,800	1,477,499	1,501,859	1,555,898
Income from Operations	224,761	355,005	399,058	355,845
Other Expenses				
Interest	15,946	16,715	14,033	25,379
Pretax Income	208,815	338,290	385,025	330,466
Income Taxes	–	–	–	–
Net Income	208,815	338,290	385,025	330,466

Balance Sheet Information

	20X1	20X2	20X3	20X4
Current Assets	387,593	805,785	504,862	722,974
Fixed Assets (Net)	63,277	30,303	43,895	33,091
Other Tangible Assets	1,300	597	597	729
Current Liabilities	19,413	17,841	19,485	21,444
Long-Term Liabilities	133,141	199,114	287,732	254,202

Normalization Adjustments and Other Information

Income Statement

	20X1	20X2	20X3	20X4
Historic Net Income	208,815	338,290	385,025	330,466
Officers' Compensation	(57,068)	(109,744)	(142,180)	(166,672)
Other Expenses	19,538	21,023	16,043	93,642
Adjusted Pretax Income	171,285	249,569	258,888	257,436
Income Taxes	55,798	88,955	91,022	90,911
Adjusted Net Income	115,487	160,614	167,866	166,525

Case Study: ABC Dental Care, Inc.
Historical Income Statements
for the Years Ended December 31, (continued)
Normalization Adjustments and Other Information

	20X1	20X2	20X3	20X4
Balance Sheet				
Fixed Assets				
Depreciated Replacement Cost				102,000
Liquidation Value				
Orderly				62,000
Forced				31,000
Rates as of December 31, 20X4				
20-Year Treasury Bonds				5.50%
Equity Risk Premium				7.00%
Micro-Cap Equity Risk Premium				3.50%
Prime Rate				3.75%
Industry Return of Net Assets				9.00%
Specific Company Risk Premium				2.00%
Increment to Convert Cash Flow to Earnings				3.00%
Long-Term Growth Rates				
Revenues				3.00%
Net Income				4.00%
Net Cash Flow				5.00%

42. Calculate the equity discount rate to be applied to net income using the buildup method.

   a. 17.50%.
   b. 18.00%.
   c. 21.00%.
   d. 19.00%.

43. Assume that the average of the most recent two years is expected to resemble the forecasted net income for the company. Calculate the value of equity, using a single-period capitalization model.

   a. $983,500.
   b. $1,023,000.
   c. $1,242,000.
   d. $1,288,000.

44. Assuming that depreciation and interest expense is at a normalized amount, calculate normalized EBIT for 20X4.

    a. $388,734.
    b. $224,793.
    c. $315,704.
    d. $282,815.

45. If forecasts prepared by the client seem unreliable, the valuation analyst should:

    a. Use the forecasts anyway; the client knows their business the best.
    b. Use the forecasts and add a limiting condition to the report.
    c. Prepare a forecast independently.
    d. Eliminate the use of this method.

46. Which of the following is important in applying a terminal-year value in the discounted cash flow method?

    a. Book value.
    b. Using anticipated inflation plus population growth as the growth rate.
    c. Normalizing depreciation and capital expenditures.
    d. Using real GDP as the growth rate.

CHAPTER 13

Discount and Capitalization Rates

In this chapter, I explained discount and capitalization rates in general, the use of pretax or after-tax rates, the factors that affect the selection of a discount rate, the components of a discount rate, the buildup method, the capital asset pricing model (CAPM), alternatives to the buildup method and CAPM, the factors that affect the selection of a capitalization rate, and the data sources for discount and capitalization rates.

1. Which of the following is a primary source of data on beta?

   a. *Stocks, Bonds, Bills, and Inflation Yearbook*.
   b. *Mergerstat Review*.
   c. Institute of Business Appraisers (IBA) market database.
   d. *Value Line Investment Survey*.

2. Which of the following factors will have the most influence in estimating company-specific risk using the capital asset pricing model (CAPM)?

   a. The ability of the management team to execute on key deliverables.
   b. Unanticipated capital expenditures.
   c. Restrictions on the transferability of the common shares.
   d. Macroenvironmental forces, including economic and political forces.

3. In estimating a discount rate, which of the following attributes would probably give rise to an increased premium for industry risk?

   a. Low barriers to entry.
   b. High product switching costs.
   c. Lack of foreseeable substitute products.
   d. Low bargaining power of the subject company's suppliers.

4. In general, why does company-specific risk assessment matter more in valuing small companies than in valuing larger ones?

   a. Research shows that size of firm and risk vary inversely.
   b. Risk decreases as company size decreases.
   c. Risk and size of company are positively correlated.
   d. Company-specific risk is inherent in a beta adjustment and the small stock premium.

5. Which of the following characteristics is associated with the arithmetic average equity risk premium?

   a. It does not account for the uncertainty of returns.
   b. It represents the compound average historical return.
   c. Each year's return is independent of the other years' returns.
   d. It tends to be smaller than the geometric equity risk premium.

6. At the macroenvironmental level, unsystematic risk is a function of all of the following except:

   a. Economic risk.
   b. Demographic risk.
   c. Political risk.
   d. Management risk.

7. Evaluating a subject company's unsystematic risk at the macroenvironmental level includes considering all of the following except:

   a. Demographic risk.
   b. Rivalry among competitors.
   c. Sociocultural trends.
   d. Technological forces.

8. Which of the following statements is generally true regarding the selection of the proper capital structure to be used in a fair market value calculation of weighted average cost of capital (WACC)?

   a. One should use the company's actual debt in place when valuing a control interest.
   b. One should use the industry's debt structure when valuing a minority interest.
   c. One should use the company's actual debt in place when valuing a minority interest.
   d. One should not use the industry's capital structure.

9. When deriving a discount rate by using the CAPM, which of the following items does beta represent?

   a. A measure of covariance or measure of systematic risk.
   b. A measure of covariance or measure of unsystematic risk.
   c. A measure of variance or measure of market risk.
   d. A measure of variance or measure of company-specific risk.

10. Which of the following is an example of systematic risk?

    a. An expected downward industry trend.
    b. Customer concentration risk.
    c. Product obsolescence.
    d. Interest rate risk.

11. Which of the following is commonly adjusted for prior to applying beta in the capital asset pricing model?

    a. Different financial reporting services provide different estimates of beta for the same industry and for the same individual security.

    b. Published betas for publicly traded stocks reflect the actual capital structure of each respective company.

    c. Financial reporting services use different market indexes of the market risk premium.

    d. Measurement intervals vary.

12. The valuation assignment requires the value of a company with three equal and unrelated shareholders for the estate tax return of one of the shareholders. Determine the weighted average cost of capital using the following assumptions and the CAPM applicable to this assignment.

    Assumptions:

    Tax rate—40%

    Industry beta—1.2

    Risk-free rate—4.0%

    Prime interest rate—6.0%

    Small stock premium—6.0%

    Equity risk premium—7.0%

    Industry capital structure—20% debt

    Book value—$50.0 million

    Interest-bearing debt—$10.0 million

    Company's weighted average cost of debt—7.5%

    Market value of total invested capital—$80.0 million

    a. 14.5%.

    b. 15.6%.

    c. 16.7%.

    d. 17.0%.

13. If a security has a price below the security market line, it represents:

    a. An appropriately priced security.

    b. The expected return on the market.

    c. A price based on inefficient capital markets.

    d. The expected return for the individual security.

14. Which of the following statements regarding the security market line is true?

    a. The security market line assumes efficient capital markets.

    b. A security is mispriced if it lies on the security market line.

    c. The CAPM is not relevant to the security market line.

    d. The security market line is a regression of the standard deviation of returns.

15. Using the CAPM with a risk-free rate of 6.0%, a market equity risk premium of 8.0%, a size premium of 2.0%, and a beta of 0.9, to what extent is the expected return adjusted for the investment's systematic risk?
    a. –0.60%.
    b. –0.80%.
    c. –1.40%.
    d. –1.60%.

16. Jones Corporation issued preferred stock that pays $0.75 each quarter. The issue is currently trading at $75 per share. Jones Corporation's common stock has a dividend of $0.25 per quarter, and it is currently trading at $45 per share. What is the return on the preferred stock that would be a component of Jones Corporation's WACC?
    a. 2.22%.
    b. 3.33%.
    c. 4.00%.
    d. 6.67%.

17. Which of the following is not an expected rate of return?
    a. WACC.
    b. Discount rate.
    c. Capitalization rate.
    d. All of the above are expected rate of returns.

18. Which of the following statements is true?
    a. As the discount rate increases, the entity value increases.
    b. As the discount rate decreases, the entity value decreases.
    c. As the discount rate increases, the entity value decreases.
    d. As the growth rate increases, the capitalization rate increases.

The following information provided for ABC, Inc. should be used for questions 19 and 20.

Risk-free rate—4%

Expected rate of inflation—2%

Return on the stock market—12%

Size premium—5%

Specific company risk—2%

Expected growth rate—5%

19. What is the equity risk premium of ABC, Inc.?
    a. 4%.
    b. 6%.
    c. 8%.
    d. 12%.

20. What is the discount rate of ABC, Inc.?
    a. 14%.
    b. 19%.
    c. 21%.
    d. 23%.

21. According to the Duff and Phelps study, high financial risk includes all of the following except:
    a. Companies that are in bankruptcy or liquidation.
    b. Companies that show a loss in the most recent year.
    c. Companies that have negative book value.
    d. Companies that have a debt-to-capital ratio greater than 80%.

The following information provided for XYZ, Inc. should be used for questions 22 and 23.

	XYZ, Inc.	Public Co., Inc.
Total Debt	$4,000,000	$25,000,000
Total Equity	$6,000,000	$42,000,000
Levered Beta	unknown	1.2

Both XYZ, Inc. and Public Co., Inc. have a marginal tax rate of 40% and expected growth of 5%.

22. Using the Hamada formula, what is the unlevered beta of Public Co., Inc.?
    a. 0.72.
    b. 0.75.
    c. 0.88.
    d. 0.79.

23. Assuming the unlevered beta is calculated to be 0.95, what is the levered beta of XYZ, Inc.?
    a. 0.68.
    b. 0.70.
    c. 1.33.
    d. 1.17.

24. CAPM includes all of the following assumptions except:
    a. Investors are risk averse.
    b. All investors have different investment time horizons.
    c. There are no investment-related taxes or transaction costs.
    d. Investors seek to hold efficient portfolios.

25. Which of the following is not a component of weighted average cost of capital?
    a. Cost of debt capital.
    b. Growth.
    c. Percentage of equity capital.
    d. Effective income tax rate.

The following information is for questions 26 and 27.

ABC Company has current-year normalized net income of $125,000 and net cash flow of $175,000. Further, the discount rate for the equity was determined to be 22% and the growth rate is assumed to be 4%.

26. What is the calculated value using a capitalization method?

  a. $934,829.
  b. $827,273.
  c. $972,222.
  d. $1,011,111.

27. What is the discount rate for earnings?

  a. 11.7%.
  b. 15.7%.
  c. 18.0%.
  d. 22.0%.

28. Which of the following investments requires the highest rate of return?

  a. Treasury bills.
  b. Venture capital.
  c. Small-cap stocks.
  d. Junk bonds.

29. When selecting the risk-free rate of return, what term do most valuation analysts consider when selecting the Treasury bond rate?

  a. 3 months.
  b. 1 year.
  c. 10 years.
  d. 20 years.

The information provided next is for ABC, Inc. and is used for question 30.

Risk-free rate—5%

Return on the stock market—135%

Industry risk premium—2%

Size premium—5%

Specific company risk—3%

Expected growth rate—5%

Beta—1.3

30. What is the discount rate of ABC, Inc. using the modified CAPM for closely held companies?

  a. 21.0%.
  b. 23.4%.
  c. 24.9%.
  d. 25.4%.

31. Which of the following is not a component of the modified CAPM for closely held companies?

    a. Risk-free rate.
    b. Specific company risk.
    c. Specific industry risk.
    d. Beta.

32. Private Co., Inc. has an unlevered beta of 1.2, debt of $4,000,000, equity of $12,000,000, a tax rate of 40%, and expected growth of 5%. What is Private Co., Inc.'s levered beta using the Hamada formula?

    a. 0.96.
    b. 1.00.
    c. 1.44.
    d. 1.60.

33. ABC, Inc. participates in the widget production industry. The widget production industry has a price-to-earnings ratio of 5. ABC, Inc. expects continued growth to be 4%. Which of the following is correct?

    a. ABC, Inc.'s capitalization rate is 24%.
    b. ABC, Inc.'s discount rate is 20%.
    c. ABC, Inc.'s capitalization rate is 20%.
    d. ABC, Inc.'s discount rate is 16%.

The information provided next is for questions 34–36.

    XYZ's Company's interest rate is 10% and its tax rate is 35% with a long-term expected annual growth rate of 4%. The company's total notes payable is $5,000,000 and its total stockholders' equity (book) is $7,000,000. The market value of equity equals twice its total debt.

34. What is XYZ Company's capitalization rate using WACC assuming the cost of equity is 20%?

    a. 10.37%.
    b. 11.50%.
    c. 14.37%.
    d. 15.50%.

35. What is XYZ Company's discount rate using WACC, assuming the cost of equity is 25%?

    a. 14.84%.
    b. 17.29%.
    c. 18.67%.
    d. 18.84%.

36. Capitalization rates are founded on which principle?

    a. The principle of supply and demand.
    b. The principle of alternatives.
    c. The principle of substitution.
    d. The principle of future benefits.

37. The Harris-Pringle formulas are consistent with the theory that:
    a. Discount rate used to calculate the tax shield equals the cost of debt capital (the tax shield has the same risk as debt).
    b. Debt capital has negligible risk that interest payments and principal repayments will not be made when owed, which infers that tax deductions on the interest expense will be realized in the period in which the interest is paid (beta of debt capital equals zero).
    c. The market value of debt capital remains at a constant percentage of equity capital, which is equivalent to saying that debt increases in proportion to the net cash flow of the firm (net cash flow to invested capital) in every period.
    d. Value of the tax shield is proportionate to the value of the market value of debt capital (value of tax shield).

CHAPTER 14

Premiums and Discounts (Valuation Adjustments)—Part I

In this chapter, I explained valuation premiums and discounts in general, control premiums, lack of control (minority) discounts, discounts from net asset value, discounts for embedded capital gains, and nonvoting stock discounts.

1. Which is not a true statement about control premiums derived from *Mergerstat Review*?

   a. The value of synergies is included in the *Mergerstat Review* control premiums.

   b. *Mergerstat Review* data include compiled information on actual completed transactions by industry.

   c. The control premiums derived from *Mergerstat Review* should be applied to the subject company's market value of total invested capital.

   d. The control premium should not be added to a value indication from a discounted cash flow analysis that adds the controlling shareholder's perquisites.

2. Which factor determines whether the income approach produces a controlling or minority value?

   a. The equity risk premium.

   b. The level of the cash flows.

   c. The discount rate used.

   d. The interest being valued.

3. A control premium is often applied in the valuation of equity interests representing more than 50% ownership but less than absolute control. Which of the following factors will not typically affect the size of the control premium in such a valuation?

   a. Cumulative versus noncumulative voting rights.

   b. The distribution of equity ownership.

   c. State statutes in the state of incorporation.

   d. Historical levels of dividend distributions.

4. Which of the following is not a valuation adjustment considered in business valuations?

   a. Control discount.
   b. Embedded capital gains discount.
   c. Blockage discount.
   d. Nonvoting stock discount.

5. The type of value estimate yielded by the adjusted book value method is:

   a. Minority and marketable.
   b. Control and marketable.
   c. Minority and nonmarketable.
   d. Control and nonmarketable.

6. Which formula is used to convert a control premium into a lack of control discount?

   a. $1 - [1/(1 - \text{Control premium})]$.
   b. $1 + [1/(1 + \text{Control premium})]$.
   c. $1 - [1/(1 + \text{Control premium})]$.
   d. $1 + [1/(1 - \text{Control premium})]$.

7. The discount for embedded capital gains came to the forefront in valuation as a result of which of the following?

   a. The 1986 Tax Reform Act.
   b. Revenue Ruling 59-60.
   c. The same tax act that reduced capital gains taxes to 15%.
   d. Revenue Ruling 04-177.

8. Nonvoting stock at the minority level is subject to a large discount:

   a. Because voting is an important aspect of stock ownership.
   b. Rarely.
   c. Almost always.
   d. Because voting premiums are large.

9. The type of value estimate yielded by the guideline company method is:

   a. Minority and marketable.
   b. Control and marketable.
   c. Minority and nonmarketable.
   d. Control or minority and marketable.

10. Which of the following is not a prerogative of control?

   a. The ability to determine management compensation and perquisites.
   b. The ability to liquidate, dissolve, sell out, or recapitalize the company.
   c. The ability to initiate a shareholder oppression lawsuit.
   d. The ability to sell or acquire treasury shares.

11. If the control value equals $125 and the control premium equals 30%, the minority interest value would be:

    a. $87.50.
    b. $95.00.
    c. $96.15.
    d. $125.00.

12. A discount from net asset value is commonly applied to which of the following?

    a. An operating company in liquidation.
    b. A controlling interest valuation of a holding company.
    c. A minority interest in a holding company.
    d. An operating company valued as a going concern.

13. Court cases that established precedents on embedded capital gains tax with C corporations include all of the following except:

    a. *Estate of Davis.*
    b. *Estate of Hall.*
    c. *Estate of Dunn.*
    d. *Estate of Jelke.*

CHAPTER 15

Premiums and Discounts (Valuation Adjustments)—Part II

In this chapter, I explained discounts for lack of marketability, private company discounts, key person discounts, blockage discounts, other discounts and premiums, and the application of discounts and premiums.

1. The value of a 100% interest in a company is $100,000 on a marketable, minority basis, before consideration of a control premium and a discount for lack of marketability (DLOM). The control premium is determined to be 10%. The applicable discount for lack of marketability is determined to be 10%. What is the value of a 100% interest in the company on a nonmarketable basis?

   a. $100,000.
   b. $99,000.
   c. $90,000.
   d. $81,000.

2. In which situation is a blockage discount most appropriate?

   a. In the valuation of a closely held company.
   b. When 1,000,000 shares of a publicly traded stock are owned and can be sold without causing the price per share to drop.
   c. When 10,000 shares of a publicly traded stock are owned and the sale will cause the price to decline due to the average share volume being 200 shares per day.
   d. A blockage discount is not appropriate for any valuation.

3. All of the following statements are true regarding the small company discount except:

   a. Small companies sell for higher multiples than larger companies.
   b. Closely held companies may be perceived as riskier because they do not make as much reliable information available to the willing buyer as public companies do.
   c. Small companies may be less marketable because of the lack of an institutional following.
   d. The small company discount may already have been considered in the selection of multiples or capitalization rates and may be inappropriate.

4. Which of the following was not one of the major factors cited by the court in its assessment of the "discount for marketability" in the 1995 *Mandelbaum* case?

   a. Studies of equity risk premiums and size risk premiums.
   b. Restricted stock studies and preinitial public offering studies.
   c. The company's dividend policy.
   d. The strength of the company's management team.

5. Which of the following factors is generally not considered when estimating the discount for lack of marketability?

   a. A stock's potential swing vote.
   b. Prospects of sale for the interest being valued.
   c. The stockholders' agreement.
   d. The size of the interest being valued.

6. Which of the following issues would most likely result in the lowest lack of marketability discount for a limited partnership interest in a family limited partnership (FLP) that owns 100% of an S corporation?

   a. The S corporation makes quarterly income distributions.
   b. The S corporation capital expenditures are minimal.
   c. The FLP distributes most of its annual income.
   d. The FLP does not have an operating agreement.

7. Which of the following statements related to DLOM is true?

   a. A DLOM for a controlling interest will generally be lower than a DLOM for a minority interest.
   b. A DLOM for a controlling interest will generally be higher than a DLOM for a minority interest.
   c. A DLOM for a controlling interest will generally be the same as a DLOM for a minority interest.
   d. DLOMs are generally not appropriate for valuing small companies.

8. After analysis, you determine that the proper discount for lack of control is 20% and the discount for lack of marketability is 30%. The total effect of the two discounts on the subject interest being valued is:

   a. 20%.
   b. 30%.
   c. 44%.
   d. 50%.

9. Which of the following is not a restricted stock study that is commonly used to assist in determining a discount for lack of marketability?

   a. Mergerstat study.
   b. Moroney study.
   c. Willamette Management Associates study.
   d. Gelman study.

10. Rule 144 changed the holding period for nonissuers to one year effective:
    a. February 15, 2008.
    b. April 1, 1990.
    c. April 29, 1997.
    d. September 23, 1983.

11. Which of the following factors has the greatest impact on the size of the DLOM?
    a. Debt ratio.
    b. Stock volume.
    c. Trading exchange.
    d. Volatility.

12. Which of the following was not a reason for transactions to be eliminated from the fair market value (FMV) DLOM study?
    a. The private placement was of debt, preferred stock, convertible preferred stock, or some kind of hybrid equity-derivative security.
    b. The private placement was issued as part of a stock-warrant unit or had warrants attached, or detachable warrants or options were issued with the common stock.
    c. The transaction did not close.
    d. The stock was traded on a domestic exchange.

13. The quantitative marketability discount model (QMDM) indicates that the minority investor must be compensated relative to the enterprise discount rate for which of the following?
    a. Likelihood of interim cash flows.
    b. Prospects for marketability.
    c. Uncertainty regarding a favorable exit.
    d. All of the above.

14. According to the Stout DLOM study, the magnitude of the DLOM is negatively correlated with:
    a. The issuing firm's stock price volatility.
    b. The issuing firm's total assets.
    c. The block size of the placement, described as a percentage of the total ownership.
    d. The level of market volatility prevailing as of the transaction date, as measured by the VIX.

15. The QMDM contains all of the following enterprise-level assumptions except:
    a. Capitalization rate.
    b. Projected terminal value.
    c. Projected interim cash flows.
    d. Forecast period.

16. The following are all quantitative models used for measuring the DLOM except:
    a. Black-Scholes.
    b. Longstaff.
    c. Valuation Advisors.
    d. LEAPS.

17. Which of the following approaches to value apply to a stock option?
    a. Asset-based.
    b. Income.
    c. Market.
    d. None of the above.

18. Which of the following factors was not considered by Moroney in the application of a DLOM?
    a. Discount rate.
    b. Swing vote.
    c. Prospects of the corporation.
    d. High dividend yield.

19. Key person attributes include all of the following except:
    a. Strong relationships with customers.
    b. Employee loyalty to the key person.
    c. Hard work ethic.
    d. Unique marketing vision, insight, and ability.

20. Which of the following was not a reason for transactions to be eliminated from the Stout DLOM study?
    a. The private placement was of debt, preferred stock, convertible preferred stock, or some kind of hybrid equity-derivative security.
    b. The private placement was issued as part of a stock-warrant unit or had warrants attached, or detachable warrants or options were issued with the common stock.
    c. The transaction did not close.
    d. The stock was traded on a domestic exchange.

CHAPTER 16

Revenue Ruling 59-60

In this chapter, I reviewed Revenue Ruling 59-60 in detail.

1. Revenue Ruling 59-60 provides guidance primarily in the area of:
   a. The valuation approaches and methods that are always appropriate to use in valuing a business interest.
   b. The factors to be used in the determination of the marketability discount.
   c. The factors to be considered in the valuation of any business interest.
   d. The use of public company comparables as the favored method of valuation of a business contract.

2. Which of the following statements is not included in Revenue Ruling 59-60?
   a. The fair market value of specific shares of stock will remain the same as economic conditions change from "normal" to "boom" to "depression."
   b. Valuation is not an exact science. A sound valuation will be based upon all the relevant facts, but the elements of common sense, informed judgment, and reasonableness must enter into the process.
   c. Valuation of securities is, in essence, a prophecy as to the future and must be based on facts available at the required date of appraisal.
   d. The purpose of this Revenue Ruling is to outline and review in general the approach, methods, and factors to be considered in valuing shares of the capital stock of closely held corporations.

3. Which of the following statements is true according to Revenue Ruling 59-60?
   a. Valuation is a prophecy as to the future.
   b. Relying on history alone is the best predictor of value.
   c. Analysts can rely on the prices of all actively traded stocks that are selling in a free and open market.
   d. A closely held stock is traded frequently, and these transactions are the best indication of value.

4. With respect to the factor of dividend paying capacity, Revenue Ruling 59-60 states:

   a. Dividends paid in the past should be given primary consideration when valuing a controlling interest.

   b. Dividend-paying capacity should be given primary consideration when valuing a controlling interest.

   c. Dividends paid are a more reliable criterion of fair market value than other applicable factors.

   d. Revenue Ruling 59-60 does not address dividend-paying capacity.

5. Which of the following is not a consideration of fair market value conditions?

   a. There must be a willing and able buyer.

   b. There must be a willing and able seller.

   c. A reasonable period of exposure on the market.

   d. Only the seller having reasonable knowledge of the property.

6. Revenue Ruling 59-60 sets out relevant factors to consider in the valuation of the stock of closely held corporations. Which of the following is not a factor?

   a. Up to five years of prior audited financial statements.

   b. Earning capacity of the company.

   c. Book value of the stock.

   d. Size of the block of stock to be valued.

7. According to Revenue Ruling 59-60, which of the following statements is the most accurate regarding the practice of averaging different valuation methods?

   a. A prescribed formula is the most accurate method of averaging various methods of valuation.

   b. Numerical weighting of applicable methods based on identified criteria is required.

   c. No useful purpose is served by weighting or averaging several factors.

   d. Weighting is specifically prohibited by Revenue Ruling 59-60.

CHAPTER 17

The Valuation Report

In this chapter, I discussed the components of a valuation report, the types of valuation reports, the preparation of the business valuation report, the defense of the business valuation report, and common errors in business valuation reports.

1. Pursuant to Rule 26 of the Federal Rules of Civil Procedure, which of the following written disclosures is required in connection with expert testimony?
   a. The total number of hours worked on the engagement.
   b. Copies of all work papers used in developing an opinion.
   c. A list of all publications authored by the witness within the last 10 years.
   d. The name, address, age, and Social Security number of the witness.

2. Under which of the following circumstances would providing an oral report be insufficient?
   a. Deposition testimony.
   b. Consultation or special use report.
   c. Report for a sophisticated client user.
   d. Expert opinion subject to Rule 26 of the Federal Rules of Civil Procedure.

3. As defined by the Statement on Standards for Valuation Services (SSVS) No. 1, all of the following are types of written reports except:
   a. Appraisal report.
   b. Detailed report.
   c. Summary report.
   d. Calculation report.

4. All of the following sections are required in a detailed valuation report by SSVS except:
   a. Assumptions and limiting conditions.
   b. Subsequent events.
   c. Valuation approaches and methods considered.
   d. Qualifications of the valuation analyst.

5. As defined by SSVS, what type of report should be issued for a calculation engagement?

   a. Valuation report.
   b. Calculation report.
   c. Detailed report.
   d. Summary report.

6. All of the following should be included in the description of the assignment section of the report except:

   a. Analysis of the subject entity.
   b. A complete description of the appraisal subject.
   c. Effective date of the appraisal.
   d. Purpose and function of the appraisal.

7. Which of the following is not a common error in a business valuation report?

   a. Using a capitalization rate of 75% but properly including an argument for its validity.
   b. Using guideline public companies that are so much larger than the appraisal subject that a true comparison cannot be made.
   c. Reaching a conclusion that does not make sense.
   d. Excluding financial analysis from the report.

8. Which of the following is considered the best way to reconcile the values?

   a. Take a straight mathematical average of all methods.
   b. Consider only the method that results in the highest value.
   c. Weight the valuation method(s) that is/are most appropriate.
   d. Consider only the method that results in the lowest value.

9. What is the intent of the Uniform Standards of Professional Appraisal Practice (USPAP)?

   a. To ensure that valuation analysts properly communicate their findings in a thorough manner.
   b. To determine which valuation methods and approaches the valuation analyst must apply.
   c. To improve the consistency and quality of practice among AICPA members performing business valuations.
   d. To provide a comprehensive set of standards for business appraisers.

10. Which section of the valuation analyst's report is considered the disclaimer?

   a. Introduction.
   b. Description of the assignment.
   c. Assumptions and limiting conditions.
   d. Analysis of the subject entity.

11. Which of the following should not be included in the sources of information section of the report?

   a. Names and titles of all people interviewed.
   b. Description of entity facilities visited.

    c. Shareholders' agreements.

    d. Owners' individual income tax returns.

12. Which type of valuation report is not allowed for a conclusion of value per SSVS?

    a. Detailed report.

    b. Calculation report.

    c. Summary report.

    d. Oral report.

13. Which of the following is the highest-level report per SSVS?

    a. Detailed report.

    b. Calculation report.

    c. Summary report.

    d. Restricted use report.

14. Which type of report is used for an agreed-upon procedures assignment?

    a. Detailed report.

    b. Calculation report.

    c. Summary report.

    d. Restricted use report.

15. All of the following are tools recommended by the author to strengthen the analyst's valuation report except:

    a. Quoting other experts.

    b. Use of pictures and logos.

    c. Use of graphs and charts.

    d. Use of color printers.

16. Which SSVS report type is equivalent to the USPAP's restricted use report?

    a. Detailed report.

    b. Calculation report.

    c. Summary report.

    d. Oral report.

17. Oral reports are allowed for which type of engagement under SSVS?

    a. Conclusion of value only.

    b. Calculation of value only.

    c. Either conclusion or calculation of value.

    d. Neither conclusion nor calculation of value.

18. Which of the following would typically not be a section of a valuation report?

    a. Applicable premise of value.

    b. Valuation date.

    c. Explanation of dates not used.

    d. Disclosure of subsequent events in certain circumstances.

CHAPTER 18

Valuation of Pass-Through Entities

In this chapter, I explained the characteristics of pass-through entities, the issues surrounding the valuation of pass-through entities, theoretical and empirical evidence of a premium for pass-through status, key court cases, and models developed to measure the value of pass-through entities.

1. The Tax Court's decision in *Gross v. Commissioner* indicated which of the following?
   a. S corporations are worth more than C corporations due to tax attributes.
   b. The hypothetical buyer would not pay a premium for S corporation stock.
   c. Normalization adjustments should be made to the earnings stream of an S corporation as if C corporation income taxes were paid.
   d. The judge in the case complied with the position of the IRS articulated in the *IRS Valuation Training for Appeals Officers Coursebook*.

2. Which of the following is not a benefit of being an S corporation?
   a. Avoiding double taxation.
   b. Obtaining minimal legal protection of operation as a corporation.
   c. Not being questioned by the IRS about reasonable compensation.
   d. Not being subject to the accumulated earnings tax if dividends are not paid.

3. Key U.S. Tax Court cases regarding S corporation issues include all of the following except:
   a. *Gross v. Commissioner.*
   b. *Heck v. Commissioner.*
   c. *Mandlebaum v. Commissioner.*
   d. *Adams v. Commissioner.*

4. Factors that an appraiser should consider in determining if an S election adds value include all of the following except:
   a. Control versus minority.
   b. Distributing versus nondistributing.
   c. Future tax rates.
   d. Holding period of the investment.

5. Various models have been developed for S corporation value determination. The authors of these models include all of the following except:
   a. Mercer.
   b. Grabowski.
   c. Treharne.
   d. Fannon.

6. The value of S corporation benefits is applicable only to U.S. Tax Court cases.
   a. True.
   b. False.

7. Empirical studies testing S corporation premiums have revealed the following results:
   a. 12 to 17% premiums.
   b. C corporations sold at higher premiums than S corporations.
   c. There was no difference in the premiums.
   d. All of the above.

8. Which of the following is not a benefit of owning a pass-through entity according to Grabowski?
   a. Income is taxed once.
   b. Owners may receive a step-up in basis.
   c. Owners' compensation is not looked at by the IRS.
   d. Owners may realize more proceeds in the event of a sale.

CHAPTER 19

Valuation in Financial Reporting

In this chapter, I explained the primary reasons for fair value measurements in financial reporting, the accounting standards that are applicable to fair value measurements, how to apply fair value measurements in business combinations, how to apply fair value measurements in impairment testing, where to find the profession's best practices in this area, how to work with management's outside auditor in defending the reasonableness of your conclusions, the new Mandatory Performance Framework, and identifying intangible assets for financial reporting.

1. Financial Accounting Standards Board (FASB) ASC 820 took the place of which of the following?

   a. SFAS No. 141.
   b. SFAS No. 142.
   c. SFAS No. 144.
   d. SFAS No. 157.

2. Assume that XYZ Corporation acquires DEF Corporation in a business combination. On its balance sheet, DEF has an investment in the common stock of ABC Company, a publicly traded company that is listed on the New York Stock Exchange (NYSE) and London Stock Exchange as follows:

Exchange	Price	Transaction Costs	Net
NYSE	$42	$6	$36
London	$40	$2	$38

   What is the fair value of the common stock of ABC Company if the principal market is neither the NYSE nor London?

   a. $42.
   b. $40.
   c. $38.
   d. $36.

3. The FASB ASC glossary defines market participants as buyers and sellers in the principal (or most advantageous) market for the asset or liability that has all of the following characteristics except:

   a. Independent of the reporting entity (that is, they are not related parties).

   b. Knowledgeable (having a reasonable understanding about the asset or liability and the transaction based on all available information, including information that might be obtained through due diligence efforts that are usual and customary).

   c. Unable to transact for the asset or liability.

   d. Willing to transact for the asset or liability

4. Applying the acquisition method under FASB ASC 805 requires all of the following except:

   a. Identifying the target.

   b. Determining the acquisition date.

   c. Recognizing and measuring the identifiable assets acquired, the liabilities assumed, and any noncontrolling interest in the acquiree.

   d. Recognizing and measuring goodwill or a gain from a bargain purchase.

5. FASB ASC 350 took the place of which of the following?

   a. SFAS No. 141.

   b. SFAS No. 142.

   c. SFAS No. 144.

   d. SFAS No. 157.

6. Trade dress falls under which class of intangible?

   a. Contract based.

   b. Marketing related.

   c. Customer related.

   d. Artistically related.

7. Franchise agreements falls under which class of intangible?

   a. Contract based.

   b. Marketing related.

   c. Customer related.

   d. Artistically related.

CHAPTER 20

Valuing Intangible Assets:
An Overview

In this chapter, I explained some ideas about separable intangible assets and why this area is emerging as a bona fide specialty area of business valuation and financial reporting. The topics covered included the basic types of intangible assets, how intangible assets are used by the owners of these assets, some of the common valuation assignments requiring this type of analysis, some legal cases addressing royalty rate calculations for patent infringement cases, some of the background of valuing intangibles independently, issues of remaining useful life (RUL) and intangible life cycles, where to look for market information on royalty rates, some of the emerging concepts of fair value in financial reporting, how an allocation assignment of separable intangible assets is distinguished from unallocated goodwill, and personal goodwill for income tax purposes.

Use the following information for questions 1–4.

ID Secure is a provider of encryption software, which allows its customers to provide a secure means to accept credit card payments over the Internet. On June 1, 20X6, ID Secure acquired all of the assets of Webpay, a small start-up software company that has developed a next generation of encryption technology. The purchase price was $5 million in cash. In addition, ID Secure assumed all of the current liabilities of Webpay. In an announcement, ID Secure's president stated that the reason for the acquisition was to incorporate Webpay's technology into ID Secure's new software.

Webpay was formed in August 20X3 and became profitable in 20X5. Webpay's strategy is to license its technology to only a select few customers in targeted industries. Webpay receives a fee for the use of its software of 10% of the revenue generated by the customers. As of the date of acquisition, Webpay had five customers, including ID Secure.

As of the date of acquisition, Webpay had seven employees:

Employee	Age	Position
John Roberts	33	CEO and Cofounder
Jim Brown	32	VP Technology and Cofounder
Sara Grey	30	VP Marketing
Bill Edwards	29	Chief Programmer
Susan Harris	28	Programmer
Linda Smith	27	Programmer
Gary Jones	29	Programmer

A valuation analyst has been retained by the management of ID Secure to assist with the allocation of the purchase price of Webpay under ASC 805. Management has provided information related to three identified intangible assets: developed technology, customer list, and assembled workforce.

Using a relief from royalty method, the fair value of the developed technology is estimated to be $782,000. The estimated fair value of the assembled workforce and the customer list needs to be determined.

Management provided the financial position of Webpay in the following two tables.

Webpay, Inc.
Balance Sheet

	May 31, 20X6	December 31, 20X5	December 31, 20X4
Assets			
Current Assets			
Cash	$ 250,000	$ 225,000	$ 100,000
Accounts Receivable	350,000	275,000	–
Inventory	200,000	225,000	100,000
Total Current Assets	$ 800,000	$ 725,000	$ 200,000
Fixed Assets			
Computer Equipment	$ 300,000	$ 300,000	$ 250,000
Furniture and Fixtures	150,000	150,000	75,000
Software	100,00	100,00	50,00
Gross Fixed Assets	$ 550,00	$ 550,00	$ 375,00
Accumulated Depreciation	(150,00)	(125,00)	(45,00)
Net Fixed Assets	$ 400,00	$ 425,00	$ 330,00
Total Assets	$1,200,000	$1,150,000	$ 530,000
Liabilities and Owners' Equity			
Current Liabilities			
Accounts Payable	$ 159,000	$ 200,000	$ 100,000
Accrued Expenses	230,000	230,000	130,000
Total Current Liabilities	$ 389,000	$ 430,000	$ 230,000
Long-Term Debt			
Stockholders' Equity			
Preferred Stock	$ 500,000	$ 500,000	$ 500,000
Common Stock	500,000	500,000	500,000
Retained Earnings	(189,000)	(280,000)	(700,000)
Total Stockholders' Equity	811,000	720,000	300,000
Total Liabilities and Stockholders' Equity	$1,200,000	$1,150,000	$ 530,000

Webpay, Inc.
Statement of Income

	Five Months Ending May 31, 20X6	Year Ending December 31, 20X5	Inception to December 31, 20X4
Net Revenue	$ 400,000	$ 2,000,000	$ –
Cost of Goods Sold	100,000	500,000	–
Gross Profit	$ 300,000	1,500,000	$ –
Research and Development	$ 50,000	$ 250,000	$ 250,000
Sales and Marketing	50,00	250,000	200,000
General and Administrative	60,000	300,000	250,000
Total Operating Expenses	$ 160,000	$ 800,000	$ 700,000
Income (Loss) Before Taxes	$ 140,000	$ 700,000	$ (700,000)
Taxes	49,000	(280,000)	–
Net Income (Loss)	$ 91,000	$ 420,000	$ (700,000)

Webpay's management has prepared a set of revenue projections for the company. Discussions with management indicate the technology is expected to be obsolete at the end of 20X9. The valuation analyst calculated the fair value of the technology using the relief from royalty method. As part of the analysis, the valuation analyst calculated an amortization benefit factor of 1.1.

Webpay, Inc.
Estimate of the Fair Value of Developed Technology

	Seven Months Ending December 31, 20X6	20X7	20X8	20X9
Net Revenue	$ 3,000,000	$ 4,000,000	$ 5,000,000	$ 5,500,000
Royalty Rate	10%	10%	10%	10%
A	$ 300,000	$ 400,000	$ 500,000	$ 550,000
Less Taxes @ 35%	(105,000)	(140,000)	(175,000)	(192,500)
Discount Period	0.50	1.50	2.50	3.50
Present Value Factor @ 25%	0.8945	0.7156	0.5724	0.4579
Present Value	$ 174,428	$ 186,056	$186,030	$ 163,928
Sum of Present Values	$ 710,441			
Times Amortization Benefit Factor	1.1			
	$ 781,485			
	$ 781,000 Rounded			

Webpay's management has provided the following information related to the assembled workforce.

Webpay, Inc.
Assembled Workforce

Employee	Salary and Benefits	Hiring Costs	Training Costs
John Roberts	$150,000	$25,000	$25,000
Jim Brown	150,000	25,000	25,000
Sara Grey	100,000	10,000	15,000
Bill Edwards	75,000	5,000	13,000
Susan Harris	60,000	5,000	12,500
Linda Smith	57,000	5,000	12,500
Gary Jones	55,000	5,000	12,500
		$80,000	$115,000

Amortization benefit factor 1.1.
Hiring costs = Search fees plus interview time.
Training costs = Estimate lost productivity while training for the position.

The information provided below should be used for question 1.

As a part of the acquisition of Webpay, ID Secure acquires the existing customer relationships of Webpay. Discussion with Webpay's management indicates the company has open-ended contractual relationships with its five customers. Management indicates that all the sales and marketing expenses incurred by the company from inception to the date of acquisition are representative of the replacement costs to develop the customer relationships. Sales and marketing expenses include all of the vice president of marketing's salary and benefits, marketing materials, and marketing related to travel as follows:

Inception to December 31, 20X4 $200,000

Year ending December 31, 20X5 $250,000

Five months ending May 31, 20X6 $50,000

1. Excluding considerations of the income tax amortization factor, what is the fair value of the Webpay customer relationships?
   a. $400,000.
   b. $440,000.
   c. $500,000.
   d. $550,000.

2. Which of the following best describes the fair value estimated from the relief from royalty method in estimating the value of the developed technology?
   a. The Webpay technology has value only because it can be licensed in the marketplace.
   b. Webpay receives a royalty for its technology, which is assumed to be a market rate.

    c. Webpay owns the technology; therefore, the company is relieved from having to pay another party to use the technology.

    d. The replacement cost of the technology of Webpay is directly related to royalties that the company would receive in the marketplace from exploiting the technology.

3. The net working capital and net fixed assets on the most recent balance sheet of Webpay are representative of its respective fair values as of the date of acquisition by ID Secure. What is the residual purchase price to be allocated between identified intangible assets and goodwill resulting from ID Secure's acquisition of Webpay?

    a. $3,650,000.
    b. $3,800,000.
    c. $3,811,000.
    d. $4,189,000.

4. Assuming a fair value of the assembled workforce of $100,000 and a fair value of the customer relationships of $350,000, what is the amount that should be allocated to goodwill in the acquisition of Webpay?

    a. $2,957,000.
    b. $3,057,000.
    c. $3,407,000.
    d. $4,189,000.

5. Which of the following best describes the economic remaining life of an intangible asset?

    a. The period the intangible asset generates positive cash flow.
    b. The contractual term of the intangible asset.
    c. The period until limitations are developed in the technology.
    d. A statistical analysis of turnover trends.

6. Intangible assets have all of the following characteristics except:

    a. Intangible assets may be bought, sold, licensed, or rented and are subject to the rights of private ownership.
    b. Intangible assets are developed through the passage of time and are not created at an identifiable time.
    c. Intangible assets have a determinate life established by law, by contract, or by economic behavior.
    d. Intangible assets can be purchased or developed internally.

7. The cost approach to valuing intangible assets is generally used to value which of the following?

    a. An assembled workforce.
    b. Covenants not to compete.
    c. Customer-related intangibles.
    d. Internet domain names.

8. Royalty rates are usually stated as a:

   a. Percentage of revenue.
   b. Capitalization rate.
   c. Discount rate.
   d. Percentage of the remaining useful life.

9. ABC Sales Company needs to determine the fair market value of an employment and confidentiality agreement. It estimates that its revenue will be $10,000,000 with after-tax income of $1,000,000 with an agreement in place. The company also anticipates that revenues will be $7,500,000 and after-tax income will be $750,000 without an agreement in place. What is the net difference due to competition?

   a. $2,500,000.
   b. $1,000,000.
   c. $250,000.
   d. $750,000.

10. Which method is the primary approach for brand names?

   a. Income approach.
   b. Market approach.
   c. Cost approach.
   d. Other.

11. Which method is the primary approach for internally developed software?

   a. Income approach.
   b. Market approach.
   c. Cost approach.
   d. Other.

12. Which of the following is not a financial reporting purpose for valuing intangible assets?

   a. Purchase price allocation.
   b. Financing.
   c. Goodwill impairment.
   d. Impairment on disposal of long-lived assets.

13. Which of the following statements is false?

   a. Market forces, obsolescence, replacements, and operation enhancements deteriorate the value of intangible assets.
   b. Legal, regulatory, or contractual provisions may limit the intangible asset's useful life.
   c. Like fixed assets, intangibles wear out.
   d. Intangible value appreciates over time and there is no useful life.

14. Which of the following qualifies as an intangible asset?

   a. High market share.
   b. High profitability.
   c. Trained and assembled workforce.
   d. Monopoly position.

15. Under the income approach to valuing intangibles, the method that "estimates cost savings based on avoided third-party license payments for the right to employ the asset to earn benefits" is referred to as:

   a. Capitalization of earnings method.
   b. Multiperiod discounting method.
   c. Relief from royalty method.
   d. Excess earnings method.

   The following information relates to questions 16–18.
   ABC, Inc. is trying to determine the value of its customer list using the replacement cost method. It is estimated that 80% of its selling costs are related directly to the acquisition of new clients. ABC, Inc.'s tax rate is 40%. Its revenue, selling costs, and new customer information are as follows:

Year	Reported Revenues	Selling Costs	New Customers
2X11	$4,000,000	$425,000	210
2X10	$3,750,000	$350,000	152
2X09	$3,100,000	$300,000	140

16. What is the total after-tax selling cost for new customers from 2X09 through 2X11?

   a. $1,075,000.
   b. $860,000.
   c. $645,000.
   d. $516,000.

17. What is the cost per new customer (after-tax) in 2X11?

   a. $2,024.
   b. $1,619.
   c. $971.
   d. $1,214.

18. If the company has 2,500 current customers, what is the total replacement cost of customers using 2X09 through 2X11 data?

   a. $5,353,586.
   b. $4,282,869.
   c. $2,569,721.
   d. $2,427,500.

19. ABC Software, Inc. has a program containing 20,000 lines of code. The company's programmers can program 10 lines of code per hour at a rate of $100 per hour. The obsolescence factor is 15%, inflation is 3%, and the company's tax rate is 40%. What is the after-tax value of the produced software?

   a. $200,000.
   b. $170,000.
   c. $120,000.
   d. $102,000.

20. Which method is the primary approach for valuing patents?
    a. Income approach.
    b. Market approach.
    c. Cost approach.
    d. Excess earnings approach.

21. Which method is the primary approach for Federal Communications Commission licenses?
    a. Income approach.
    b. Market approach.
    c. Cost approach.
    d. Excess earnings approach.

22. Which court case created the 15 factors to consider in determining reasonable royalty rates?
    a. *Georgia Pacific v. U.S. Plywood.*
    b. *Mad Auto Wrecking v. IRS Commissioner.*
    c. *Panduit Corp. v. Stahlin Bros.*
    d. *Bernard Mandelbaum et al. v. Commissioner.*

CHAPTER 21

Estate and Gift Valuations

In this chapter, I explained the valuation rules for estate and gift tax purposes, valuing family limited partnerships (and similar entities) for estate and gift tax purposes, and how the valuation analyst should do the job the right way.

1. In order to obtain discounts for lack of control or marketability when valuing limited partnership interests in a family limited partnership (FLP), the partnership agreement need not be:

   a. A bona fide business arrangement.
   b. Restrictive as to the admissibility of corporate partners.
   c. Comparable to arm's-length arrangements found between nonrelated parties.
   d. A testamentary device to transfer property for less than adequate consideration.

2. Before performing a business valuation for estate and gift tax purposes, the valuation analyst should be familiar with all of the following except:

   a. Local case laws.
   b. Internal Revenue codes.
   c. Revenue Rulings.
   d. Tax Court decisions.

3. The 2006 Pension Protection Act added a new penalty for any person who prepares a property appraisal where the value results in a substantial or gross valuation misstatement. What is the amount of the penalty?

   a. $1,000.
   b. The lesser of (1) the greater of (a) 10% of the underpayment or (b) $1,000, or (2) 125% of the gross income received for the appraisal services.
   c. The greater of (1) $10,000 or (2) 100% of the fees charged for the appraisal services.
   d. The lesser of $10,000 or 125% of the gross income received for the appraisal services.

4. Which of the following is not an advantage of an FLP?

   a. It provides a high degree of protection against personal creditors.
   b. The gifting or transfer of an ownership interest may be made at a lower value than that interest's pro rata share of net asset value.
   c. The FLP pays tax in a lower tax bracket than most individuals.
   d. The assets can be kept in the family by placing restrictions on the transfer of interests.

5. Which of the following methods is inappropriate in valuing an FLP?

   a. Asset-based approach.
   b. Income-based approach.
   c. Market approach.
   d. All of these approaches are appropriate.

6. When using the market approach to value an FLP, what is the most appropriate multiple?

   a. Price to earnings.
   b. Price to revenue.
   c. Price to dividends.
   d. Market value of invested capital to revenue.

7. When comparing an FLP to a real estate limited partnership (RELP), RELP factors to consider include all of the following except:

   a. The location of the real estate.
   b. The type of real estate owned.
   c. The reputation, integrity, and perceived competence of the management and general partner.
   d. Liquidity factors such as the number of partners and the number of transactions.

8. Which of the following factors is most likely to reduce a discount for lack of marketability?

   a. No partner or assignee has the right to withdraw from the FLP prior to dissolution and liquidation.
   b. The FLP has a history of paying dividends to its partners.
   c. No partner or assignee may transfer all or any part of their interest without prior written consent.
   d. A transferee is not entitled to the rights that the assignee holds.

9. IRC Section 6662 provides for penalties against taxpayers for undervaluation of assets on estate and gift tax returns. What is the maximum penalty a taxpayer can receive?

   a. 0%.
   b. 10%.
   c. 20%.
   d. 40%.

10. What is the main fight with the IRS relating to FLP values?

   a. The size of marketability and control discounts.
   b. Whether an income approach or market approach is more reliable.
   c. The application of discount or capitalization rates.
   d. What should and should not be included in the valuation report.

11. Which of the following is a document that is typically not needed to prepare the valuation report for a family limited partnership?

    a. Financial statements and tax returns for a reasonable number of years.
    b. A summary of the qualifications of the general partner.
    c. A list of distributions made to all partners.
    d. The Agreement of Partnership and Certificate of Limited Partnership.

12. Which of the following court cases does not deal with applications issues relating to Sections 2703 and 2704 of the Internal Revenue Code?

    a. *Baine P. Kerr, et ux. v. Commissioner.*
    b. *Estate of Albert Strangi v. Commissioner.*
    c. *Bernard Mandelbaum, et al. v. IRS Commissioner.*
    d. *Church v. United States.*

13. Which of the following is a potential Section 2036 mistake?

    a. Excluding a personal residence from an FLP.
    b. Transferring business assets to an FLP.
    c. Timing distributions to coincide with the limited partners' financial obligations.
    d. Hiring an outside party to be the general partner of the FLP.

14. Which of the following is not an common source for determining the discount for lack of control when valuing an FLP owning primarily real estate?

    a. Mergerstat.
    b. Real estate limited partnerships.
    c. Real estate investment trusts.
    d. Partnership Profile's *Direct Investment Spectrum.*

15. Which of the following factors is most likely to increase the discount for lack of marketability?

    a. High volatility in the value of the underlying assets.
    b. A proven and stabilized history of income.
    c. Favorable outlook for future growth.
    d. Limited time period on restriction of ability to sell the interest.

CHAPTER 22

Divorce Valuations

In this chapter, I explained the role of the valuation analyst in divorce assignments, standards of value and their unique aspects in divorce assignments, different valuation dates used in these assignments, how the normalization process differs in divorce assignments, valuing professional practices for divorce assignments, personal versus enterprise goodwill, and how noncompete agreements affect values in the distribution of marital property.

1. Assuming no material mistakes were made, a court will generally rely mostly on which expert's report?
   a. The business owner's expert.
   b. The non–business owner's expert.
   c. The court-appointed expert.
   d. The court generally determines its own value and does not rely on one expert in particular.

2. Which standard of value should be selected for equitable distribution purposes?
   a. Fair market value.
   b. Fair value.
   c. Investment value.
   d. The definition of value dictated by the court with jurisdiction over the matter.

3. The business owner who is going through a divorce will not be selling the business, and therefore there will be no hypothetical transaction. Instead, the owner will continue to receive the benefits of ownership into the future. The definition of value based on this premise is:
   a. Fair market value.
   b. Fair value.
   c. Intrinsic value.
   d. Going concern value.

4. Which of the following subsequent events would affect the business valuation?

   a. A fire burns down the main facility the day after the valuation date.

   b. The company sells for two times earnings three months after the valuation date.

   c. The company's key officer dies in an automobile accident two weeks after the date of valuation.

   d. Prior to the date of valuation, the company announces that it will be adding 12 additional locations in the following year.

5. In most divorce valuations, when is it appropriate to make discretionary normalization adjustments to the income statement when valuing a minority interest?

   a. Discretionary adjustments can always be made for minority interests.

   b. Discretionary adjustments can never be made for minority interests.

   c. Discretionary adjustments should be made if a hypothetical minority interest buyer would eliminate the discretionary items.

   d. Discretionary adjustments are generally appropriate when valuing a minority interest in a family-owned business.

6. Which of the following is not a normal adjustment when valuing professional practices?

   a. Goodwill.

   b. Cash versus accrual accounting.

   c. Contingencies.

   d. Work in process.

7. Which type of goodwill is generally associated with an individual?

   a. Practice goodwill.

   b. Professional goodwill.

   c. Commercial goodwill.

   d. Business goodwill.

8. A well-known California case, *Lopez. v. Lopez*, pointed out several factors affecting professional goodwill; which of the following factors is not included in that court case?

   a. The age and health of the professional.

   b. The number of hours the professional works per week.

   c. The professional's past earning power.

   d. The professional's reputation in the community for judgment, skill, and knowledge.

CHAPTER 23

Professional Practice Valuations

In this chapter, I explained the reasons for valuing professional practices, the characteristics of a professional practice, the differences between professional practice valuations and valuations of other types of businesses, and engagement-specific matters.

1. Which of the following is not considered a professional practice?
   a. Law firm.
   b. Real estate agency.
   c. Accounting firm.
   d. Doctor's practice.

2. Which of the following is not generally a reason for valuing a professional practice?
   a. Fair value reporting.
   b. Mergers and acquisitions.
   c. Stockholder and partner disputes.
   d. Damages litigation.

3. Which of the following is not a characteristic of a professional practice?
   a. In general, professional practices have significant amounts of tangible assets and few intangible assets.
   b. In general, professional practices depend on a strong relationship between the professional and the client or patient that is based off reputation.
   c. In general, professional practices are licensed, regulated, or certified by a governmental or regulatory agency or professional organization.
   d. In general, most professionals are required to obtain an undergraduate degree as well as maintain some level of continuing education to keep their licenses.

4. Which of the following statements is true?
   a. Valuations of professional practices will generally lead toward the use of an asset-based method.
   b. Professional practices will generally be valued using the excess earnings approach.
   c. Valuations of professional practices using the excess earnings approach will be lower than valuations using the income approach.
   d. Valuations of professional practices will be much more oriented toward a market or income approach.

5. Which of the following is least likely to be considered in the valuation of a professional practice?

   a. Buy-sell agreements.
   b. Internal transactions.
   c. External transactions.
   d. Subsequent event transactions.

6. Which of the following is not a key consideration of a professional practice?

   a. Cash versus accrual method of accounting.
   b. Consideration of the asset costs.
   c. Consideration of the professional's attributes.
   d. Consideration of the professional's licensing requirements.

CHAPTER 24

Ownership Disputes

In this chapter, I explained what causes ownership disputes, the difference between dissenting and oppression cases, the impact of case law on the standard of value and valuation adjustments, and valuation methodologies accepted by the courts.

1. In the Revised Model Business Corporation Act definition of the term *fair value*, which of the following statements is correct?
   a. Value occurs immediately after the corporate action.
   b. Value is determined only with the dissenter's approval.
   c. Value is determined at the occurrence of the corporate action, unless inequitable.
   d. Value changes in anticipation of the corporate action are excluded, unless inequitable.

2. Fair value is defined in the Model Business Corporation Act as:
   a. The amount at which property would change hands between a willing seller and a willing buyer when neither is acting under compulsion and when both have reasonable knowledge of the relevant facts.
   b. The value of the shares immediately before the effectuation of a corporate action to which the dissenter objects, excluding any appreciation or depreciation in anticipation of the corporate action unless exclusion would be inequitable.
   c. The specific value of goods or services to a particular investor based on individual investment requirements.
   d. An analytical judgment of value based on the perceived characteristics inherent in the investment, not tempered by characteristics peculiar to any one investor, but rather tempered by how these perceived characteristics are interpreted by one analyst versus another.

3. Oppressed shareholders' statutes or dissolution statutes provide minority shareholders with remedies for actions against controlling stockholders for all of the following except:
   a. Selling their interest in the company.
   b. Fraud.
   c. Abusive behavior.
   d. Mismanagement.

4. Which of the following is not generally a remedy to a minority shareholder oppression case?

a. The minority interest sells their shares back to the company for fair value.
b. The minority interest is entitled to compensation as a measure of damages.
c. The company is forced to liquidate.
d. The minority interest is entitled to purchase the shares of the controlling shareholders and keep the company.

5. Which of the following statements is true regarding fair value and fair market value?

a. At all times, the true value of what a shareholder is giving up is equal to the fair market value of the interest.
b. Fair value will usually be the same as fair market value.
c. The estimation of fair market value and fair value of a minority shareholder's stock may include both a discount for lack of marketability and a discount for minority ownership.
d. The methodology used in a fair value appraisal may be different than in a fair market value appraisal.

6. In his discussion of the *Lawson Mardon Wheaton, Inc. v. Smith* and *Emanuel Balsamides, Sr., et al. v. Protameen Chemicals, Inc.* cases, the author is trying to illustrate which of the following?

a. That the court is looking for all shareholders to be treated fairly, regardless of the circumstances.
b. That a discount for lack of marketability should always be applied in fair value cases.
c. That a discount for lack of marketability should never be applied in fair value cases.
d. That under the same standard of value, all valuations must be performed in the same manner.

7. Which of the following is not a step in the Delaware block method?

a. Derive separate values using methods under the income, asset, and market approaches.
b. Apply weights to each of the methods depending upon the type of business being valued.
c. Apply a discount for the lack of marketability.
d. Add the results of the weighted values to determine the final estimate of value.

8. Which of the following is not a common exercisable right of a majority shareholder?

a. Appoint or change members of the board of directors.
b. Liquidate the company.
c. Distribute and purchase additional common shares to increase ownership.
d. Declare and pay cash dividends.

9. The standard of value in most dissenting shareholder cases is:

   a. Fair market value.
   b. Fair value.
   c. Intrinsic value.
   d. Going concern value.

10. In fair value valuations, which of the following is correct?

    a. Discounts for lack of marketability are not applicable.
    b. Discounts for lack of marketability are applicable.
    c. Discounts for lack of control are applicable.
    d. Discounts for both lack of marketability and lack of control are applicable.

11. In general, what will the date of valuation be for a dissenting shareholder case?

    a. The day of trial.
    b. The day the motion is filed.
    c. The day after the meeting of shareholders at which the action dissented from was opposed.
    d. The day prior to the meeting of shareholders at which the action dissented from was opposed.

12. Which of the following states has heavily influenced judicial precedents?

    a. Delaware.
    b. New Jersey.
    c. Florida.
    d. California.

CHAPTER 25

Other Valuation Assignments

In this chapter, I explained some general information on specialized valuation assignments that valuation analysts often encounter. This chapter discussed valuation issues related to stock options, warrants, preferred stock, debt, and the valuation of early-stage companies.

1. With respect to the valuation of an option using the Black-Scholes option pricing model, which of the following is true?

   a. Dividends are ignored.
   b. Black-Scholes values an American option.
   c. The value of the option decreases as the time to maturity increases.
   d. The value of the option decreases as the volatility of the underlying stock increases.

2. Generally, the most significant factor to consider in the valuation of a preferred stock is:

   a. The preferred stock's redemption rights.
   b. The company's fixed charge coverage ratio.
   c. The preferred stock's dividend rate.
   d. The preferred stock's liquidation preference.

3. Which of the following statements about a stock option is most correct?

   a. It gives the holder the right to sell the underlying stock by a certain date at a certain price.
   b. It can be exercised only on the option expiration date.
   c. It is exercisable at any time up to the expiration date.
   d. It is a derivative security whose value is contingent on the price of a stock.

4. A firm has Series A convertible preferred stock with no dividend rights and a face value of $20,000,000 and similar Series B preferred stock with a face value of $35,000,000. The Series A stock has liquidation priority over the Series B stock. At what total equity value would the common equity begin to participate in the value of the company?

   a. $0.
   b. $20,000,000.
   c. $35,000,000.
   d. $55,000,000.

5. Put the following business securities in order from the least risky to the most risky.

   I. Common stock
   II. Short-term debt
   III. Nonconvertible preferred stock
   IV. Long-term debt

   a. II, IV, III, I
   b. II, IV, I, III
   c. IV, II, III, I
   d. I, III, IV, II

6. Which of the following is an important **difference** between debt and preferred stock?

   a. May be convertible into common stock.
   b. Typically offers contractual periodic cash flows.
   c. Offers tax advantages to the issuer.
   d. Has liquidation seniority to common stock.

7. Assume a particular debt security has a face value of $100 and a coupon of 5%, is neither convertible, nor callable, nor redeemable. Which of the following statements is true?

   a. If the required market yield is 4%, then the fair market value of the debt will be less than $100.
   b. If the required market yield is 5%, then the fair market value of the debt will be less than face value.
   c. If the required market yield is 6%, then the fair market value of the debt will be less than face value.
   d. None of the above.

8. Which of the following is not a factor identified in IRS Revenue Ruling 83-120 as relevant to the valuation of preferred stock?

   a. How long the preferred stock has been outstanding.
   b. Whether dividends are cumulative.
   c. Whether credit ratio analysis indicates the issuer can pay the stated dividends.
   d. Whether the preferred stock has any voting rights.

9. The Black-Scholes option pricing model is based on discrete mathematics.
   a. True.
   b. False.

10. The most common procedure used to value debt securities is which of the following?
   a. Discounted value of contractual interest and principal payments.
   b. The Black-Scholes option pricing method.
   c. Credit analysis to determine a market yield for the subject debt.
   d. Both a and c.

11. Which of the following characteristics would be expected to decrease the value of a share of preferred stock?

    a. A conversion feature.
    b. A below-market dividend yield.
    c. A participation feature.
    d. Voting rights.

12. The owner of a call option has the right, but not the obligation, to sell the underlying asset at a specified price on or before a specified date in time.

    a. True.
    b. False.

13. Consider a European call option for 100 shares of McDonald's stock for $180 that matures in 24 months. What does this option entitle the holder to do?

    a. Sell 100 shares of McDonald's stock between now and the maturity date.
    b. Purchase 100 shares of McDonald's stock between now and the maturity date.
    c. Purchase 100 shares of McDonald's stock at the maturity date.
    d. Sell 100 shares of McDonald's stock at the maturity date.

Consider the following information for questions 14–20.

- The stock price of the company is $125
- The exercise price of a call option is $135
- The volatility of the underlying stock is 25%
- The risk-free rate is 2.50%
- The stock does not pay a dividend
- The investor paid $4 for the stock option

14. What is the maximum amount that the purchaser of the call option can lose?

    a. $4.
    b. $25.
    c. $35.
    d. $0.

15. Based on the information given, this call option would be considered to be in the money.

    a. True.
    b. False.

16. Using an online Black-Scholes option pricing calculator, what is the value of this call option assuming there are six months left to maturity?

    a. $5.50.
    b. $13.84.
    c. $16.00.
    d. $9.54.

17. Which of the following statements is incorrect regarding this option?

    a. An increase in the price of the stock would make this option more valuable.
    b. The option would become more valuable as it gets closer to the expiration date.
    c. If the volatility on this option were 35%, the option would be more valuable.
    d. A decrease in the risk-free rate would make this option less valuable.

18. If the stock paid dividends, what impact would it have on the value of the option?

    a. The option would become more valuable.
    b. Dividends have no impact on the value of an option.
    c. The option would become less valuable.
    d. None of the above.

19. Suppose this security was a warrant as opposed to a call option. Which of these adjustments would have to be made from a valuation perspective?

    a. The dilutive effect of the warrant.
    b. The terms of the warrant agreement.
    c. Both a and b.
    d. No adjustments need to be made.

20. Suppose this option was an American option as opposed to a European option. Which of the following statements is correct?

    a. The Black-Scholes option pricing model should be used to value the option.
    b. The binomial option pricing model should be used to value the option.
    c. The option cannot be exercised until the maturity date.
    d. All of the above.

Consider the following information for questions 21–26.

- Par value of the bond equals $1,000
- The coupon rate for the bond is 5%
- Based on an analysis of rates of return for similar debt issues, the valuation analyst determined that the going rate of interest for similar securities was 8%
- The bond matures in 10 years
- The yield on a 10-year Treasury bond is 2.5%
- The yield on Moody's AAA bonds was 6.8%

21. Based on the information given:

    a. The market value of the bond is below par value.
    b. The market value of the bond is above par value.
    c. The market value of the bond is equal to par value.
    d. It is not possible to determine from the information given.

22. Based on the information given, what is the value of the bond?

    a. $872.40.
    b. $1,218.80.
    c. $798.70.
    d. $1,231.65.

23. Suppose the time to maturity was reduced to eight years. What would the impact be on the value of the bond?

    a. Increase.
    b. Decrease.
    c. No change.

24. Suppose the coupon rate was 10% as opposed to 5%. Which of the following statements is correct?

    a. The market value of the bond would be above par value.
    b. The market value of the bond would be below par value.
    c. The market value of the bond would not change.

25. If the market rate of interest increases, which of the following is true?

    a. This is an example of default risk, and the value of the bond would decrease.
    b. This is an example of interest rate risk, and the value of the bond would increase.
    c. This is an example of reinvestment risk, and the value of the bond would increase.
    d. This is an example of interest rate risk, and the value of the bond would decrease.

26. If this were a callable bond, which of these statements would be true?

    a. The bond would be subject to a higher level of default risk and prepayment risk.
    b. The bond would be subject to a higher level of reinvestment risk and prepayment risk.
    c. The bond would be subject to a higher level of interest rate risk and default risk.
    d. The bond would be subject to a higher level of interest rate risk and reinvestment risk.

27. Which of the following statements is true with respect to reinvestment risk?

    a. Reinvestment risk increases in a rising interest rate environment.
    b. Reinvestment risk is the risk that an increase in interest rates would reduce the market value of a security.
    c. Reinvestment risk increases in a declining interest rate environment.
    d. Reinvestment risk is not impacted by interest rates.

28. Default risk does which of the following?

    a. Increases in a rising interest rate environment.
    b. Relates to the credit quality of the issuer.
    c. Is higher for callable bonds.
    d. Decreases in a declining interest rate environment.

29. Suppose a group of investors purchased a 25% preferred stock interest in an early-stage company for $50 million. Which of the following statements is true?

    a. The implied value of the company is $200 million.
    b. An asset-based approach would better capture the implied value of the company.
    c. An alternative approach, such as the back-solve method would be needed to determine the implied value of the company.
    d. Since the transaction involved preferred stock, this transaction should be ignored and an income approach should be performed to determine the value of the common stock.

CHAPTER 26

Economic Damages

In this chapter, I explained the similarities of an economic damages analysis to a business valuation assignment, types of economic damages claims, how to perform a lost profits analysis, different methodologies available to perform a lost profits analysis, and other types of damages measurements.

1. A business enterprise may suffer lost profits when, as a result of someone's actions, any of the following takes place except:

   a. Revenues are lower than they would have been had the act not occurred.
   b. Revenues are higher than they would have been had the act not occurred.
   c. Costs are higher than they would have been had the act not occurred.
   d. Some combination of revenues being lower and costs being higher.

2. Compensatory damages are considered all of the following except:

   a. General damages.
   b. Special damages.
   c. Consequential damages.
   d. Punitive damages.

3. Which of the following is not one of the three generally accepted methods to calculate lost profits?

   a. Income method.
   b. The before and after method.
   c. The yardstick method.
   d. The "but for" method.

CHAPTER 27

My Favorite Court Cases

In this chapter I reviewed some of my favorite court cases. They are all available as a download from the Business Valuation Resources website that was set up to accompany the textbook (AICPAStore.com/UBV). Reading each of these cases will serve as your refresher for this chapter.

CHAPTER 28

Interactive Case Study

This chapter presents one interactive case study that can be woven throughout the valuation course. In addition to the materials that are included in this chapter, there are various appendices that should be downloaded (only when instructed to do so) from a special workbook folder at www.AICPAStore.com/UBV. There are suggested solutions available for instructors and for those individuals who are using this workbook to study for the ABV examination. If you are a student, you really do not want the answers until you have done the exercises.

EXERCISE 1: DEFINING THE VALUATION ASSIGNMENT

Your assignment is to define the valuation assignment. You may use the exercise tables following the exhibits to record your work. Additionally, determine whether you will need a tangible asset appraisal. Do not spend too much time reviewing the financial statements at this point. Concentrate on answering the questions that follow.

INITIAL DESCRIPTION OF THE PROBLEM

(a) The Initial Inquiry Situation   You have just met with an attorney who is soliciting a proposal from you regarding the valuation of a privately held computer company. The attorney explains that the controlling shareholder is currently involved in a litigation, and, due to many circumstances, the valuation date is far in the past. The subject is a company called Quimby's Computer Solutions, Inc.

Your assignment, should your proposal be accepted, will be to value a 90% controlling interest as of December 29, 1995.

(b) The Client's Situation   The name of the subject is Quimby's Computer Solutions, Inc. ("The Company" or "Quimby's"), which was founded in 1979 by Roger Smith. The Company's principal business was originally as a midrange computer reseller, but more recently it has changed primarily to an IBM distributor of various types of computer equipment and peripherals.

Company sales are made to corporate America, and The Company has no retail operations. Over the years, The Company has grown from one employee to approximately 120 employees with sales exceeding $100 million. The Company's market is the entire United States.

Quimby's Computer Solutions, Inc.
Schedule 1: Annual Historical Balance Sheets
as Reported
Fiscal Years Ended August 31,

	1991	1992	1993	1994	1995
Current Assets					
Cash	$ 10,647	$ 2,148	$ 69,266	$ 544,500	$ 1,118,697
Marketable Securities	35,233	–	52,886	–	–
Accounts Receivable	313,751	797,374	971,565	3,963,550	4,589,646
Inventories	50,100	189,224	270,233	1,814,009	3,693,293
Prepaid Expenses	–	–	–	24,396	15,484
Other Current Assets	–	3,348	–	–	–
Total Current Assets	$ 409,731	$ 992,094	$ 1,363,950	$ 6,346,455	$ 9,417,120
Net Fixed Assets	$ 66,947	$ 7,619	$ 18,048	$ 43,021	$ 316,784
Other Assets					
Security Deposits	$ 8,391	$ 8,391	$ 11,393	$ –	$ 11,301
Stockholder Loans	56,446	–	–	34,996	229,246
Employee Advances	15,620	–	–	–	96,687
Other Assets	12,668	–	21,160	35,384	51,302
Total Other Assets	$ 93,125	$ 8,391	$ 32,553	$ 70,380	$ 388,536
TOTAL ASSETS	$ 569,803	$ 1,008,104	$ 1,414,551	$ 6,459,856	$ 10,122,440
Current Liabilities					
Accounts Payable	$ 363,408	$ 848,670	$ 1,071,061	$ 1,686,380	$ 1,361,785
Accrued Expenses	–	–	36,181	398,617	704,373
Income Taxes Payable	–	–	–	306,000	–
Due to Stockholder	–	56,582	115,004	–	–
Revolving Credit Line	411,775	372,270	290,977	3,603,175	6,540,143
Total Current Liabilities	$ 775,183	$ 1,277,522	$ 1,513,223	$ 5,994,172	$ 8,606,301
Stockholders' Equity					
Common Stock	$ 865	$ 865	$ 865	$ 865	$ 865
Retained Earnings	(206,245)	(270,283)	(99,537)	464,819	1,515,274
Total Stockholders' Equity	$ (205,380)	$ (269,418)	$ (98,672)	$ 465,684	$ 1,516,139
TOTAL LIABILITIES AND STOCKHOLDERS' EQUITY	$ 569,803	$ 1,008,104	$ 1,414,551	$ 6,459,856	$ 10,122,440

Quimby's Computer Solutions, Inc.
Schedule 2: Annual Historical Income Statements
as Reported
Fiscal Years Ended August 31,

	1991	1992	1993	1994	1995
Revenues	$ 5,008,819	$ 5,813,102	$ 11,825,174	$ 22,285,781	$ 40,945,386
Cost of Sales	4,405,459	5,064,854	9,775,873	18,276,690	33,588,165
Gross Profit	$ 603,360	$ 748,248	$ 2,049,301	$ 4,009,091	$ 7,357,221
Operating Expenses					
Accounting	$ 67,565	$ 9,619	$ –	$ –	$ –
Advertising	19,913	28,071	38,892	–	–
Auto Expense	19,440	20,361	27,831	14,984	17,578
Bad Debts	(11,440)	–	–	8,348	16,580
Bank Charges	33,029	–	733	–	–
Charitable Contributions	–	–	–	–	1,150
Commissions	–	–	401,553	662,400	2,188,422
Data Processing	–	–	–	70,685	–
Depreciation	8,150	5,996	4,212	23,758	77,199
Employee Benefits Programs	23,254	11,539	–	–	52,890
Entertainment	19,314	16,315	14,852	62,326	6,747
Officers' Compensation	130,108	196,078	184,784	617,559	1,235,045
Capitalized 263A Costs	–	–	–	–	(40,521)
Insurance—Group	7,950	7,193	62,762	33,799	47,950
Insurance—Life	11,025	9,570	2,016	2,016	7,279
Licenses and Fees	–	–	7,274	3,859	–
Miscellaneous	–	–	18,981	20,549	60,406
Office Expenses	26,832	17,966	41,078	50,073	348,761
Outside Services	28,798	40,124	–	–	–
Computer Expenses	–	–	14,742	61,439	–
Pension, Profit-Sharing Plans	–	–	1,200	343	32,688
Postage and Delivery	7,385	10,035	47,232	11,089	–
Professional Fees	–	–	7,137	96,020	97,868
Rents	43,801	47,298	121,530	49,425	92,724
Repairs and Maintenance	6,529	4,269	11,615	–	26,319
Equipment Rental	–	1,324	3,738	–	26,716
Salaries and Wages	95,400	103,115	466,009	592,724	653,575
Seminars and Meetings	–	–	375	35,113	31,425
Taxes—Payroll	36,610	44,364	50,847	155,841	179,557
Telephone	97,031	100,738	113,365	143,044	186,042
Travel	4,687	1,727	31,865	15,582	85,891
Utilities	7,868	6,318	5,843	7,892	13,946
Lead Expense	6,072	7,566	–	–	–

Dues and Subscriptions	$ 7,629	$ 5,180	$ –	$ 4,739	$ 11,706
Finders Fees	–	–	130,813	275,468	–
Recruiting	–	–	12,064	8,108	23,250
Education	–	–	–	1,240	–
Technical Support	–	–	–	500	13,295
Temporary Help	1,368	788	22,281	81,889	63,056
Selling Expenses/ Promotional	13,607	17,379	10,401	38,191	108,624
Total Operating Expenses	$ 711,925	$ 712,933	$ 1,856,025	$ 3,149,003	$ 5,666,168
Operating Income (Loss)	$ (108,565)	$ 35,315	$ 193,276	$ 860,088	$ 1,691,053
Other Income					
Interest Income	$ 2,146	$ 2,081	$ 647	$ 7,054	$ 32,558
Dividend Income	520	–	–	249	3,114
Gain on Sale of Assets	(543)	–	–	–	–
Rental Income	(7,933)	1,055	–	–	–
Other Income	269	–	–	17,480	78,596
Other Income	6,161	–	–	–	–
Total Other Income	$ 620	$ 3,136	$ 647	$ 24,783	$ 114,268
Other Expenses					
Interest Expense	$ 43,813	$ 67,256	$ 41,829	$ 139,909	$ 199,028
Loss on Sale of Assets	–	35,233	2,508	–	–
Total Other Expenses	$ 43,813	$ 102,489	$ 44,337	$ 139,909	$ 199,028
Total Other Income (Expenses)	$ (43,193)	$ (99,353)	$ (43,690)	$ (115,126)	$ (84,760)
Income (Loss) Before Taxes	$ (151,758)	$ (64,038)	$ 149,586	$ 744,962	$ 1,606,293
Income Taxes	–	–	–	262,000	–
NET INCOME (LOSS)	$ (151,758)	$ (64,038)	$ 149,586	$ 482,962	$ 1,606,293

Quimby's Computer Solutions, Inc.
Notes to Financial Statements
August 31, 1995 and 1994

(1) ORGANIZATION

Quimby's Computer Solutions, Inc. ("The Company") was incorporated in the State of Delaware in August 1983 and has operated primarily in the State of Florida. The

Company is a distributor of computers and computer-related products and provides its products to commercial enterprises throughout the United States.

(2) SUMMARY OF SIGNIFICANT ACCOUNTING POLICIES

(a) Cash and Cash Equivalents   Cash and cash equivalents are generally comprised of bank accounts and highly liquid investments with an initial maturity of less than three months. Substantially all cash and cash equivalents at August 31, 1995, are interest bearing.

(b) Inventories   Inventories consist of new and refurbished computers and peripheral products that are valued at the lower of historical cost (on a first in, first out basis) or market cost. At August 31, components of inventories are as follows:

	1995	1994
New Products	$1,798,231	$1,734,809
Refurbished Products	341,553	79,200
	$2,139,784	$1,814,009

(c) Property and Equipment   Property and equipment are carried at cost. Depreciation is recorded using the straight-line method over the estimated lives of the related assets. Such lives range from 5 to 10 years for office furniture, equipment, and computer software. Leasehold improvements are depreciated over approximately 1.5 years.

(d) Income Taxes   Prior to January 1, 1995, The Company accounted for income taxes in accordance with Statement of Financial Accounting Standards No. 109 ("SFAS 109"), "Accounting for Income Taxes." SFAS 109 utilizes the liability method, and deferred taxes are determined based on the estimated future tax effects of differences between the financial statement and tax bases of assets and liabilities given the provisions of enacted tax laws. Deferred income tax provisions and benefits are based on the changes to the asset or liability from period to period.

   During fiscal 1995, The Company, with the consent of its shareholders, elected under the Internal Revenue Code to be an S corporation. In lieu of corporate income taxes, the shareholders of an S corporation are taxed on their proportionate share of The Company's taxable income. Therefore, no provision or liability for federal income taxes has been included *in* these financial statements subsequent to January 1, 1995, the effective date of the election. The provision for income taxes included in the accompanying statement of income for fiscal 1995 reflects income taxes on earnings attributable to the four months ended December 31, 1994.

(e) Fair Value of Financial Instruments   Statement of Financial Accounting Standards No. 107 ("SFAS 107"), "Disclosures about Fair Value of Financial Instruments," requires disclosure of the fair value of certain financial instruments. Cash and cash equivalents, accounts receivable, prepaid expenses, and other current assets, due from shareholders, along with notes payable, accounts payable, accrued expenses, and income tax payable are reflected in the financial statements at cost, which approximates fair value.

(f) Financial Statement Presentation   The preparation of financial statements in conformity with generally accepted accounting principles requires management to make estimates and assumptions that affect the reported amounts of assets and liabilities and disclosures of contingent assets and liabilities at the date of the financial statements and the reported amounts of revenues and expenses during the reporting period. Actual results could differ from these estimates.

(3) DUE FROM SHAREHOLDERS

Due from shareholders represents loans made to The Company's shareholders. Such loans bear interest at 7% per annum and are repayable upon maturity on August 31, 2005. The loans are personally guaranteed by the shareholders.

(4) PROPERTY AND EQUIPMENT

Property and equipment consist of the following:

	1995	1994
Furniture and Equipment	$355,559	$102,495
Computer Software	68,550	45,259
Leasehold Improvements	31,850	–
Total Property and Equipment	$455,959	$147,754
Less Accumulated Depreciation	140,382	98,526
Property and Equipment, Net	$315,577	$49,228

(5) NOTES PAYABLE

The Company has entered into a "Wholesale Financing Flexible Payment Plan" (the "Plan") with a financing subsidiary of its major supplier to finance certain inventory purchases. The Company can borrow up to $25 million for purchases of inventory and working capital requirements. Borrowings for inventories accrue interest at prime plus 1.5% (10.875% at August 31,1995) and are generally repayable within 70 days of the date of the related invoice. Borrowings for working capital requirements accrue interest at prime plus 1.75% (11.125% at August 31,1995) and are generally repayable within 180 days of the related advance. Borrowings are collateralized by substantially all of The Company's assets.

(6) INCOME TAXES

Provision for income taxes consists of the following for the years ended August 31, 1995 and 1994, respectively.

	1995	1994
Current		
Federal	$48,538	$262,000
State	7,901	44,000
Deferred	24,397	67,000
Total Provision for Income Taxes	$80,836	$373,000

The difference between the expected 1994 provision for income taxes using the statutory federal rate and The Company's actual provision results primarily from the effect of state income taxes and the utilization of net operating loss carry forward.

At August 31, 1994, a deferred tax asset in the amount of $24,397 related primarily to differences in the reporting of accounts receivable allowances for financial statement and income tax purposes was recorded. During fiscal 1995, as a result of the change in tax status, such deferred tax asset was removed from the books and is reflected in the deferred tax provision for the year ended August 31, 1995.

(7) COMMITMENTS AND CONTINGENCIES

Operating Leases   The Company conducts its operations principally from corporate and sales offices that are leased under an operating lease agreement that expires in July 1996. Rental expense under this agreement was $78,745 and $49,425 for the years ended August 31, 1995, and 1994, respectively.

The Company also leases certain equipment under operating lease agreements. Rental expense under these agreements was $44,745 and $30,984 for the years ended August 31, 1995, and 1994, respectively.

REPORT OF INDEPENDENT PUBLIC ACCOUNTANTS

We have audited the accompanying balance sheets of Quimby's Computer Solutions, Inc. (a Delaware corporation) as of August 31, 1995, and 1994 and the related consolidated statements of operations, shareholders' equity, and cash flows for the years then ended. These financial statements are the responsibility of The Company's management. Our responsibility is to express an opinion on these financial statements based on our audits.

We conducted our audits in accordance with generally accepted auditing standards. Those standards require that we plan and perform the audit to obtain reasonable assurance about whether the financial statements are free of material misstatement. An audit includes examining, on a test basis, evidence supporting the amounts and disclosures in the financial statements. An audit also includes assessing the accounting principles used and significant estimates made by management, as well as evaluating the overall financial statement presentation. We believe that our audits provide a reasonable basis for our opinion.

In our opinion, the financial statements referred to above present fairly, in all material respects, the financial position of Quimby's Computer Solutions, Inc. and subsidiaries as of August 31, 1995, in conformity with generally accepted accounting principles.

Final Four Accounting Firm
Chicago, Illinois
October 28, 1995

EXERCISE 1: DEFINING THE APPRAISAL ASSIGNMENT

What is being appraised?

When is the appraisal as-of date?

_____

_____

Why are the appraisals being performed (the function)?

_____

_____

How is value to be defined?

_____

_____

_____

How will the appraisal be performed (the scope)?

_____

_____

Who is the client?

_____

_____

EXERCISE 1: PRACTICAL ASSIGNMENT CONSIDERATIONS

Tangible asset appraisal? _____

EXERCISE 2: THE ENGAGEMENT LETTER

Review the following engagement letter for points that you would change. You may use the exercise table to record your thoughts.

Date XXXXXXX XX, XXXX

Mr. John Burns, Controller
Quimby's Computer Solutions, Inc.
1204 State Street, Suite 3700
Chicago, IL 30303

Dear Mr. Burns:

This letter outlines our understanding of the terms and objectives of the valuation engagement. We will perform a valuation to estimate the value of (1) a block of 77,850 shares representing a 90% controlling interest in Quimby's. The date of the appraisal will be as of December 29, 1995. The standard of value employed will be "fair market value," which we define as follows:

The amount at which property would change hands between a willing seller and a willing buyer when neither is acting under compulsion and when both have reasonable knowledge of the relevant facts on or about the valuation date.

The scope of this assignment will involve a comprehensive level of due diligence and the issuance of a formal report. We understand that our valuation conclusion will be used for Mr. Smith's litigation. These reports will not be distributed to outside parties to obtain credit or for any other purposes. If for any reason we are unable to complete the valuation engagement, we will not issue these reports.

We have no responsibility to update our valuation reports for events and circumstances that occur after the valuation date or the date of its issuance. We expect to begin this engagement on XXXXX XX, XXXX and barring any unforeseen problems, we expect to complete the valuation portion of our assignment by XXXXX XX, XXXX.

Our method of valuation of security interests in going concerns follows the guidelines set forth by the Internal Revenue Service in its Revenue Ruling 59-60 as subsequently modified, as well as conforming to the ethics and valuation standards promulgated by the American Institute of Certified Public Accountants (AICPA) and the Appraisal Foundation under its *Uniform Standards of Professional Appraisal Practice.*

In performing our valuation, we will be relying on the accuracy and reliability of your historical financial statements, forecasts of future operations, or other financial data of your company. We will not audit, compile, or review your financial statements, forecasts, or other data, and we will not express an opinion or any form of assurance on them. At the conclusion of the engagement, we will ask you to sign a representation letter on the accuracy and reliability of the financial information used in the engagement. Our engagement cannot be relied on to disclose errors, irregularities, or illegal acts, including fraud or defalcation that may exist.

In developing our value estimate, we may use the services of an independent asset appraisal firm to establish the value of the real estate owned by The Company and its machinery and equipment, which is estimated to cost $X,XXX. We estimate that our fee for this service will be $X,XXX. If we encounter unusual circumstances that would require us to expand the scope of the engagement, we will discuss this with you before doing the additional work. We will require a retainer of $X,XXX at the execution of this agreement. The remainder of our fees will be rendered on a monthly basis and are payable upon receipt. Our valuation reports will state that our fee is not contingent on the values determined by this engagement. In addition, the fee estimate is for the valuation and valuation reports and does not include any services that may be required defending our valuation reports in litigation, including conferences, depositions, court appearances, and testimony. Fees for such services will be billed at our standard hourly rates.

We have attached to this Engagement Letter (1) our initial Limiting Conditions (which are an integral part of our valuation assignment and may be subsequently modified should circumstances warrant) and (2) our initial request for Company information. If you agree with the foregoing terms, please sign the copy of this letter in the space provided and return the letter to us along with you retainer check and requested preliminary information.

We sincerely appreciate this opportunity to be of service to you.

Brown Business Valuation Services
Karen Brown, ASA, CPA/ABV, CBA, CVA, CFA
Principal

This letter correctly sets forth the understanding of Quimby's Computer Solutions, Inc.

Signature   _____

Title   _____

Date   _____

(EXERCISE 2): PROBLEMS WITH THE ENGAGEMENT LETTER

_____

_____

_____

_____

_____

_____

_____

_____

_____

_____

_____

_____

_____

_____

_____

_____

_____

_____

EXERCISE 3: ANALYSIS OF GENERAL ECONOMIC DATA

Appendix 1 (to be downloaded) contains a selection of articles from various periodicals concerning the status and outlook of the general economy as of December 29, 1995.

Your assignment is to read this material and then identify the most relevant factors and trends that influence the value of Quimby's Computer Solutions, Inc. You must also be able to state how these relevant factors or trends will affect value.

The following page provides a basic table for you to list these factors and their potential qualitative impact on the subject Company's value. Use a + or + + for factors that enhance potential future returns or reduce investment risk, use a 0 for important factors that are currently having a neutral impact, and use a - or – – for factors that detract from potential future returns or increase investment risk.

(EXERCISE 3) GENERAL ECONOMIC ANALYSIS CONCLUSIONS

	Impact on Value
Observations	+ / 0 / –
_____	_____
_____	_____
_____	_____
_____	_____
_____	_____
_____	_____
_____	_____
_____	_____
_____	_____
_____	_____
_____	_____
_____	_____
_____	_____
_____	_____
_____	_____

EXERCISE 4: ANALYSIS OF SPECIFIC INDUSTRY DATA

Appendix 2 (to be downloaded) contains a selection of articles from various periodicals concerning the status and outlook of the specific industry as of December 1995. Your assignment is to read this material and then identify the most relevant factors and trends that influence the value of Quimby's Computer Solutions, Inc. You must also be able to state how these relevant factors or trends will affect value.

The following provides a basic table for you to list these factors and their potential qualitative impact on the subject Company's value. Use a + or ++ for factors that enhance potential future returns or reduce investment risk, use a 0 for important factors that are currently having a neutral impact, and use a - or - - for factors that detract from potential future returns or increase investment risk.

(EXERCISE 4) SPECIFIC INDUSTRY ANALYSIS CONCLUSIONS

Observations	Impact on Value + / 0 / –
_____	_____
_____	_____
_____	_____
_____	_____
_____	_____
_____	_____
_____	_____
_____	_____
_____	_____
_____	_____
_____	_____
_____	_____
_____	_____
_____	_____

EXERCISE 5: COMPARISON OF SUBJECT COMPANY FINANCIALS TO INDUSTRY DATA

Exhibit 1 provides a description of SIC# 5045 and 7373 under which we might classify the business of Quimby's Computer Solutions, Inc. Prior to performing the management interview, the appraiser went out onto the Internet and reviewed The Company's website. Initially, it seemed that The Company performed systems integration and other such services, leading the appraiser to believe that SIC# 7373 was the correct classification. According to management, however, while they would like to perform this type of work, 95% of The Company's revenue comes from the sale of computer hardware. Therefore, it was decided to use SIC# 5045.

Exhibit 2 provides Integra comparative industry data (SIC# 5045 for sales volume of $25 million to $49.999 million) for the years 1993 through 1997.

Schedules 1 through 6 provide historical financial data of Quimby's as reported for the fiscal years ended August 31, 1991, through August 31, 1995. There are no financial statements through December 1995. These schedules also include comparative financial analysis between the subject Company and Integra industry data.

Your assignment is to review this material and then identify the most relevant factors and trends that influence the value of Quimby's. You must also be able to state how these relevant factors or trends affect value. Express an opinion of the analytical strength/weight that the Integra data should be given in this case. Finally, develop a list of adjustments that you believe may be appropriate for the subject Company's financial statements that you want to discuss with management. Provide your answers on the exercise tables.

Exhibit 1

Occupational Safety & Health Administration (OSHA), U.S. Department of Labor

SIC Description for 5045

Division F: *Wholesale Trade*

Major Group 50: *Wholesale Trade—Durable Goods*

Industry Group 504: *Professional and Commercial Equipment and Supplies*

5045 Computers and Computer Peripheral Equipment and Software

Establishments primarily engaged in the wholesale distribution of computers, computer peripheral equipment, and computer software. These establishments frequently also may sell related supplies, but establishments primarily engaged in wholesaling supplies are classified according to the individual product (for example, computer paper in Industry 5112). Establishments primarily engaged in the wholesale distribution of modems and other electronic communications equipment are classified in Industry 5065. Establishments primarily engaged in selling computers and computer peripheral equipment and software for other than business or professional use are classified in Retail Trade, Industry 5734.

- Computer terminals—wholesale
- Computers—wholesale
- Disk drives—wholesale
- Keying equipment—wholesale
- Peripheral equipment computer—wholesale
- Printers computer—wholesale
- Software computer—wholesale

Exhibit 1 *(continued)*

Occupational Safety and Health Administration (OSHA), U.S. Department of Labor

SIC Description for 7373

Division I: *Services*

Major Group 73: *Business Services*

Industry Group 737: *Computer Programming, Data Processing, and Other Computer-Related Services*

7373 Computer Integrated Systems Design

Establishments primarily engaged in developing or modifying computer software and packaging or bundling the software with purchased computer hardware (computers and computer peripheral equipment) to create and market an integrated system for specific application. Establishments in this industry must provide each of the following services: (1) the development or modification of the computer software; (2) the marketing of purchased computer hardware; and (3) involvement in all phases of systems development from design through installation. Establishments primarily engaged in selling computer hardware are classified in Wholesale Trade, Industry 5045, and Retail Trade, Industry 5734; and those manufacturing computers and computer peripheral equipment are classified in Manufacturing, Industry Group 357.

- Computer-aided design (CAD) systems services
- Computer-aided engineering (CAE) systems services
- Computer-aided manufacturing (CAM) systems services
- Local area network (LAN) systems integrators
- Network systems integration, computer
- Office automation, computer systems integration
- Systems integration, computer
- Turnkey vendors, computer systems
- Value-added resellers, computer systems

Exhibit 2: Integra Comparative Industry Data (SIC# 5045) for the Years 1992–1995

(Permission for use granted by Integra.)

Business Profiler - SIC Description

SIC: 5045   **Wholesale Trade - Computers, peripherals & software**

Establishments primarily engaged in the wholesale distribution of computers, computer peripheral equipment, and computer software. These establishments frequently also may sell related supplies, but establishments primarily engaged in wholesaling supplies are classified according to the individual product (for example, computer paper in industry 5112). Establishments primarily engaged in the wholesale distribution of modems and other electronic communications equipment are classified in Industry 5065. Establishment primarily engaged in selling computers and computer peripheral equipment and software for other than business or professional use are classified in Retail Trade, Industry 5734.

5045

Wholesale Trade
Computers, peripherals & software

Sales Range	Business Count
All Sales Ranges	8,614
Less Than $250,000	2,182
$250,000 - $499,999	456
$500,000 - $999,999	1,562
$1,000,000 - $2,499,999	1,898
$2,500,000 - $4,999,999	977
$5,000,000 - $9,999,999	771
$10,000,000 - $24,999,999	501
$25,000,000 - $49,999,999	149
$50,000,000 - $99,999,999	62
$100,000,000 - $249,999,99	54
$250,000,000 - $499,999,99	0
More Than $500,000,000	2

INTEGRA
I N F O R M A T I O N

BUSINESS
PR⚙FILER™

Business Prof⚙ - Summary Financials

Profile Name:		SIG:	5045
Date:	6-19-00	Description:	Wholesale Trade - Computers, peripherals & software
Database #:	77	Sales Range:	$25,000,000 - $49,999,999
Profile Type:	Industry Profile	Final Year Business Count:	149

Database Expired - Please contact Integra Information for the most recent database update.

(Dollars in Thousand)

Income Statement	1993	1994	1995	1996	1997
Revenue	22,824	23,972	28,351	31,130	33,743
Cost of Sales	18,383	19,180	22,783	25,030	27,091
Gross Margin	4,440	4,792	5,568	6,100	6,653
Operating Expenses	3,921	4,166	4,871	5,292	5,714
Operating Income	519	626	697	808	939
Pre-Tax Income	377	403	485	511	574
Net Income	233	249	301	314	358

Balance Sheet	1993	1994	1995	1996	1997
Assets					
Cash & Equivalents	613	648	749	821	887
Accounts Receivable, net	3,472	3,675	4,251	4,654	5,027
Inventory	4,153	4,397	5,088	5,572	6,020
Other Current Assets	359	382	466	516	575
Total Current Assets	8,597	9,101	10,554	11,564	12,509
Fixed Assets, net	682	692	813	842	917
Intangible Assets, net	128	131	159	174	191
Depletable Assets, net					
Other Assets/Investments	444	474	564	609	680
Total Assets	9,851	10,398	12,090	13,189	14,298
Liabilities & Net Worth					
Notes Payable	1,824	1,920	2,274	2,526	2,692
Accounts Payable	2,731	2,899	3,569	3,963	4,368
Other Current Liabilities	814	844	1,040	1,154	1,272
Total Current Liabilities	5,369	5,663	6,883	7,643	8,333
Long Term Debt	1,192	1,294	1,558	1,692	1,892
Other Liabilities/Shareholder Loans	166	174	207	228	242
Total Long Term Liabilities	1,359	1,467	1,765	1,920	2,133
Total Liabilities	6,728	7,130	8,648	9,564	10,466
Total Net Worth	3,124	3,268	3,442	3,626	3,832
Total Liabilities & Net Worth	9,851	10,398	12,090	13,189	14,298

INTEGRA
I N F O R M A T I O N™

BUSINESS
PROFILER™

Business Profiler - Summary Financials

Profile Name:		SIC:	5045
Date:	6-19-00	Description:	Wholesale Trade - Computers, peripherals & software
Database #:	77	Sales Range:	$25,000,000 - $49,999,999
Profile Type:	Industry Profile	Final Year Business Count:	149

Database Expired - Please contact Integra Information for the most recent database update.

Income Statement

	1993	1994	1995	1996	1997
Revenue	100.0%	100.0%	100.0%	100.0%	100.0%
Cost of Sales	80.5%	80.0%	80.4%	80.4%	80.3%
Gross Margin	19.5%	20.0%	19.6%	19.6%	19.7%
Operating Expenses	17.2%	17.4%	17.2%	17.0%	16.9%
Operating Income	2.3%	2.6%	2.5%	2.6%	2.8%
Pre-Tax Income	1.6%	1.7%	1.7%	1.6%	1.7%
Net Income	1.0%	1.0%	1.1%	1.0%	1.1%

Balance Sheet

	1993	1994	1995	1996	1997
Assets					
Cash & Equivalents	6.2%	6.2%	6.2%	6.2%	6.2%
Accounts Receivable, net	35.2%	35.3%	35.2%	35.3%	35.2%
Inventory	42.2%	42.3%	42.1%	42.2%	42.1%
Other Current Assets	3.6%	3.7%	3.9%	3.9%	4.0%
Total Current Assets	87.3%	87.5%	87.3%	87.7%	87.5%
Fixed Assets, net	6.9%	6.7%	6.7%	6.4%	6.4%
Intangible Assets, net	1.3%	1.3%	1.3%	1.3%	1.3%
Depletable Assets, net					
Other Assets/Investments	4.6%	4.5%	4.7%	4.6%	4.8%
Total Assets	100.0%	100.0%	100.0%	100.0%	100.0%
Liabilities & Net Worth					
Notes Payable	18.5%	18.5%	18.8%	19.1%	18.8%
Accounts Payable	27.7%	27.9%	29.5%	30.0%	30.5%
Other Current Liabilities	8.3%	8.1%	8.6%	8.8%	8.9%
Total Current Liabilities	54.5%	54.5%	56.9%	57.9%	58.3%
Long Term Debt	12.1%	12.4%	12.9%	12.6%	13.2%
Other Liabilities/Shareholder Loans	1.7%	1.7%	1.7%	1.7%	1.7%
Total Long Term Liabilities	13.8%	14.1%	14.6%	14.6%	14.9%
Total Liabilities	68.3%	68.6%	71.5%	72.5%	73.2%
Total Net Worth	31.7%	31.4%	28.5%	27.5%	26.8%
Total Liabilities & Net Worth	100.0%	100.0%	100.0%	100.0%	100.0%

INTEGRA
INFORMATION™

BUSINESS
PRØFILER

Business Profiler - Income Statement

Profile Name:		SIC:	5045
Date:	6-19-00	Description:	Wholesale Trade - Computers, peripherals & software
Database #:	77	Sales Range:	$25,000,000 - $49,999,999
Profile Type:	Industry Profile	Final Year Business Count:	149

Database Expired - Please contact Integra Information for the most recent database update.

(Dollars in Thousands)

Income Statement	1993	1994	1995	1996	1997
Revenue	22,824	23,972	28,351	31,130	33,743
Cost of Sales	18,383	19,180	22,783	25,030	27,091
Gross Margin	4,440	4,792	5,568	6,100	6,653
Selling, General & Administrative	2,970	3,140	3,686	4,010	4,317
Officer Compensation	278	300	343	364	398
Pension & Benefits	80	84	94	100	105
Advertising & Sales	210	233	275	302	341
Bad Debts	91	96	113	121	128
Rents Paid	148	153	170	187	196
Depreciation & Amortization	144	161	190	209	229
Operating Expenses	3,921	4,166	4,871	5,292	5,714
Operating Income	519	626	697	808	939
Interest Income	32	34	39	43	47
Interest Expense	(240)	(324)	(326)	(427)	(503)
Total Other Inc(Exp)	66	67	76	87	91
Pre-Tax Income	377	403	486	511	574
Income Taxes *	(144)	(153)	(184)	(196)	(216)
Net Income	233	249	301	314	358

* Income taxes are derived by applying
a 38% tax rate to pre-tax income.

BUSINESS
PROFILER™

Business Profiler - Income Statement

Profile Name:			SIC:	5045
Date:	6-19-00		Description:	Wholesale Trade - Computers, peripherals & software
Database #:	77		Sales Range:	$25,000,000 - $49,999,999
Profile Type:	Industry Profile		Final Year Business Count:	149

Database Expired - Please contact Integra Information for the most recent database update.

Income Statement	1993	1994	1995	1996	1997
Revenue	100.0%	100.0%	100.0%	100.0%	100.0%
Cost of Sales	80.5%	80.0%	80.4%	80.4%	80.3%
Gross Margin	19.5%	20.0%	19.6%	19.6%	19.7%
Selling, General & Administrative	13.0%	13.1%	13.0%	12.9%	12.8%
Officer Compensation	1.2%	1.2%	1.2%	1.2%	1.2%
Pension & Benefits	0.4%	0.4%	0.3%	0.3%	0.3%
Advertising & Sales	0.9%	1.0%	1.0%	1.0%	1.0%
Bad Debts	0.4%	0.4%	0.4%	0.4%	0.4%
Rents Paid	0.7%	0.6%	0.6%	0.6%	0.6%
Depreciation & Amortization	0.6%	0.7%	0.7%	0.7%	0.7%
Operating Expenses	17.2%	17.4%	17.2%	17.0%	16.9%
Operating Income	2.3%	2.6%	2.5%	2.6%	2.8%
Interest Income	0.1%	0.1%	0.1%	0.1%	0.1%
Interest Expense	-1.1%	-1.3%	-1.2%	-1.4%	-1.5%
Total Other Inc(Exp)	0.3%	0.3%	0.3%	0.3%	0.3%
Pre-Tax Income	1.6%	1.7%	1.7%	1.6%	1.7%
Income Taxes *	-0.6%	-0.6%	-0.7%	-0.6%	-0.6%
Net Income	1.0%	1.0%	1.1%	1.0%	1.1%

* Income taxes are derived by applying
a 38% tax rate to pre-tax income.

INTEGRA
INFORMATION*

BUSINESS PROFILER™

Business Profiler - Balance Sheet

Profile Name:			SIC:		5045
Date:	6-19-00		Description:		Wholesale Trade - Computers, peripherals & software
Database #:	77		Sales Range:		$25,000,000 - $49,999,999
Profile Type:	Industry Profile		Final Year Business Count:	149	

Database Expired - Please contact Integra Information for the most recent database update.

(Dollars in Thousands)

Balance Sheet	1993	1994	1995	1996	1997
Assets					
Cash	546	581	675	744	805
Marketable Securities	66	67	74	77	82
Accounts Receivable	3,505	3,710	4,293	4,702	5,078
less Allowance for Bad Debt	(33)	(35)	(43)	(48)	(52)
Accounts Receivable, net	3,472	3,675	4,251	4,654	5,027
Raw Material					
Work In Process					
Finished Goods					
Inventory	4,153	4,397	5,088	5,572	6,020
Other Current Assets	359	382	466	516	575
Total Current Assets	8,597	9,101	10,554	11,564	12,509
Property, Plant & Equipment	1,485	1,570	1,882	1,960	2,194
less Accumulated Depreciation	(803)	(878)	(1,069)	(1,117)	(1,277)
Property, Plant & Equipment, net	682	692	813	842	917
Intangible Assets, net	128	131	159	174	191
Depletable Assets, net					
Investments	310	324	393	416	466
Other Assets	134	150	172	191	214
Total Assets	9,851	10,398	12,090	13,189	14,298
Liabilities & Net Worth					
Short Term Debt	1,824	1,920	2,274	2,526	2,692
Accounts Payable	2,731	2,899	3,569	3,963	4,368
Other Current Liabilities	814	844	1,040	1,154	1,272
Total Current Liabilities	5,369	5,663	6,883	7,643	8,333
Long Term Debt	1,192	1,294	1,558	1,692	1,892
Loans from Shareholders	0	0	0	0	0
Other Liabilities	166	174	207	228	242
Total Long Term Liabilities	1,359	1,467	1,765	1,920	2,133
Total Liabilities	6,728	7,130	8,648	9,564	10,466
Total Net Worth	3,124	3,268	3,442	3,626	3,832
Total Liabilities & Net Worth	9,851	10,398	12,090	13,189	14,298

Integra Business Profiler is a proprietary financial analysis tool and database developed by Integra Information, Inc. (Integra). Integra shall exercise its best efforts to furnish accurate and reliable information but does not warranty the correctness, currency or completeness of such deliverables regardless of media i.e. electronic/printed material. Integra will not be liable for any loss or injury to the client that arises out of any errors or inaccuracies in the information and/or reports delivered.

INTEGRA INFORMATION™

BUSINESS
PRƆFILER™

Business Profiler - Balance Sheet

Profile Name:	
Date:	6-19-00
Database #:	77
Profile Type:	Industry Profile

SIC:	5045
Description:	Wholesale Trade - Computers, peripherals & software
Sales Range:	$25,000,000 - $49,999,999
Final Year Business Count:	149

Database Expired - Please contact Integra Information for the most recent database update.

Balance Sheet	1993	1994	1995	1996	1997
Assets					
Cash	5.5%	5.6%	5.6%	5.6%	5.6%
Marketable Securities	0.7%	0.6%	0.6%	0.6%	0.6%
Accounts Receivable	35.6%	35.7%	35.5%	35.7%	35.5%
less Allowance for Bad Debt	-0.3%	-0.3%	-0.4%	-0.4%	-0.4%
Accounts Receivable, net	35.2%	35.3%	35.2%	35.3%	35.2%
Raw Material					
Work In Process					
Finished Goods					
Inventory	42.2%	42.3%	42.1%	42.2%	42.1%
Other Current Assets	3.6%	3.7%	3.9%	3.9%	4.0%
Total Current Assets	87.3%	87.5%	87.3%	87.7%	87.5%
Property, Plant & Equipment	15.1%	15.1%	15.6%	14.9%	15.3%
less Accumulated Depreciation	-8.2%	-8.4%	-8.8%	-8.5%	-8.9%
Property, Plant & Equipment, net	6.9%	6.7%	6.7%	6.4%	6.4%
Intangible Assets, net	1.3%	1.3%	1.3%	1.3%	1.3%
Depletable Assets, net					
Investments	3.2%	3.1%	3.3%	3.2%	3.3%
Other Assets	1.4%	1.4%	1.4%	1.4%	1.5%
Total Assets	100.0%	100.0%	100.0%	100.0%	100.0%
Liabilities & Net Worth					
Short Term Debt	18.5%	18.5%	18.8%	19.1%	18.8%
Accounts Payable	27.7%	27.9%	29.5%	30.0%	30.5%
Other Current Liabilities	8.3%	8.1%	8.6%	8.8%	8.9%
Total Current Liabilities	54.5%	54.5%	56.9%	57.9%	58.3%
Long Term Debt	12.1%	12.4%	12.9%	12.8%	13.2%
Loans from Shareholders					
Other Liabilities	1.7%	1.7%	1.7%	1.7%	1.7%
Total Long Term Liabilities	13.8%	14.1%	14.6%	14.6%	14.9%
Total Liabilities	68.3%	68.6%	71.5%	72.5%	73.2%
Total Net Worth	31.7%	31.4%	28.5%	27.5%	26.8%
Total Liabilities & Net Worth	100.0%	100.0%	100.0%	100.0%	100.0%

BUSINESS
PROFILER™

Business Profiler - Cash Flow Analysis

Profile Name:		SIC:	5045
Date:	6-19-00	Description:	Wholesale Trade - Computers, peripherals & software
Database #:	77	Sales Range:	$25,000,000 - $49,999,999
Profile Type:	Industry Profile	Final Year Business Count:	149

(Dollars in Thousands)

Analysis of Cash Flow	1994	1995	1996	1997
Operating Cash Flow				
Net Income	249	301	314	358
Adjustments to reconcile net income to net cash provided by operating activities:				
Depreciation and Amortization	161	190	209	229
Change in Accounts Receivable, net	(203)	(576)	(404)	(372)
Change in Inventory	(244)	(691)	(485)	(448)
Change in Accounts Payable	168	670	394	405
Change in Other Operating Activities	(1)	123	66	50
Total Adjustments	(119)	(284)	(219)	(136)
Cash Provided by Operating Activities	131	17	95	221
Investing Activities				
Capital Expenditures	(173)	(339)	(253)	(322)
Change in Marketable Securities	(1)	(7)	(3)	(5)
Change in Investments	(14)	(66)	(25)	(46)
Cash Provided by Investing Activities	(188)	(416)	(281)	(375)
Financing Activities				
Change in Short Term Debt	95	355	252	166
Change in Long Term Debt	102	265	134	199
Change in Loans from Shareholders	0	0	0	0
Cash Provided by Financing Activities	197	619	386	366

Note: The intent of the Cash Flow Analysis is to reflect operating performance. It does not address investments or changes in capital structure which can vary significantly from firm to firm. When evaluating cash flow, this information should be used in conjunction with specifics around an individual firm's capital structure.

BUSINESS PROFILER™

Business Profiler - Ratios

Profile Name:		SIC:	5045
Date:	6-19-00	Description:	Wholesale Trade - Computers, peripherals & software
Database #:	77	Sales Range:	$25,000,000 - $49,999,999
Profile Type:	Industry Profile	Final Year Business Count:	149

Liquidity / Solvency

	1993	1994	1995	1996	1997
Quick Ratio	0.76	0.76	0.73	0.72	0.71
Current Ratio	1.60	1.61	1.53	1.51	1.50
Days Accounts Receivable Outstanding	56	54	51	52	52
Days Accounts Payable	54	54	56	57	58
Days Working Capital	52	51	46	45	44
Days Inventory	82	84	82	81	81
Accounts Receivable to Sales	15%	15%	14%	14%	15%
Accounts Payable to Sales	12%	12%	11%	12%	12%
Current Liabilities to Net Worth	171.9%	173.3%	200.0%	210.8%	217.5%
Current Liabilities to Inventory	x1.29	x1.29	x1.35	x1.37	x1.38
Cost of Sales to Payables	x6.73	x6.62	x6.38	x6.32	x6.20

Turnover

	1993	1994	1995	1996	1997
Receivables Turnover	x6.57	x6.71	x7.16	x6.99	x6.97
Cash Turnover	x41.77	x41.27	x41.99	x41.82	x41.91
Inventory Turnover	x4.43	x4.49	x4.60	x4.70	x4.67
Current Asset Turnover	x2.66	x2.63	x2.69	x2.69	x2.70
Working Capital Turnover		x7.19	x7.98	x8.20	x8.34
Fixed Asset Turnover	x33.45	x34.65	x34.89	x36.95	x36.79
Total Asset Turnover	x2.32	x2.31	x2.35	x2.36	x2.36

Debt

	1993	1994	1995	1996	1997
Debt Service Coverage - EBITDA	x0.32	x0.37	x0.40	x0.38	x0.39
Debt Service Coverage - Pre-Tax	x0.37	x0.41	x0.45	x0.42	x0.43
Debt Service Coverage - After-Tax	x0.30	x0.34	x0.36	x0.35	x0.36
Interest Coverage	x2.16	x1.93	x2.13	x1.89	x1.87
Current Assets to Short Term Debt	x4.71	x4.74	x4.64	x4.58	x4.65
Accounts Payable to Total Debt	40.6%	40.7%	41.3%	41.4%	41.7%
Short Term Debt to Total Debt	27.1%	26.9%	26.3%	26.4%	25.7%
Long Term Debt to Total Assets	12.1%	12.4%	12.9%	12.8%	13.2%
ST Debt plus LT Debt to Net Worth	96.6%	98.3%	111.3%	116.3%	119.6%
Total Debt to Assets	68.3%	68.6%	71.6%	72.5%	73.2%
Total Debt to Inventory	x1.62	x1.62	x1.70	x1.72	x1.74
Total Debt to Net Worth	x2.15	x2.18	x2.51	x2.64	x2.73

Risk

	1993	1994	1995	1996	1997
Z Score	4.03	4.08	3.73	3.66	3.62
Fixed Assets to Net Worth	x0.22	x0.21	x0.24	x0.23	x0.24

BUSINESS PROFILER

Business Profiler - Ratios

Profile Name:				SIC:	5045
Date:	6-19-00			Description:	Wholesale Trade - Computers, peripherals & software
Database #:	77			Sales Range:	$25,000,000 - $49,999,999
Profile Type:	Industry Profile			Final Year Business Count:	149

Profitability	1993	1994	1995	1996	1997
Gross Margin	19.5%	20.0%	19.6%	19.6%	19.7%
EBITDA to Sales	2.9%	3.3%	3.1%	3.3%	3.5%
Operating Margin	2.3%	2.6%	2.5%	2.6%	2.8%
Operating Cash Flow to Sales		0.5%	0.1%	0.3%	0.7%
Pre-Tax Return on Assets	3.8%	3.9%	4.0%	3.9%	4.0%
After-Tax Return on Assets	2.4%	2.4%	2.5%	2.4%	2.5%
Pre-Tax Return on Net Worth	12.1%	12.3%	14.1%	14.1%	15.0%
After-Tax Return on Net Worth	7.5%	7.6%	8.7%	8.7%	9.3%
Pre-Tax Return on Sales	1.6%	1.7%	1.7%	1.6%	1.7%
After-Tax Return on Sales	1.0%	1.0%	1.1%	1.0%	1.1%

Working Capital	1993	1994	1995	1996	1997
Working Capital	$3,228	$3,439	$3,671	$3,921	$4,176
Working Capital to Sales	14.1%	13.9%	12.5%	12.2%	12.0%
Net Income to Working Capital	7.2%	7.3%	8.2%	8.0%	8.6%
Inventory to Working Capital	128.7%	127.9%	138.6%	142.1%	144.1%
Short Term Debt to Working Capital	56.5%	55.8%	62.0%	64.4%	64.5%
Long Term Debt to Working Capital	36.9%	37.6%	42.5%	43.2%	45.3%

Operating Efficiency	1993	1994	1995	1996	1997
Operating Expenses to Gross Margin	88.3%	86.9%	87.5%	86.8%	85.9%
Operating Expenses to Sales	17.2%	17.4%	17.2%	17.0%	16.9%
Depreciation & Amortization to Sales	0.6%	0.7%	0.7%	0.7%	0.7%
Total Assets to Sales	43.2%	43.4%	42.6%	42.4%	42.4%
Sales to Net Worth	x7.31	x7.34	x8.24	x8.59	x8.81
Sales to Fixed Assets	3345.2%	3465.1%	3466.7%	3695.0%	3676.5%
Inventory to Cost of Sales	22.6%	22.9%	22.3%	22.3%	22.2%
Intangible Assets to Sales	0.6%	0.5%	0.6%	0.6%	0.6%
Capital Expenditures to Sales		0.7%	1.2%	0.8%	1.0%

Growth (CAGR 5 Years)	1997
Sales	10.3%
Operating Income	16.0%
Pre-Tax Profit	11.1%
Net Income	11.3%
Assets	9.8%
Liabilities	11.7%
Net Worth	5.2%

SCHEDULES 3 THROUGH 8:
QUIMBY'S FINANCIAL STATEMENTS AS REPORTED WITH INTEGRA
FOR THE FISCAL YEARS ENDED 8/31/91–95

Quimby's Computer Solutions, Inc.
Schedule 3: Annual Historical Balance Sheets as Reported
Fiscal Years Ended August 31,

	1991	1992	1993	1994	1995
Current Assets					
Cash	$ 10,647	$ 2,148	$ 69,266	$ 544,500	$ 1,118,697
Marketable Securities	35,233	–	52,886	–	–
Accounts Receivable	313,751	797,374	971,565	3,963,550	4,589,646
Inventories	50,100	189,224	270,233	1,814,009	3,693,293
Prepaid Expenses	–	–	–	24,396	15,484
Other Current Assets	–	3,348	–	–	–
Total Current Assets	$ 409,731	$ 992,094	$ 1,363,950	$ 6,346,455	$ 9,417,120
Net Fixed Assets	$ 66,947	$ 7,619	$ 18,048	$ 43,021	$ 316,784
Other Assets					
Security Deposits	$ 8,391	$ 8,391	$ 11,393	–	$ 11,301
Stockholder Loans	56,446	–	–	34,996	229,246
Employee Advances	15,620	–	–	–	96,687
Other Assets	12,668	–	21,160	35,384	51,302
Total Other Assets	$ 93,125	$ 8,391	$ 32,553	$ 70,380	$ 388,536
TOTAL ASSETS	$ 569,803	$ 1,008,104	$ 1,414,551	$ 6,459,856	$ 10,122,440
Current Liabilities					
Accounts Payable	$ 363,408	$ 848,670	$ 1,071,061	$ 1,686,380	$ 1,361,785
Accrued Expenses	–	–	36,181	398,617	704,373
Income Taxes Payable	–	–	–	306,000	–
Due to Stockholder	–	56,582	115,004	–	–
Revolving Credit Line	411,775	372,270	290,977	3,603,175	6,540,143
Total Current Liabilities	$ 775,183	$ 1,277,522	$ 1,513,223	$ 5,994,172	$ 8,606,301
Stockholders' Equity					
Common Stock	$ 865	$ 865	$ 865	$ 865	$ 865
Retained Earnings	(206,245)	(270,283)	(99,537)	464,819	1,515,274
Total Stockholders' Equity	$ (205,380)	$ (269,418)	$ (98,672)	$ 465,684	$ 1,516,139
TOTAL LIABILITIES AND STOCKHOLDERS' EQUITY	$ 569,803	$ 1,008,104	$ 1,414,551	$ 6,459,856	$ 10,122,440

Quimby's Computer Solutions, Inc.
Schedule 4: Historical Income Statements as Reported
Fiscal Years Ended August 31,

	1991	1992	1993	1994	1995
Revenues	$ 5,008,819	$ 5,813,102	$11,825,174	$ 22,285,781	$ 40,945,386
Cost of Sales	$ 4,405,459	$ 5,064,854	$ 9,775,873	$ 18,276,690	$ 33,588,165
Gross Profit	$ 603,360	$ 748,248	$ 2,049,301	$ 4,009,091	$ 7,357,221
Operating Expenses					
Accounting	$ 67,565	$ 9,619	$ –	$ –	$ –
Advertising	19,913	28,071	38,892	–	–
Auto Expense	19,440	20,361	27,831	14,984	17,578
Bad Debts	(11,440)	–	–	8,348	16,580
Bank Charges	33,029	–	733	–	–
Charitable Contributions	–	–	–	–	1,150
Commissions	–	–	401,553	662,400	2,188,422
Data Processing	–	–	–	70,685	–
Depreciation	8,150	5,996	4,212	23,758	77,199
Employee Benefits	23,254	11,539	–	–	52,890
Entertainment	19,314	16,315	14,852	62,326	6,747
Officers' Compensation	130,108	196,078	184,784	617,559	1,235,045
Capitalized 263A Costs	–	–	–	–	(40,521)
Insurance—Group	7,950	7,193	62,762	33,799	47,950
Insurance—Life	11,025	9,570	2,016	2,016	7,279
Licenses and Fees	–	–	7,274	3,859	–
Miscellaneous	–	–	18,981	20,549	60,406
Office Expenses	26,832	17,966	41,078	50,073	348,761
Outside Services	28,798	40,124	–	–	–
Computer Expenses	–	–	14,742	61,439	–
Pension Plan	–	–	1,200	343	32,688
Postage and Delivery	7,385	10,035	47,232	11,089	–
Professional Fees	–	–	7,137	96,020	97,868
Rents	43,801	47,298	121,530	49,425	92,724
Repairs and Maintenance	6,529	4,269	11,615	–	26,319
Equipment Rental	–	1,324	3,738	–	26,716
Salaries and Wages	95,400	103,115	466,009	592,724	653,575
Seminars and Meetings	–	–	375	35,113	31,425
Taxes—Payroll	36,610	44,364	50,847	155,841	179,557
Telephone	97,031	100,738	113,365	143,044	186,042

Quimby's Computer Solutions, Inc.
Schedule 4: Historical Income Statements as Reported
Fiscal Years Ended August 31, *(continued)*

	1991	1992	1993	1994	1995
Travel	4,687	1,727	31,865	15,582	85,891
Utilities	7,868	6,318	5,843	7,892	13,946
Lead Expense	6,072	7,566	–	–	–
Dues and Subscriptions	7,629	5,180	–	4,739	11,706
Finders Fees	–	–	130,813	275,468	–
Recruiting	–	–	12,064	8,108	23,250
Education	–	–	–	1,240	–
Technical Support	–	–	–	500	13,295
Temporary Help	1,368	788	22,281	81,889	63,056
Selling Expenses	13,607	17,379	10,401	38,191	108,624
Total Operating Expenses	$ 711,925	$ 712,933	$ 1,856,025	$ 3,149,003	$ 5,666,168
Operating Income (Loss)	$ (108,565)	$ 35,315	$ 193,276	$ 860,088	$ 1,691,053
Other Income					
Interest Income	$ 2,146	$ 2,081	$ 647	$ 7,054	$ 32,558
Dividend Income	520	–	–	249	3,114
Gain on Sale of Assets	(543)	–	–	–	–
Rental Income	(7,933)	1,055	–	–	–
Other Income	269	–	–	17,480	78,596
Other Income	6,161	–	–	–	–
Total Other Income	$ 620	$ 3,136	$ 647	$ 24,783	$ 114,268
Other Expenses					
Interest Expense	$ 43,813	$ 67,256	$ 41,829	$ 139,909	$ 199,028
Loss on Sale of Assets	–	35,233	2,508	–	–
Total Other Expenses	$ 43,813	$ 102,489	$ 44,337	$ 139,909	$ 199,028
Total Other (Expenses)	$ (43,193)	$ (99,353)	$ (43,690)	$ (115,126)	$ (84,760)
Income (Loss) Before Taxes	$ (151,758)	$ (64,038)	$ 149,586	$ 744,962	$ 1,606,293
Income Taxes	–	–	–	262,000	–
NET INCOME (LOSS)	$ (151,758)	$ (64,038)	$ 149,586	$ 482,962	$ 1,606,293

Quimby's Computer Solutions, Inc.
Schedule 5: Common Size Historical Financial Statement Comparison
Fiscal Years Ended August 31,

	1991		1992		1993		1994		1995	
	Integra	Quimby's	Integra	Quimby's	Integra	Quimby's	Integra	Quimby's	Integra	Quimby's
Assets										
Cash	0.0%	1.9%	5.5%	0.2%	5.6%	4.9%	5.6%	8.4%	5.6%	11.1%
Marketable Securities	0.0%	6.2%	0.7%	0.0%	0.6%	3.7%	0.6%	0.0%	0.6%	0.0%
Accounts Receivable	0.0%	55.1%	35.6%	79.1%	35.7%	68.7%	35.5%	61.4%	35.5%	45.3%
Less Allowance for Bad Debt	0.0%	0.0%	-0.3%	0.0%	-0.4%	0.0%	-0.4%	0.0%	-0.4%	0.0%
Accounts Receivable (Net)	0.0%	55.1%	35.3%	79.1%	35.3%	68.7%	35.2%	61.4%	35.2%	45.3%
Inventory	0.0%	8.8%	42.2%	18.8%	42.3%	19.1%	42.1%	28.1%	42.1%	36.5%
Other Current Assets	0.0%	0.0%	3.6%	0.3%	3.7%	0.0%	3.9%	0.4%	3.9%	0.2%
Total Current Assets	0.0%	71.9%	87.3%	98.4%	87.5%	96.4%	87.3%	98.2%	87.3%	93.0%
Fixed Assets										
Property, Plant, and Equipment	0.0%	11.8%	15.1%	0.8%	15.1%	1.3%	15.6%	0.7%	15.6%	3.1%
Accumulated Depreciation	0.0%	0.0%	-8.2%	0.0%	-8.4%	0.0%	-8.8%	0.0%	-8.8%	0.0%
Net Fixed Assets	0.0%	11.8%	6.9%	0.8%	6.7%	1.3%	6.7%	0.7%	6.7%	3.1%
Other Assets										
Intangible Assets (Net)	0.0%	0.0%	1.3%	0.0%	1.3%	0.0%	1.3%	0.0%	1.3%	0.0%
Depletable Assets (Net)	0.0%	0.0%	0.0%	0.0%	0.0%	0.0%	0.0%	0.0%	0.0%	0.0%
Investments	0.0%	11.4%	3.2%	0.8%	3.1%	0.8%	3.3%	0.5%	3.3%	2.4%

Quimby's Computer Solutions, Inc.
Schedule 5: Common Size Historical Financial Statement Comparison
Fiscal Years Ended August 31, (continued)

	1991		1992		1993		1994		1995	
	Integra	Quimby's	Integra	Quimby's	Integra	Quimby's	Integra	Quimby's	Integra	Quimby's
Other Assets	0.0%	5.0%	1.4%	0.0%	1.4%	1.5%	1.4%	0.6%	1.4%	1.5%
Total Other Assets	0.0%	16.3%	5.8%	0.8%	5.8%	2.3%	6.0%	1.1%	6.0%	3.8%
TOTAL ASSETS	0.0%	100.0%	100.0%	100.0%	100.0%	100.0%	100.0%	100.0%	100.0%	100.0%
Liabilities and Net Worth										
Notes Payable—Banks	0.0%	0.0%	18.5%	0.0%	18.5%	0.0%	18.8%	0.0%	18.8%	0.0%
Accounts Payable	0.0%	63.8%	27.7%	84.2%	27.9%	75.7%	29.5%	26.1%	29.5%	13.5%
Other Current Liabilities	0.0%	72.3%	8.3%	42.5%	8.1%	31.3%	8.6%	66.7%	8.6%	71.6%
Total Current Liabilities	0.0%	136.0%	54.5%	126.7%	54.5%	107.0%	56.9%	92.8%	56.9%	85.0%
Long-Term Liabilities										
Long-Term Debt	0.0%	0.0%	12.1%	0.0%	12.4%	0.0%	12.9%	0.0%	12.9%	0.0%
Loans from Stockholders	0.0%	0.0%	0.0%	0.0%	0.0%	0.0%	0.0%	0.0%	0.0%	0.0%
Other Liabilities	0.0%	0.0%	1.7%	0.0%	1.7%	0.0%	1.7%	0.0%	1.7%	0.0%
Total Long-Term Liabilities	0.0%	0.0%	13.8%	0.0%	14.1%	0.0%	14.6%	0.0%	14.6%	0.0%
Total Liabilities	0.0%	136.0%	68.3%	126.7%	68.6%	107.0%	71.5%	92.8%	71.5%	85.0%
Total Net Worth	0.0%	-36.0%	31.7%	-26.7%	31.4%	-7.0%	28.5%	7.2%	28.5%	15.0%
TOTAL LIABILITIES AND NET WORTH	0.0%	100.0%	100.0%	100.0%	100.0%	100.0%	100.0%	100.0%	100.0%	100.0%

Quimby's Computer Solutions, Inc.
Schedule 6: Common Size Financial Statement Comparison
Fiscal Years Ended August 31,

	1991		1992		1993		1994		1995	
	Integra	Quimby's	Integra	Quimby's	Integra	Quimby's	Integra	Quimby's	Integra	Quimby's
Revenue	0.0%	100.0%	100.0%	100.0%	100.0%	100.0%	100.0%	100.0%	100.0%	100.0%
Cost of Sales	0.0%	88.0%	80.5%	87.1%	80.0%	82.7%	80.4%	82.0%	80.4%	82.0%
Gross Margin	0.0%	12.1%	19.5%	12.9%	20.0%	17.3%	19.6%	18.0%	19.6%	18.0%
Operating Expenses	0.0%	14.2%	17.2%	12.3%	17.4%	15.7%	17.2%	14.1%	17.2%	13.8%
Operating Income	0.0%	-2.2%	2.3%	0.6%	2.6%	1.6%	2.5%	3.9%	2.5%	4.1%
Interest Expense	0.0%	0.9%	-1.1%	1.2%	-1.4%	0.4%	-1.2%	0.6%	-1.2%	0.5%
Total Other Income (Expenses)	0.0%	0.0%	0.4%	-0.6%	0.4%	0.0%	0.4%	0.1%	0.4%	0.3%
Pretax Income (Loss)	0.0%	-3.0%	1.7%	-1.1%	1.7%	1.3%	1.7%	3.3%	1.7%	3.9%
Income Taxes	0.0%	0.0%	-0.6%	0.0%	-0.6%	0.0%	-0.7%	1.2%	-0.7%	0.0%
NET INCOME (LOSS)	**0.0%**	**-3.0%**	**1.0%**	**-1.1%**	**1.0%**	**1.3%**	**1.1%**	**2.2%**	**1.1%**	**3.9%**

Quimby's Computer Solutions, Inc.
Schedule 7: Historical Ratios Comparison to Integra Industry
Benchmark Data as of August 31,

	1992	1993	1994	1995
LIQUIDITY/SOLVENCY				
Quick Ratio	0.63	0.72	0.75	0.66
Quick Ratio—Integra	0.76	0.76	0.73	0.73
Current Ratio	0.78	0.90	1.06	1.09
Current Ratio—Integra	1.60	1.61	1.53	1.53
Days Accounts Receivables Outstanding	34.88	27.30	40.41	38.12
Days Accounts Receivables Outstanding—Integra	55.56	54.40	50.98	50.98
Days Accounts Payable	43.67	35.84	27.53	16.56
Days Accounts Payable—Integra	27.11	53.57	51.81	57.18
Days Working Capital	(20.43)	(6.71)	1.66	5.18
Days Working Capital—Integra	–	50.76	45.74	45.74
Days Inventory Sales	8.62	8.58	20.81	29.92
Days Inventory Sales—Integra	82.39	81.29	76.04	76.04
TURNOVER				
Receivables Turnover	10.46	13.37	9.03	9.57
Receivables Turnover—Integra	6.57	6.71	7.16	7.16
Cash Turnover	908.65	331.17	72.62	49.24
Cash Turnover—Integra	41.77	41.27	41.99	41.99
Inventory Turnover	42.33	42.55	17.54	12.20
Inventory Turnover—Integra	4.43	4.49	4.80	4.80
Current Asset Turnover	8.29	10.04	5.78	5.19
Current Asset Turnover—Integra	2.66	2.63	2.69	2.69
Working Capital Turnover	(17.86)	(54.41)	219.55	70.41
Working Capital Turnover—Integra	–	7.19	7.98	7.98
Fixed Asset Turnover	155.92	921.43	729.86	227.60
Fixed Asset Turnover—Integra	33.45	34.65	34.89	34.89
Total Asset Turnover	7.37	9.76	5.66	4.94
Total Asset Turnover—Integra	2.32	2.31	2.35	2.35
Payables Turnover	8.36	10.18	13.26	22.04
Payables Turnover—Integra	13.46	6.81	7.04	6.38
SG&A Expense to Cash	111.44	51.98	10.26	6.81
SG&A Expense to Cash—Integra	14.36	7.39	7.76	7.22

DEBT

Times Interest Earned	0.05	4.58	6.32	9.07
Times Interest Earned—Integra	2.16	1.93	2.13	2.13
Total Liabilities to Total Assets	1.27	1.07	0.93	0.85
Total Liabilities to Total Assets—Integra	0.68	0.69	0.72	0.72
Total Liabilities to Equity	(4.74)	(15.34)	12.87	5.68
Total Liabilities to Equity—Integra	2.15	2.18	2.51	2.51
Short-Term Debt to Equity	–	–	–	–
Short-Term Debt to Equity—Integra	0.58	0.59	0.66	0.66
Long-Term Debt to Equity	–	–	–	–
Long-Term Debt to Equity—Integra	0.38	0.40	0.45	0.45
Total Interest-Bearing Debt to Equity	–	–	–	–
Total Interest-Bearing Debt to Equity— Integra	0.97	0.98	1.11	1.11
Total Assets to Equity	(3.74)	(14.34)	13.87	6.68
Total Assets to Equity—Integra	3.15	3.18	3.51	3.51
Total Liabilities to Invested Capital	(4.74)	(15.34)	12.87	5.68
Total Liabilities to Invested Capital— Integra	1.10	1.10	1.19	1.19
Net Fixed Assets to Equity	(0.03)	(0.18)	0.09	0.21
Net Fixed Assets to Equity—Integra	0.22	0.21	0.24	0.24

PROFITABILITY

EBITDA Return on Total Assets	4.10%	13.96%	13.68%	17.47%
EBITDA Return on Total Assets—Integra	6.73%	7.57%	7.34%	7.34%
EBIT Return on Assets	3.50%	13.66%	13.31%	16.71%
EBIT Return on Assets—Integra	6.26%	6.99%	6.72%	6.72%
Pretax Return on Assets	-6.35%	10.57%	11.53%	15.87%
Pretax Return on Assets—Integra	2.40%	2.40%	2.50%	2.50%
After-Tax Return on Assets	-6.35%	10.57%	7.48%	15.87%
After-Tax Return on Assets—Integra	12.10%	12.30%	14.10%	14.10%
EBITDA Return on Equity	-15.33%	-200.15%	189.80%	116.63%
EBITDA Return on Equity—Integra	21.22%	24.08%	25.77%	25.77%
EBIT Return on Equity	-13.11%	-195.88%	184.69%	111.54%
EBIT Return on Equity—Integra	19.75%	22.25%	23.62%	23.62%
Pretax Return on Equity	23.77%	-151.60%	159.97%	105.95%
Pretax Return on Equity—Integra	7.50%	7.60%	8.70%	8.70%
After-Tax Return on Equity	23.77%	-151.60%	103.71%	105.95%
After-Tax Return on Equity—Integra	1.60%	1.70%	1.70%	1.70%
EBITDA Return on Net Sales	0.71%	1.67%	3.97%	4.32%

Quimby's Computer Solutions, Inc.
Schedule 7: Historical Ratios Comparison to Integra Industry
Benchmark Data
as of August 31, *(continued)*

	1992	1993	1994	1995
EBITDA Return on Net Sales—Integra	2.90%	3.28%	3.13%	3.13%
EBIT Return on Net Sales	0.61%	1.63%	3.86%	4.13%
EBIT Return on Net Sales—Integra	2.70%	3.03%	2.87%	2.87%
Pretax Return on Net Sales	−1.10%	1.26%	3.34%	3.92%
Pretax Return on Net Sales—Integra	1.00%	1.00%	1.10%	1.10%
After-Tax Return on Net Sales	−1.10%	1.26%	2.17%	3.92%
After-Tax Return on Net Sales—Integra	1.00%	1.00%	1.10%	1.10%
EBITDA Return on Invested Capital	−15.33%	−200.15%	189.80%	116.63%
EBITDA Return on Invested Capital—Integra	10.80%	12.14%	12.19%	12.19%
EBIT Return on Invested Capital	−13.11%	−195.88%	184.69%	111.54%
EBIT Return on Invested Capital—Integra	10.05%	11.22%	11.18%	11.18%
Pretax Return on Invested Capital	23.77%	−151.60%	159.97%	105.95%
Pretax Return on Invested Capital—Integra	6.14%	6.22%	6.67%	6.67%
After-Tax Return on Invested Capital	23.77%	−151.60%	103.71%	105.95%
After-Tax Return on Invested Capital—Integra	3.79%	3.84%	4.14%	4.14%
WORKING CAPITAL				
Working Capital ($000)	−285.43	−149.27	352.28	810.82
Working Capital ($000)—Integra	3.23	3.44	3.67	3.67
Short-Term Debt to Working Capital	–	–	–	–
Short-Term Debt to Working Capital—Integra	0.57	0.56	0.62	0.62
Long-Term Debt to Working Capital	–	–	–	–
Long-Term Debt to Working Capital—Integra	0.37	0.38	0.43	0.43
OPERATING EFFICIENCY				
Operating Expense to Sales	12.26%	15.70%	14.13%	13.84%
Operating Expense to Sales—Integra	17.20%	17.40%	17.20%	17.20%
Depreciation and Amortization to Sales	0.10%	0.04%	0.11%	0.19%
Depreciation and Amortization to Sales—Integra	0.60%	0.70%	0.70%	0.70%
Capital Expenditures to Sales	−1.02%	0.09%	0.11%	0.67%
Capital Expenditures to Sales—Integra	0.00%	0.70%	1.20%	1.20%

INDUSTRY GROWTH

Revenue	16.06%	103.42%	88.46%	83.73%
Revenue—Integra	0.00%	5.03%	18.27%	0.00%
Net Income	−57.80%	−333.59%	222.87%	232.59%
Net Income—Integra	0.00%	6.87%	20.88%	0.00%

OTHER

Officers' Compensation/Sales	0.03	0.02	0.03	0.03
Officers' Compensation/Sales—Integra	0.01	0.01	0.01	0.01
Size of Revenues ($000)	5,813.10	11,825.20	22,285.80	40,945.4
Size of Revenues ($000)—Integra	22,824	23,972	28,351	28,351
Earnings ($000)	−64	150	483	1606
Earnings ($000)—Integra	233	249	301	301
3-Year Compound Growth Rate—EPS		0.00%	0.00%	227.21%
3-Year Compound Growth Rate—Revenues		53.65%	95.80%	86.08%
3-Year Compound Growth Rate—EPS—Integra			13.66%	9.95%
3-Year Compound Growth Rate—Revenues—Integra			11.45%	8.75%

Quimby's Computer Solutions, Inc.
Schedule 8: Extended Dupont Analysis Unadjusted

| | Profitability × | | | | Turnover | | × Solvency | = ROE |
| | Taxes | Financing | Operations | | | | | |
	Income / EBT	× EBT / EBIT	× EBIT / Sales	= Income / Sales	× Sales / Total Assets	= Net Income / Total Assets	Total Assets / Common Equity	Net Income / Common Equity
Quimby's								
1995	100.00%	94.99%	4.13%	3.92%	404.50%	15.87%	667.65%	105.95%
1994	64.83%	86.61%	3.86%	2.17%	344.99%	7.48%	1387.18%	103.71%
1993	100.00%	77.40%	1.63%	1.26%	835.97%	10.57%	-1433.59%	-151.60%
1992	100.00%	-181.33%	0.61%	-1.10%	576.64%	-6.35%	-374.18%	23.77%
Integra								
1995	62.06%	59.66%	2.87%	1.06%	234.50%	2.49%	351.25%	8.74%
1994	62.06%	59.66%	2.87%	1.06%	234.50%	2.49%	351.25%	8.74%
1993	61.79%	55.43%	3.03%	1.04%	230.54%	2.39%	318.18%	7.62%
1992	61.80%	61.10%	2.70%	1.02%	231.69%	2.37%	315.33%	7.46%

[1]Note: Integra figures may not match Integra ratios due to rounding.

(EXERCISE 5) COMPARATIVE FINANCIAL ANALYSIS "AS REPORTED"

Observations

Impact
on Value
+ / 0 / −

_____   _____

_____   _____

_____   _____

_____   _____

_____   _____

_____   _____

_____   _____

_____   _____

_____   _____

_____   _____

_____   _____

_____   _____

_____   _____

_____   _____

Strength of Integra Comparison

_____

_____

_____

Possible Adjustments

_____

_____

_____

_____

CASE STUDY EXERCISE 6: PREPARATION FOR MANAGEMENT INTERVIEW

In preparation for the management interview, create a list of specific questions about which your curiosity has been raised from the information you have been given. A worksheet is provided for your issues.

(EXERCISE 6) PREPARATION FOR MANAGEMENT INTERVIEW

Specific Inquiries

_____

_____

_____

_____

_____

_____

_____

CASE STUDY EXERCISE 7: ASSESSMENT OF THE MANAGEMENT INTERVIEW

Exhibit 3 provides Quimby's response to the Company Questionnaire and results of the interview.

Your assignment is to review this material and then identify the most relevant factors and trends that influence the value of Quimby's. You must also be able to state how these relevant factors or trends will affect value. Additionally, note items that you would adjust in the historical financial statements to value the controlling interest. A worksheet is provided for your thoughts. Please use the same method of noting whether the influence on value is positive or negative.

Exhibit 3: Quimby's Computer Solutions, Inc. Management Interview

COMPANY AND INDUSTRY BACKGROUND INFORMATION FORM
BUSINESS VALUATION ENGAGEMENTS
(ANSWERS PROVIDED BY COMPANY MANAGEMENT)

Company Name: Quimby's Computer Solutions, Inc.

Completed by: Karen Brown

Date: XXXXX XX, XXXX

Instructions: This form covers the data typically needed to obtain an understanding of The Company being valued and its industry. The questions have been grouped into sections. You may complete only those sections that apply.

Provide the requested information in the appropriate spaces. Attach additional sheets if necessary. If the information is not relevant, write N/A in that space.

COMPANY BACKGROUND

1. Describe The Company's legal structure.

Company's legal name:	**Quimby's Computer Solutions, Inc.**
Type of entity (corp., partnership, proprietorship)	C corporation
Date of incorporation or formation	1983
State incorporated	Delaware
Number of common shares authorized	100,000 shares
Par value	$1.00 par value
Number of shares issued and outstanding	86,500 shares
Briefly describe other types of stock	None

2. List the major stockholders, partners, or owners of the company and their percentage of ownership or number of shares owned.

Name	Number of Shares Owned	Percentage Ownership
Mr. Smith	77,850 shares	90% interest
Mr. Skinner	8,650 shares	10% interest

3. List all known related parties (subsidiaries, affiliates, or relatives) that the company does business with.

None

4. List each location maintained by the company and the primary activity at each, (executive office, plant, sales office, etc.).

Location	Activity
1234 Main Street, Boca Raton, FL (100,000 sq. ft.)	Corporate offices
6225 Ellwood Avenue, Louisville, KY (25,000 sq. ft.)	Warehouse

5. Discuss The Company's history and the evolution of its (a) product lines, (b) customer base, (c) locations, (d) marketing activities, (e) distribution methods, (f) employees, (g) acquisitions, and (h) ownership.

(a) Evolution of Company Products   Quimby's Computer Solutions, Inc. originally operated as a mid-range computer reseller. Operations consisted of purchasing used, mid-range computers, disassembling them, and selling the parts to maintenance companies. These maintenance companies would use the parts to repair mid-range computers that were in place. According to the president of Quimby's, Mr. Skinner, "Prior to 1992, Quimby's was basically a used equipment broker in the midrange market."

In 1992, there were some dramatic changes in the computer resale industry. Louis Gerstner took the reins of IBM and began using distribution channels to get IBM products to customers, whereas prior to this time, IBM had sold most of its products directly to customers. IBM began using value-added resellers and distributors like Quimby's to get its products out into the market. In 1992, The Company formed a strategic alliance with IBM and became an IBM business partner, which allowed Quimby's to distribute IBM terminals (dumb terminals that hook up to midrange or mainframe machines). During this time frame, Quimby's also established its relationship with IBM Credit Corp. This strategic alliance marked the beginning of Quimby's extraordinary growth. By establishing this strategic alliance with IBM, The Company opened a door leading to future opportunities with IBM and its extensive product line.

Quimby's began selling dumb terminals in 1992, while at the same time continuing to broker used midrange computers. As time progressed, opportunities arose to distribute new products. As the salespeople of Quimby's established customer contacts and put hardware in place, they began getting requests for more, and different, hardware. Working with IBM and its customers, Quimby's increased product offerings. The Company expanded its product lines to include printers, modems, and controllers utilizing its existing customer base. Quimby's was able to increase revenues with the addition of each product line. According to Mr. Skinner, "We went from terminals to printers, and then from printers to modems, and from modems to controllers, and you can see a definite spike [in revenues]."

During 1995, Quimby's entered into discussions with IBM regarding the distribution of storage devices. The Industry Remarketer Business Plan lists Quimby's experience in computer equipment distribution and details how The Company plans to distribute storage products. Storage products are much more costly items than the peripheral hardware distributed by Quimby's. Regarding the opportunities available selling storage, Mr. Skinner noted, "So, now instead of selling things that cost at most $20,000, now you're selling something that could cost $1 million." Distributing storage products would dramatically increase the revenues of Quimby's, and the addition of this new product would mark the beginning of a strong growth period for The Company.

(b) **Evolution of Company Customer Base**   Quimby's originally sold its midrange computer parts to maintenance companies located in the southeastern region of the United States. The Company's customer base expanded little during the 1980s. The majority of the business was dependent upon established relationships with existing customers.

Subsequent to Quimby's strategic alliance with IBM in 1992, The Company's customer base changed significantly. As Quimby's began to distribute dumb terminals, it still maintained its original customer base by continuing its brokering of parts. However, as The Company's operations shifted focus to the distribution for computer hardware and peripherals, Quimby's expanded its geographic customer base to the national level. In addition, value-added resellers also became an integral part of Quimby's customer base.

(c) **History of Company Locations**   The Company started in a rented warehouse in 1979. This site was located in Hollywood, Florida, and consisted of 19,000 square feet. The Company's offices remained at this location until 1987, when Quimby's began leasing office space in Boca Raton, Florida. The Company continued to lease the warehouse until 1990. At this time, Quimby's moved its warehouse facilities to Louisville, Kentucky. This new warehouse consists of 25,000 square feet. In addition, several small offices are leased for salespersons throughout the country.

(d) Evolution of Company Marketing Activities According to Quimby's Industry Remarketer Business Plan:

Quimby's, with its additional influx of products and relationships, began undergoing rapid growth. In 1993 The Company began updating all of its internal systems, increased its office space and sales force, and began formulating new and innovative strategies to increase business while achieving the highest attainable levels of employee, vendor, and customer satisfaction.

Today, Quimby's is the recognized leader in network marketing with almost 50,000 contacts, including approximately 37,000 end-user sites, more than 4,800 customers, and over 7,700 IBM Marketing Representatives and Business Partners who turn to Quimby's for solutions. Quimby's has consistently lead the Authorized Distributor channel since its inception and continues to be the number one IBM products and services provider while expanding to accommodate customer needs.

In addition, its established telemarketing resources have been described as follows:

Quimby's is a telemarketing- and consulting-based business staffed with more than 60 professionals who field over 2,800 outgoing calls and more than 800 incoming calls per day, promoting the sale and support of IBM hardware peripheral products to midrange system users.

(e) Evolution of Company Distribution Methods Warehouse distribution activities are performed at The Company's Louisville, Kentucky, warehouse. Sales to resellers are shipped to their locations. Sales to end users are shipped directly to their facilities.

(f) Evolution of Company Employee Base The Company started in 1979 with just a handful of employees. As of December 29, 1995, it employed approximately 60 employees. There are no unions representing the employees.

(g) History of Company Acquisitions As of the valuation date, Quimby's has not made any business acquisitions.

(h) History of Company Ownership For the first 14 years of The Company's operations, Mr. Smith owned 100% of Quimby's. In 1993, Quimby's president, Mr. Skinner, acquired a 10% ownership interest in The Company. There are several significant restrictions that limit the transferability of this interest. Specifically, Mr. Skinner is unable to liquidate his ownership until he has left Quimby's. If he is interested in selling his shares to a third party, the transaction requires the approval of Mr. Smith. This, in addition to Mr. Smith having the initial right to purchase shares significantly restricts the transferability of Mr. Skinner's interest in Quimby's.

6. Other key dates or events in company history.
   None.

PRODUCTS OR SERVICES

7. Description of the company's products or services:
   Quimby's operates as a hardware distributor specializing in IBM peripheral equipment. The Company offers IBM terminals, printers, modems, and controllers, and expects to increase its product offering to include IBM storage equipment. In addition to new equipment, Quimby's brokers used midrange computers and computer parts, including the RS/6000 and AS/400 machines.

8. How are the products or services used?

These products are primarily purchased by domestic customers involved in a variety of industries. This computer equipment is designed to fulfill the computer hardware and peripheral needs that are specific to each customer's operations.

9. Describe the company's customer base.

The Company is not dependent upon a single customer or a few customers, the loss of which would have a material adverse effect on its operations. Most corporate sales are made to end users throughout the United States.

10. Breakdown of sales by customer for the fiscal year ended August 31, 1995:

Allstate Ins. Co.	$2,989,372
State of IN Co. Offices	1,083,242
Office Depot	716,794
Intel Corporation	645,120
American Gen. Finance	558,531
Crawford & Co.	519,408
Greentree Financial	494,996
Waste Management	465,951
Skelgas, Inc.	447,405
Enterprise Rent-A-Car	427,926
Innovative Computing	419,226
Costco Wholesale	403,702
Total	$9,171,673
Percentage of Total Revenues	25%

As indicated in the table, Quimby's provided computer hardware solutions to companies such as Allstate Insurance, Office Depot, and Intel Corporation.

Mr. Skinner, who runs Quimby's daily operations, has also indicated that Quimby's provides hardware through alliances with other value-added resellers (VARs) that concentrate on selling software solutions that run on IBM hardware. Many of these companies do not have an interest in selling peripheral hardware; therefore, Quimby's has developed relationships with certain IBM VARs to provide hardware to their customers. This practice of providing hardware solutions to other IBM VAR customers has effectively increased Quimby's client base.

11. Which product line is growing fastest?

Quimby's revenues have grown approximately 92% since 1992. This growth is the result of The Company adding the distribution of hardware and eripherals to its operations. Quimby's continually adds different types of products to its distribution operations. As a result, there is not enough history of sales to enable management to confidently determine the fastest-growing product line.

In addition, due to expectations of adding other products such as IBM storage products, management would not speculate on which product lines will grow fastest in the future.

Which product line is growing the slowest?

Due to Quimby's shift in its operations, the brokerage of used computer parts is the slowest-growing product line.

12. How diversified are the product lines? Do all sales depend on the same factors?
The Company's product lines are not diversified, as they are all closely related to computer hardware. However, the customer base is very diversified. Therefore, factors affecting sales will vary depending on the customer.

13. What are the products' advantages and disadvantages versus competitors?
Advantages: The Company's primary brand, IBM, as well as others such as Hewlett-Packard, are known as premium, highly innovative manufacturers that have developed a loyal customer base.

The primary competitive factors affecting The Company's sales are customer relationships, sales strategy, price, and computer hardware and peripheral support, as well as the ability to advise, develop, and implement computer systems that are tailored to the client's specific needs.

Disadvantages: The Company believes it is very susceptible to price competition, as the majority of competitors distribute the same or similar products that can be easily substituted for Quimby's products. In addition, other services such as systems integration and support may cause customers to buy elsewhere when these sources are important.

14. Are the products proprietary? Does the company have patents, technology, or expertise that prevents others from copying the products?
The products distributed by The Company are not proprietary, and each manufacturer offers items that are very similar to one another. There is not a large amount of differentiation between the available products of the competitors. Management considers the expertise, training, and ability of its employees to implement and support The Company's products as being the characteristic that adds value above and beyond the services of competitors.

15. What other products compete with the company's products?
Since IBM's products account for 99% of Quimby's sales, other major national name-brand products with major advertising and promotion budgets such as Hewlett-Packard, Digital Equipment Corporation, and Sun Microsystems are considered as of 1995 to be competitors that produce substitutable products.

16. Are sales cyclical? What economic factors (inflation, interest rates, etc.) affect sales?
The purchases of computer hardware and peripherals are highly dependent on corporate willingness to invest in new productive capital. Recently, as the economy continues its expansion, companies are looking to enhance their productivity through the upgrading of their information technology systems. Although demand for such products would be expected to decrease in times of economic recession, the need to develop more efficient processes that will reduce

operating costs may offset such a reduction in demand as companies look to make more with less.

Companies purchasing information technology systems may utilize debt to acquire computer hardware. Rising interest rates could have an impact on corporate borrowings. Another economic factor that may affect the industry's sales is the existence of trade barriers between the United States and foreign countries.

Computer hardware and information services companies are expected to benefit from implementation of the North American Free Trade Agreements (NAFTA) and expansion of the General Agreement on Tariffs and Trade (GATT). By establishing working relationships with their counterparts overseas, U.S.-based trade associations contribute to the globalization of the information services industry. As an indication of U.S. competitiveness abroad, U.S.-controlled companies received 35% of all European revenues from computer and systems integration services.

17. Are sales seasonal?
Sales are not considered to be seasonal due to the diversification of Quimby's customer base and the nature of its products.

18. Discuss any industry technology trends.
There are several technology trends developing within Quimby's industry. These advancements are geared toward making computer equipment faster, smaller, and able to handle larger amounts of information.

19. Discuss the company's research and development (R&D) efforts, the importance of new products, and the annual cost of research and development activities.
Since The Company is a distributor of manufactured hardware and peripherals, it does not have any investment or expenses related to research and development. However, as more products are added, this may change based on the characteristics of the new products.

20. What is the size (in dollars) of the industry market?
Due to the large degree of industry overlap of Quimby's products, it is difficult to estimate the actual size of the industry market. It is estimated that the hardware and services market accounts for several hundred billion dollars in business, and is approaching trillion-dollar levels. However, while this market includes the operations of Quimby's, it also includes operations in which The Company is not involved. Therefore, no supportable estimate could be provided.

21. What is The Company's market share? How fragmented is the market? Is the market growing or shrinking?
Management has not conducted any analysis to estimate Quimby's market share as a result of the difficulty of doing so. Quimby's market consists of many companies, both small and large. With the advent of the Internet and continuing use of computers, Quimby's market is growing.

22. What distribution channels does the company use (direct sales, distributors, retailers, etc.)? How successful are they?
The Company's products are sold to a limited network of value-adding distributors that have established contacts. However, The Company's primary

distribution channel is still direct sales to end users. Both channels have been effective, although Quimby's is looking to expand its network of distributors with established contacts when it begins to sell IBM storage products in the next year to two years.

23. How are salespeople compensated?
    Salespeople are compensated on a base pay plus commission basis.

24. What is the market area? How important are freight costs?
    The primary market area is the U.S. national market. Quimby's is not currently involved in international sales, but it has potential for strong future growth.
    Freight costs are low relative to sales.

25. Are sales concentrated in a few customers? What percentage of total sales are made to five largest customers?
    Sales are spread across a large base of resellers and end users. The five largest customers account for approximately 16% of total sales.

26. How loyal are customers? That is, do they tend to buy from the same company or switch? How does pricing affect customer loyalty?
    Competitors offer the same or similar products that are sold by Quimby's. As a result, pricing is very important in maintaining customers. Also of importance are these support services offered by companies after the products have been sold. Since all these companies offer similar products, both pricing and product support are very important to continuing business from customers.

27. Does the company sell to the federal, state, or local government agencies? Are those sales likely to increase or decrease?
    No, Quimby's does not sell to government agencies.

28. What is the key selling feature—product, price, service, brand name, packaging, and so forth?
    Key selling features are price, brand name, and support services for the products.

29. How are pricing policies determined? To what degree do competitors' prices affect company policy?
    Pricing is set by continual competitive surveys; thus the market sets the price in this highly crowded marketplace.

30. What are normal sales and credit terms? Describe a typical customer contract.
    Terms to all customers are 2/10 net 30: 2% discount if paid within 10 days, or pay full amount (net) within 30 days. However, the professional market tends to take up to 60 days to pay.

31. What type of promotion and advertising methods does the company use?
    Quimby's uses in-house telemarketers and sales staff, as well as a network marketing scheme consisting of approximately 50,000 contacts, which is made up of 37,000 end-user sites, 4,800 customers, and more than 7,700 IBM marketing representatives.

32. Who are the company's major competitors? Where are they located? How big are they? What is their market share? How diverse are they? Identify those competitors (if any) that are publicly held.

    Since Quimby's products and services are diverse within the computer hardware peripheral and information services industry, there is a large amount of overlap. Therefore, the industry is not dominated by a single company or even a small number of companies. Rather, there are a large number of firms offering various products and services, all of which are very similar to one another. Several of these firms are publicly held companies. These include Scientific Computer Technologies, Integrated Microcomputers, Helos Information Technologies, Data Systems Storage, and Esterland and Norwick Solutions.

33. How does the company compare in size and market share to its competitors?

    Many of the competitors are substantially larger than The Company in total sales volume and resources.

    The Company is not among the larger companies in the industry. Nonetheless, Quimby's believes it is among the leaders in the distribution and support of IBM hardware and peripherals.

34. How easy is it to enter the industry? What are the barriers to entry?

    There are no significant capital barriers to entry, although warehouse space may be necessary to handle inventory. The primary barriers are the establishment of contacts with customers and suppliers. Customer contacts are very important as a result of competitors offering identical or similar products and the ease of switching from one firm to another. Contracts with brand-name manufacturers, such as IBM and Hewlett-Packard are vital because of the market share and recognition that these products have attained in the corporate world.

35. What are the company's competitive strengths and weaknesses?

    Strengths

    - **Proven track record.** Quimby's has proven to be the leader in all endeavors it embarks upon. Quimby's is the IBM PC company's top authorized distributor of terminal, controller, and modem products; the #1 IBM Printing Systems company printer remarketer; and IBM's top RS/6000 storage remarketer. Quimby's anticipates quickly rising to the top of the IBM industry remarketer channel.
    - **Dedicated quality assurance team.** Quimby's has a dedicated six-person, quality assurance team (QAT) that closely monitors, tracks, and follows up on every order. Additionally, Quimby's QAT adds value by assisting customers with simple configurations and suggestions to leverage the customers' hardware investment.
    - **Technical/customer support.** Quimby's provides expert pre- and post-sales support. Its support staff represents more than 100 years of combined industry and platform experience in both the AS/400 and the RS/600 environments.
    - **Systems.** Quimby's has state-of-the-art information systems that supply all tools necessary to perform a job function directly to the employees' desks,

all information is electronically online and not filed on paper, and all systems are fully integrated so that any employee of Quimby's may service any customer as though that employee has handled that account from the beginning of time. Quimby's has been publicly recognized for its use of in-house technology.

■ **Personnel.** Quimby's employees want to be a part of the IBM/Customer team and not just another vendor. Their professionalism, expertise, training, and attitude express their dedication to providing the highest level of service to their customers, referral sources, and fellow employees.

■ **Priority delivery notices.** Every order is confirmed by fax immediately upon shipment. The priority delivery notice (PDN) informs the customer as to exactly what equipment shipped, the ship-to-location, the carrier, the carrier's tracking number, and the carrier's phone number. This eliminates any problems before they occur and gives the customer control, if desired, in tracing lost shipments, if any. Additionally, the PDN contains Quimby's invoice number upon which the shipped equipment will appear.

■ **Training.** All employees at Quimby's undergo continuous and ongoing training in all facets of customer service, sales, management, and product knowledge. Each member of the sales staff is an authority on AS/400 and RS/600 platforms, a sales professional, and an expert in maintaining client satisfaction.

■ **Longevity.** Quimby's has been in the business of supplying computer peripheral products since 1979. As such, Quimby's is a recognized leader in the industry with a strong reputation for excellence. Quimby's continues to build upon this reputation with each new transaction and is poised to remain the leader as it progresses into the future.

■ **Customer base.** Quimby's has more than 4,800 dedicated and loyal customers and a database of over 35,000 qualified midrange accounts with almost 50,000 contacts. These accounts are the lifeblood of Quimby's and are treated as such. They are a consistent source of business and referrals.

■ **Understanding of IBM relationships.** Quimby's recognizes the interdependence of all IBM business partners and marketing representatives and has built tremendous loyalty in the IBM community for the services it performs. Likewise, Quimby's extends tremendous loyalty to IBM, ensuring that products only move through authorized channels, and eliminating channel conflict through the development of strategic relationships across all IBM channels.

Weaknesses

The Company's primary weakness is its dependence on its single supplier, IBM. Quimby's has enjoyed phenomenal growth over the past five years, which was due mainly to its relationship with IBM. When considering the long-term earnings potential of The Company, much consideration must be given to the strength of the relationship between these companies. IBM products account for 99% of Quimby's revenues. Although management has indicated that loss of IBM as a supplier would not have a material adverse effect on The Company's operations, the loss could affect profit margins. The Company's reputation and proven track record illustrate the picture of an excellent performer, but this single supplier dependence is a definite weakness for Quimby's.

COMPANY ORGANIZATION

36. Describe the company's organization structure (attach organization chart if available).

    Quimby's is a flat organization. Mr. Skinner runs the daily operation of The Company, with all vice presidents and managers reporting to him. There are no separate divisions within Quimby's, although there are several departments that are interdependent. These include sales, technical support, and distribution.

37. What is the relative size of the company's divisions in terms of sales and gross profits? How interrelated are the divisions? How much vertical integration is there among the divisions? How easily can a division be eliminated without affecting other operations?

    There are no separate divisions within Quimby's. However, the departments within The Company are interrelated and there is a high degree of vertical integration among them. As a result, it would be very difficult for Quimby's to eliminate any department under its corporate umbrella without a affecting other departments.

38. Describe the manufacturing or service process. Are any of the methods or equipment proprietary?

    Quimby's acquires ownership of various computer hardware and peripherals and maintains the items as inventory. At the time of sale, products are delivered and installed at the customer site. This process is supported by Quimby's quality assurance team. Once the products are operating, Quimby's provides technical and customer support through its sales support staff.

39. Are buildings and machinery owned or leased? If leased, are the leases renewable and on what terms?

    All facilities are leased with fair rental terms.

40. Briefly describe past and current employee relations (i.e., contentious, harmonious, strikes, etc.). Also discuss employee turnover and indicate whether any of the employees are unionized.

    Employee morale is good. Labor turnover is low. There are no union employees.

41. Discuss the current labor market. How easy is it to attract qualified employees?

    The greater Boca Raton, Florida, area has ample qualified employees to fulfill the needs of The Company headquarters. The Louisville, Kentucky, area has ample qualified employees for Quimby's warehouse facilities.

42. How extensively are independent contractors used?

    Quimby's uses approximately 20 to 30 independent contractors who act as agents for The Company. These independent contractors make up Quimby's reseller network and are proficient in open systems, connectivity, management, and software implementation.

43. Discuss key suppliers. Are any suppliers the sole source? Have there been major problems in getting raw materials? Are there long lead times to get the purchased goods?

The Company's primary supplier is IBM. IBM products account for 99% of Quimby's revenues. Although Quimby's does deal in other companies' products, its emphasis is clearly on IBM hardware and peripherals. This has been the case since 1992.

There are no long lead times to acquire goods because Quimby's has established inventories of the majority of products that it sells.

44. Does the company have any foreign operations? If so, does the company have any problems with any foreign governments?

As of the valuation date, Quimby's does not have any foreign operations.

MANAGEMENT

45. List key members of management.

Name	Age	Title	Year Hired
Mr. Smith	55	Chairman and CEO	1979
Mr. Skinner	33	President	1985
Mr. Murphy	41	Vice President, Sales	1990
Ms. Jones	38	Manager of Channel Operations	1994
Mr. Klein	40	Vice President, Information Systems	1994
Mr. Brockman	35	Advanced Product Manager	1994

46. Discuss the company's officers (age, health, education, experience, and current duties).

Mr. Smith, Chairman and CEO. Mr. Smith is the founder of Quimby's with over 20 years of experience in the midrange marketplace. He possesses a deep understanding of the used equipment market, customers, products, and services, particularly as a broker. Over the years, Mr. Smith had developed many contacts that allowed The Company to operate in the used equipment market. Mr. Smith became less active in The Company as the relationship with IBM continued to grow. From 1992 to 1995, there was a transformation in his role, as Quimby's went from a used equipment company to an IBM partner. Mr. Smith became less involved in the day to day operations of The Company, and was more involved with strategic decisions. Some of these decisions included structuring the management staff for the future.

Mr. Skinner, President. Mr. Edison started with The Company in 1985, right out of college. He had interned at IBM over the final two years of his studies, and developed an interest in computers. Mr. Skinner started at Quimby's as a sales associate, and over his tenure has been promoted to executive vice president and then to president. Since 1994, after becoming president, he manages the day-to-day operations of The Company, as well as the main customer and supplier relationships, and determines the product mix to be sold. He was responsible for nurturing Quimby's relationship with IBM, and continues to be Quimby's contact with IBM. Mr. Skinner's employment contract indicates that his compensation is a result of three components: salary, spread compensation, and profit-sharing spread.

Mr. Murphy, Vice President, Sales. Mr. Murphy has been employed with Quimby's since 1990, progressing from sales representative to vice president of sales. He is responsible for developing and maintaining Quimby's customer base and increasing overall sales. He is also responsible for all sales managers, consultants, and their associated training and development.

Ms. Jones, Manager of Channel Operations. Ms. Jones has been with Quimby's since about 1994, overseeing all strategic and tactical operations as they relate to partner alliances. She is responsible for all order processing, contracts, special bids, and business partner promotions.

Mr. Klein, Vice President of Sales and Information Systems. Mr. Klein has been with Quimby's since 1994, and has more than 16 years of research and marketing experience with IBM Corporation. A graduate of Hunter College, Mr. Klein was number one in sales while at IBM, averaging over $6 million in sales per year. He has achieved invention achievement awards for six patents and has published 12 technical writings. He is a recognized authority on midrange hardware and is frequently quoted in national publications.

Mr. Brockman, Advanced Product Manager. Mr. Brockman has been with Quimby's since 1994, and has more than 12 years of industry technical experience in the following areas:
- High-performance I/O subsystems
- UNIX System V
- Supercomputing
- Networking

47. Discuss compensation. Also, describe employee benefits (insurance, stock options, profit sharing, etc.).
We have retrieved the following breakdown of total officers' compensation, which has been compiled from Quimby's corporate tax returns, along with Mr. Smith's personal tax returns and Form W-2 s.

Officer Compensation

	Mr. Smith	Mr. Skinner	Total
1995	$883,945	$351,100	$1,235,045
1994	426,955	190,604	617,559
1993	184,784	0[1]	184,784
1992	196,178	0[2]	196,178
1991	130,108	0[3]	130,108

[1] Prior year's financial statements included Mr. Skinner's compensation as a nonofficer.
[2] Ibid.
[3] Ibid.

All senior management receive normal benefits, including health insurance.

48. Discuss any employment contracts.
    All senior managers have employment contracts.

49. How easily can officers be replaced? That is, is there one or a few key officers on whom the success of the company depends who cannot be easily replaced?
    There is a key person situation at The Company. Mr. Skinner is currently running day-to-day operations, and if he were to leave on an untimely basis, it would be difficult for The Company to continue in the short term.
    Mr. Smith is capable of maintaining a stable leadership as chairman and CEO but would not necessarily be able to manage Quimby's in the event that Mr. Skinner left The Company.

50. Who is on the board of directors and how actively is the board governing company activities?
    The board of directors is composed of Mr. Smith, the chairman and CEO, and Mr. Skinner, the president of Quimby's. The board is relatively inactive, as the majority of The Company's governance and planning is the responsibility of Mr. Skinner, with ultimate approval resting with Mr. Smith.

FINANCIAL

51. Provide copies of the company's year-end financial statements for the last five years (or since the inception of the company, if less than five years). Also, provide copies of any interim statements since the most recent year end. For each year-end statement, complete the following analysis:
    The Company has furnished audited annual financial statements for the fiscal years ended August 31, 1991–1995. The audits were performed by the Final Four Accounting Firm.

52. Describe the nature of any report qualifications or unusual matters noted in reviewing the company's financial statements that may affect the engagement.
    None.

53. Provide copies of the company's tax returns for the last five years (or since the date of inception if less than five years). Briefly describe any unusual matters noted in reviewing the tax returns that may require special consideration during the valuation.
    Nothing unusual is observed.

54. Obtain copies of any forecasts or budgets of future operations. Briefly describe any unusual matter that may require special consideration during the valuation. If such statements are not available, state whether they will be needed during the engagement and who will probably prepare them.
    The Company provided projected financial statements for the fiscal years ended August 31, 1996–2000. The Company experienced above-average growth over those five years, averaging 24.6% per year as it capitalized on its expansion into storage products. The outlook is for higher growth in the next few years, slowing quickly to a rate of about 5% per year.

55. Has there been any change in accounting principles during the past five years (cash to accrual, FIFO to LIFO, etc.) or similar changes that might affect the comparability of the financial statements?
There have not been any changes. The Company uses FIFO inventory accounting.

56. Describe any relevant specialized industry accounting practices or principles.
N/A.

57. Have there been any nonrecurring or extraordinary income or expenses during the last five years?
The Company received miscellaneous fees, mainly from IBM in 1994 and 1995. These are considered nonrecurring income.

58. What are the main discretionary expenses (such as bonus, profit-sharing, repairs, advertising, and R&D)? How have the levels of those expenses changed during the last five years?
See the financial statements.

59. Describe short-term sources of credit and how they were used during the last five years.
Quimby's has access to a revolving line of credit of $25 million from a financing subsidiary of IBM. This short-term debt is used to finance inventory and working capital requirements. As of the valuation date, The Company had approximately $6.5 million outstanding on this line of credit.

60. Describe long-term sources of credit and how they were used during the last five years.
Quimby's has no long-term debt.

61. Discuss the company's dividend history.
None

62. Discuss the company's dividend history.
The Company has historically not paid out dividends to its shareholders.

63. Discuss plans for major capital expenditures, how they will be financed, and how much represents expansion versus replacement of existing assets.
The plans are for slightly increased amounts of capital expenditure in the foreseeable future.

64. Discuss any contingent liabilities, including lawsuits and pending or threatened litigation.
The Company is, from time to time, engaged in litigation normally incident to the conduct of its business (including product liability cases), in some of which material damages are sought. With respect to product liability cases, The Company carries product liability insurance in amounts that it believes to be adequate. Management believes that none of the current litigation will have a material effect on The Company's financial position.

65. Describe any nonoperating assets, such as aircraft, boats, and real estate investments.
N/A.

Comments on Financial Performance for the Fiscal Year Ended August 31, 1995

Financial Condition—Liquidity and Capital Resources Working capital increased to $810,819 in 1995 from $352,283 in 1994. This increase is primarily due to results of decreased accounts payable and an increase in inventory and accounts receivable.

Capital expenditures increased from $24,973 in 1994 to $273,763 in 1995.

Results of Operations The income statement reflects a healthy, growing company. Since 1992, revenues have grown consistently as illustrated in the following table.

Revenue Growth
for the Years Ended August 31,

	1992	1993	1994	1995
Revenues	$5,813,102	$11,825,174	$22,285,781	$40,945,386
Annual Growth		103%	89%	83%
4-Year CAGR				92%

The Company has experienced extraordinary growth over the four years analyzed, highlighted by its compound annual growth rate (CAGR) of 92% over this period.

Cost of goods sold has been growing proportionally to revenues, such that Quimby's has been able to consistently obtain gross margins over 17% since 1993. Operating expenses have fluctuated, ranging from 21% to 14% of revenues in 1992 and 1995, respectively. Quimby's appears to have taken control of its operating expenses in 1994 and 1995, thus listing operating margins at 4%. The Company's net income has been steadily increasing as shown in the following table, which is a positive indicator for the future.

Net Income Analysis
for the Years Ended August 31,

	1991	1992	1993	1994	1995
Net Income	$(151,758)	$(64,038)	$149,586	$482,962	$1,606,293

Management's Discussion and Analysis of Financial Condition and Results of Operation

Financial Condition As of the valuation date, The Company reflected a book value of $1,516,139. Cash accounts have increased from a low of $2,148 to $1,118,697 as of the valuation date. Accounts receivable and inventories increased steadily with sales. As with cash, accounts receivable and inventory jumped from 1993 to 1994, and this is reflected in total current assets.

The Company had high levels of fixed assets in 1990 and 1991, which were fully depreciated and were written off the balance sheet after 1992. Since then, fixed assets have increased, but still contribute little to the asset value of Quimby's.

Other assets constitute a marginal percentage of the balance sheet, with the largest contributions from stockholder loans, employee advances, and cash surrender value of officers' life insurance, all of which appear to be nonoperating assets.

Current liabilities account for all of the liabilities listed on the balance sheet. Accounts payable has been relatively consistent, while notes payable and payroll taxes payable jumped between 1993 and 1994. In 1994 and 1995, notes payable accounted for approximately three-quarters of all liabilities, and 65% of total liabilities and stockholders' equity. Notes payable reflect a revolving line of credit that Quimby's has established with a financing subsidiary of IBM through a "Wholesale Financing Flexible Payment Plan." Through this plan, The Company can borrow up to $25,000,000 for purchases and working capital requirements. Borrowings for inventories accrue interest after 30 days at prime plus 1.5% and are generally repayable within 70 days of the date of the related invoice. Borrowings for working capital requirements accrue interest at prime plus 1.75% and are generally repayable within 180 days of the related advance. Borrowings are collateralized by substantially all of The Company's assets.

The Company's stockholder equity increased dramatically over the previous five years, from a low of negative $269,418 to a high of $2,174,535 in 1995.

COMPANY EXPECTATIONS

66. Describe relevant past and expected future trends for the company, such as growth patterns, expansion or cutbacks of business segments, possible spin-offs, mergers, or acquisitions.

    Quimby's is operating in a market of unknown potential. According to expectations of the Internet, the industry is on the brink of exceptional growth. The Company can capitalize upon these forecasts by continuing its current product distribution while adding more product lines, such as IBM storage products. These items' sale prices are significantly greater than those of other hardware and peripherals. This will result in significant revenue increases that may be comparable to those seen since 1992.

    Also pertinent to company expectations of growth is the anticipated enactment of the government's initiative to facilitate the growth of the Internet with the establishment of the National Information Infrastructure. This is expected to revolutionize communications and access to information for businesses in the United States and the rest of the world. As the effects of this initiative are realized in the future, the importance of the Internet is expected to become vital to organizations around the globe.

    Quimby's is also looking to increase the number of value-added resellers that it conducts business with. By expanding this network, The Company will gain access to additional contacts, customers, and sales. Through this, as well as the capitalization on the potential of the Internet, Quimby's expects continued growth and expansion of The Company's operations.

67. Describe the company's future expectations, goals, objectives, and long-range plans in the following areas:

    Products and Services

    Over the next two years, Quimby's is expected to begin distributing IBM storage products, which are more high-end than the products that The Company currently distributes. Quimby's also anticipates more of its operations being geared toward value-added operations, such as increased bundled product sales to end users, where the added value is completed by Quimby's. In addition, The Company expects to add support personnel related to these expanded businesses.

Marketing and Customers

The Company to continue is expected to use its direct sales force as well as increase the number of resellers in its reseller network. Since Quimby's expects to add IBM's storage products to its business, The Company will also increase its customer base. Also, as a result of increased involvement in value-added distribution, Quimby's will look to increase its number of end-user customers who previously purchased items through The Company's network of resellers.

R&D and Technology

The Company is investigating the potential of adding light manufacturing to its operations. This expansion would be related to the expansion of value-added operations. As a result, Quimby's will need to incur research, development, and technology expenses in the future, although this aspect of Quimby's business plan is still in its preliminary planning stages.

COMMENTS AND OBSERVATIONS

68. Describe any matters to be considered in applying the valuation approaches selected. Factors to consider include the following:

Growth Expectations

The Company is expecting to sustain its exceptional growth in the next several years, especially if it does add the high-end IBM storage products. Although Quimby's may not sustain the 92% growth that it realized since 1992, The Company expects growth of approximately 25 to 50% in the next three years.

Financial Condition

The Company is in excellent financial condition with over $1 million in cash and no long-term debt. Although Quimby's does have substantial short-term debt, the majority of it is owed to IBM or IBM-affiliated companies. Since Quimby's is one of the leading distributors of IBM products, there are no anticipated problems with this outstanding debt, especially after the 300% increase in net income in 1995.

Management Depth and Competence

Currently, there is only one individual qualified to run the daily operations of Quimby's, Mr. Skinner. As a result, there is a serious deficiency in executive depth and competence. On the management level, Quimby's has several capable leaders. However, these managers have only been exposed to the business of their departments, and lack management skills for other areas of The Company. In the case of Mr. Skinner leaving Quimby's, outside management from competitors should be able to manage The Company without much difficulty.

Product, Customer, and Geographic Diversification

To maintain long-term success, The Company must add IBM storage products to its existing lines as well as add to its reseller network. With the Internet explosion on the horizon, adding products specifically related to this business may be necessary. The Company does not have any international presence, although recent (as of 1995) agreements will make it easier to expand into the global market, or at least expand sales to North America.

(EXERCISE 7) ASSESSMENT OF MANAGEMENT INTERVIEW

Observations

Impact
on Value
+ / 0 / −

_____   _____

_____   _____

_____   _____

_____   _____

_____   _____

_____   _____

_____   _____

_____   _____

Recommended Adjustments

Control Value

_____   _____

_____   _____

_____   _____

_____   _____

_____   _____

_____   _____

_____   _____

_____   _____

_____   _____

EXERCISE 8: ANALYSIS OF FINANCIAL STATEMENTS WITH ADJUSTMENTS

Schedules 9 through 18 provide Quimby's historical financial data as adjusted for nonrecurring events for the fiscal years ended August 31, 1991, through August 31, 1995

Your assignment is to review this material and then identify the most relevant factors and trends that are different from the as-reported financials and that influence the value of Quimby's Computer Solutions, Inc. You must also be able to state how these relevant factors or trends affect value. Provide your answers on the exercise table.

SCHEDULES 9 THROUGH 17
QUIMBY'S COMPUTER SOLUTIONS, INC.
FINANCIAL STATEMENTS
ADJUSTED FOR NONOPERATING ITEMS
FOR THE FISCAL YEARS ENDED 8/31/91–95

Quimby's Computer Solutions, Inc.
Schedule 9: Annual Historical Balance Sheets
as Adjusted for Nonoperating Items
Fiscal Years Ended August 31,

	1991	1992	1993	1994	1995
Current Assets					
Cash	$ 10,647	$ 2,148	$ 69,266	$ 544,500	$ 1,118,697
Marketable Securities	35,233	–	52,886	–	–
Accounts Receivable	313,751	797,374	971,565	3,963,550	4,589,646
Inventories	50,100	189,224	270,233	1,814,009	3,693,293
Prepaid Expenses	–	–	–	24,396	15,484
Other Current Assets	–	3,348	–	–	–
Total Current Assets	$ 409,731	$ 992,094	$1,363,950	$6,346,455	$9,417,120
Total Fixed Assets	$ 66,947	$ 7,619	$ 18,048	$ 43,021	$ 316,784
Other Assets					
Security Deposits	$ 8,391	$ 8,391	$ 11,393	$ –	$ 11,301
Other Assets	12,668	–	21,160	35,384	51,302
Total Other Assets	$ 21,059	$ 8,391	$ 32,553	$ 35,384	$ 62,603
TOTAL ASSETS	$ 497,737	$1,008,104	$1,414,551	$6,424,860	$9,796,507
Current Liabilities					
Accounts Payable	$ 363,408	$ 848,670	$1,071,061	$1,686,380	$ 1,361,785
Accrued Expenses	–	–	36,181	398,617	704,373
Income Taxes Payable	–	–	–	306,000	–
Due to Stockholder	–	56,582	115,004	–	–
Revolving Credit Line	411,775	372,270	290,977	3,603,175	6,540,143
Total Current Liabilities	$ 775,183	$1,277,522	$1,513,223	$5,994,172	$ 8,606,301
Stockholders' Equity					
Common Stock	$ 865	$ 865	$ 865	$ 865	$ 865
Retained Earnings	(278,311)	(270,283)	(99,537)	(429,823)	(1,189,341)
Total Stockholders' Equity	$ (277,446)	$ (269,418)	$ (98,672)	$ 430,688	$ 1,190,206
TOTAL LIABILITIES AND STOCKHOLDERS' EQUITY	$ 497,737	$1,008,104	$1,414,551	$6,424,860	$9,796,507

Quimby's Computer Solutions, Inc.
Schedule 10: Annual Historical Income Statements
as Adjusted
Fiscal Years Ended August 31,

	1991	1992	1993	1994	1995
Revenues	$ 5,008,819	$ 5,813,102	$ 11,825,174	$ 22,285,781	$ 40,945,386
Cost of Sales	4,405,459	5,064,854	9,775,873	18,276,690	33,588,165
Gross Profit	$ 603,360	$ 748,248	$ 2,049,301	$ 4,009,091	$ 7,357,221
Total Operating Expenses	725,906	669,264	1,885,838	2,854,244	4,946,935
Operating Income (Loss)	$ (122,546)	$ 78,984	$ 163,463	$ 1,154,847	$ 2,410,286
Interest Expense	43,813	67,256	41,829	139,909	199,028
Total Other Income (Expenses)	620	(32,097)	(1,861)	7,303	35,672
Income (Loss) Before Taxes	$ (165,739)	$ (20,369)	$ 119,773	$ 1,022,241	$ 2,246,930
Income Taxes	(53,449)	(4,008)	33,980	384,669	845,520
NET INCOME (LOSS)	$ (112,290)	$ (16,361)	$ 85,793	$ 637,572	$ 1,401,410

Quimby's Computer Solutions, Inc.
Schedule 11: Annual Adjusted Common Size Comparison
to Integra Data

	1991	1992	1993	1994	1995	Integra
Current Assets						
Cash	2.14%	0.21%	4.90%	8.47%	11.42%	5.58%
Marketable Securities	7.08%	0.00%	3.74%	0.00%	0.00%	0.61%
Accounts Receivable	63.04%	79.10%	68.68%	61.69%	46.85%	35.51%
Allowance for Bad Debts	0.00%	0.00%	0.00%	0.00%	0.00%	−0.36%
Inventories	10.07%	77.00%	19.10%	28.23%	37.70%	42.08%
Prepaid Expenses	0.00%	0.00%	0.00%	0.38%	0.16%	0.00%
Other Current Assets	0.00%	0.33%	0.00%	0.00%	0.00%	3.85%
Total Current Assets	82.32%	98.41%	96.42%	98.78%	96.13%	87.30%
Gross Fixed Assets	13.45%	0.76%	1.28%	0.67%	3.23%	15.57%
Accumulated Depreciation	0.00%	0.00%	0.00%	0.00%	0.00%	−8.84%
Net Fixed Assets	13.45%	0.76%	1.28%	0.67%	3.23%	6.72%
Other Assets						
Intangible Assets (Net)	0.00%	0.00%	0.00%	0.00%	0.00%	1.32%
Security Deposits	1.69%	0.83%	0.81%	0.00%	0.12%	0.00%
Other Assets	2.55%	0.00%	1.50%	0.55%	0.52%	4.67%
Total Other Assets	4.23%	0.83%	2.30%	0.55%	0.64%	5.99%
TOTAL ASSETS	100.00%	100.00%	100.00%	100.00%	100.00%	100.00%

Quimby's Computer Solutions, Inc.
Schedule 11: Annual Adjusted Common Size Comparison
to Integra Data *(continued)*

	1991	1992	1993	1994	1995	Integra
Current Liabilities						
Accounts Payable	73.01%	84.18%	75.72%	26.25%	13.90%	29.52%
Long-Term Debt—Current	0.00%	0.00%	0.00%	0.00%	0.00%	18.81%
Accrued Expenses	0.00%	0.00%	2.56%	6.20%	7.19%	0.00%
Income Taxes Payable	0.00%	0.00%	0.00%	4.76%	0.00%	0.00%
Due to Stockholder	0.00%	5.61%	8.13%	0.00%	0.00%	0.00%
Revolving Credit Line	82.73%	36.93%	20.57%	56.08%	66.76%	0.00%
Other Current Liabilities	0.00%	0.00%	0.00%	0.00%	0.00%	8.60%
Total Current Liabilities	155.74%	126.73%	106.98%	93.30%	87.85%	56.93%
Long-Term Liabilities						
Long-Term Debt	0.00%	0.00%	0.00%	0.00%	0.00%	12.89%
Other Liabilities	0.00%	0.00%	0.00%	0.00%	0.00%	1.71%
Total Long-Term Liabilities	0.00%	0.00%	0.00%	0.00%	0.00%	14.60%
Total Liabilities	155.74%	126.73%	106.98%	93.30%	87.85%	71.53%
Stockholders' Equity						
Common Stock	0.17%	0.09%	0.06%	0.01%	0.01%	n/a
Retained Earnings	−55.92%	−26.81%	−7.04%	6.69%	12.14%	n/a
Total Stockholders' Equity	−55.74%	−26.73%	−6.98%	6.70%	12.15%	28.47%
TOTAL LIABILITIES AND STOCKHOLDERS' EQUITY	100.00%	100.00%	100.00%	100.00%	100.00%	100.00%

Quimby's Computer Solutions, Inc.
Schedule 12: Common Size Income Statement Adjusted
for the Years Ended August 31,

	1991	1992	1993	1994	1995	Average	Integra
Total Revenues	100.00%	100.00%	100.00%	100.00%	100.00%	100.00%	100.00%
Total Cost of Sales	87.95%	87.13%	82.67%	82.01%	82.03%	82.80%	80.36%
Gross Profit	12.05%	12.87%	17.33%	17.99%	17.97%	17.20%	19.64%
Total Operating Expenses	14.49%	11.51%	15.95%	12.81%	12.08%	12.90%	17.18%
Operating Income (Loss)	−2.45%	1.36%	1.38%	5.18%	5.89%	4.29%	2.46%
Interest Expense	0.87%	1.16%	0.35%	0.63%	0.49%	0.57%	1.16%
Total Other Income (Expenses)	0.01%	−0.55%	−0.02%	0.03%	0.09%	0.01%	0.41%
Income (Loss) Before Taxes	−3.31%	−0.35%	1.01%	4.59%	5.49%	3.73%	1.71%
Income Taxes	−1.07%	−0.07%	0.29%	1.73%	2.06%	1.41%	0.65%
NET INCOME (LOSS)	−2.24%	−0.28%	0.73%	2.86%	3.42%	2.32%	1.06%

Quimby's Computer Solutions, Inc.
Schedule 13: Normalization Adjustments

	August 31, 1991	Adjust-ments	Adjusted 1991	August 31, 1992	Adjust-ments	Adjusted 1992	August 31, 1993	Adjust-ments	Adjusted 1993	August 31, 1994	Adjust-ments	Adjusted 1994	August 31, 1995	Adjust-ments	Adjusted 1995
Current Assets															
Cash	$ 10,647	-	$ 10,647	$ 2,148	-	$ 2,148	$ 69,266	-	$ 69,266	$ 544,500	-	$ 544,500	$1,118,697	-	$1,118,697
Marketable Securities	35,233	(36,446)	35,233	-	-	-	52,886	-	52,886	-	-	-	-	-	-
Accounts Receivable	313,751	(15,620)	313,751	797,374	-	797,374	971,565	-	971,565	3,963,550	-	3,963,550	4,589,646	-	4,589,646
Allowance for Bad Debts	-		-	-		-	-		-	-		-	-		-
Inventories	50,100		50,100	189,224		189,224	270,233		270,233	1,814,009		1,814,009	3,693,293		3,693,293
Prepaid Expenses	-		-	-		-	-		-	24,396		24,396	15,484		15,484
Other Current Assets	-		-	3,348		3,348	-		-	-		-	-		-
Total Current Assets	$ 409,731	-	$ 409,731	$ 992,094	-	$ 992,094	$1,363,950	-	$1,363,950	$6,346,455	-	$6,346,455	$ 9,417,120	-	$9,417,120
Net Fixed Assets	$ 66,947	-	$ 66,947	$ 7,619	-	$ 7,619	$ 18,048	-	$ 18,048	$ 43,021	-	$ 43,021	$ 316,784	-	$ 316,784
Other Assets															
Security Deposits	$ 8,391		$ 8,391	$ 8,391		$ 8,391	$ 11,393		$ 11,393	-		-	$ 11,301		$ 11,301
Stockholder Loans	56,446	(56,446)	-	-		-	-		-	34,996	(34,996)	-	229,246	(229,246)	-
Employee Advances	15,620	(15,620)	-	-		-	-		-	-		-	96,687	(96,687)	-
Other Assets	12,668		12,668	-		-	21,160		21,160	35,384		35,384	51,302		51,302
Total Other Assets	$ 93,125	$ (72,066)	$ 21,059	$ 8,391	-	$ 8,391	$ 32,553	-	$ 32,553	$ 70,380	$ (34,996)	$ 35,384	$ 388,536	$ (325,933)	$ 62,603
TOTAL ASSETS	$ 569,803	$ (72,066)	$ 497,737	$1,008,104	-	$1,008,104	$1,414,551	-	$1,414,551	$6,459,856	$ (34,996)	$6,424,860	$10,122,440	$ (325,933)	$9,796,507

Current Liabilities														
Accounts Payable	$ 363,408	–	$ 363,408	$ 848,670	–	$ 848,670	$ 1,071,061	–	$ 1,071,061	$ 1,686,380	–	$ 1,686,380	$ 1,361,785	–	$ 1,361,785
Accrued Expenses	–	–	–	–	–	–	36,181	–	36,181	398,617	–	398,617	704,373	–	704,373
Income Taxes Payable	–	–	–	–	–	–	115,004	–	115,004	306,000	–	306,000	–	–	–
Due to Stockholder	–	–	–	56,582	–	56,582	–	–	–	–	–	–	–	–	–
Revolving Credit Line	411,775	–	411,775	372,270	–	372,270	290,977	–	290,977	3,603,175	–	3,603,175	6,540,143	–	6,540,143
Total Current Liabilities	$ 775,183	$ –	$ 775,183	$ 1,277,522	$ –	$ 1,277,522	$ 1,513,223	$ –	$ 1,513,223	$ 5,994,172	$ –	$ 5,994,172	$ 8,606,301	$ –	$ 8,606,301
Stockholders' Equity														
Common Stock	$ 865	$ –	$ 865	$ 865	$ –	$ 865	$ 865	$ –	$ 865	$ 865	$ –	$ 865	$ 865	$ –	$ 865
Retained Earnings	(206,245)	(72,066)	(278,311)	(270,283)	–	(270,283)	(99,537)	–	(99,537)	464,819	(34,996)	429,823	1,515,274	(325,933)	1,189,341
Total Stockholders' Equity	$ (205,380)	$ (72,066)	$ (277,446)	$ (269,418)	$ –	$ (269,418)	$ (98,672)	$ –	$ (98,672)	$ 465,684	$ (34,996)	$ 430,688	$ 1,516,139	$ (325,933)	$ 1,190,206
TOTAL LIABILITIES AND STOCKHOLDERS' EQUITY	$ 569,803	$ (72,066)	$ 497,737	$ 1,008,104	$ –	$ 1,008,104	$ 1,414,551	$ –	$ 1,414,551	$ 6,459,856	$ (34,996)	$ 6,424,860	$ 10,122,440	$ (325,933)	$ 9,796,507
Total Nonoperating Assets/(Liabilities)	$ –	$ 72,066	$ 72,066	$ –	$ –	$ –	$ –	$ –	$ –	$ –	$ 34,996	$ 34,996	$ –	$ 325,933	$ 325,933

Note: Stockholder loans and employee advances were considered to be nonoperating.

Quimby's Computer Solutions, Inc.
Schedule 14: Normalization of Income
for the Years Ended August 31,

	1991	1992	1993	1994	1995
Historical Net Income	$(151,758)	$(64,038)	$149,586	$482,962	$1,606,293
Adjustments					
Officers' Compensation—Add Back[1]	130,108	196,078	184,784	617,559	1,235,045
Officers' Compensation—Reasonable[2]	(144,089)	(152,409)	(214,597)	(322,800)	(515,812)
Other Income[3]				(17,480)	(78,596)
Historical Income Taxes[4]	–	–	–	262,000	–
ADJUSTED PRETAX NET INCOME	**$(165,739)**	**$(20,369)**	**$119,773**	**$1,022,241**	**$2,246,930**
Income Taxes[5]	(53,449)	(4,008)	33,980	384,669	845,520
ADJUSTED HISTORICAL NET INCOME	**$(112,290)**	**$(16,361)**	**$85,793**	**$637,572**	**$1,401,410**

[1] Officers' compensation has been added back in full, as reasonable compensation for Quimby's officers will be calculated in footnote 2.

[2] We have retrieved the following breakdown of total officers' compensation, which has been compiled from Quimby's corporate tax returns, along with Mr. Smith's personal tax returns and Form W-2s.

[3] Other income reflects miscellaneous fees received mainly from IBM. This income was nonrecurring, and has been normalized from the income statement.

[4] Historical taxes have been added back to reflect adjusted levels of pretax income.

[5] Income taxes have been recalculated using state and federal tax rates and schedules as follows:

		1991	1992	1993	1994	1995
Adjusted Pretax Net Income		$ (165,739)	$ (20,369)	$ 119,773	$ 1,022,241	$ 2,246,930
State Income Tax	6%	(9,116)	(1,120)	6,588	56,223	123,581
SUBTOTAL		**$ (156,623)**	**$ (19,249)**	**$ 113,185**	**$ 966,018**	**$ 2,123,349**
Federal Tax Calculation						
$50,000	15%	(7,500)	(2,887)	7,500	7,500	7,500
25,000	25%	(6,250)	–	6,250	6,250	6,250
25,000	34%	(8,500)	–	8,500	8,500	8,500
235,000	39%	−22,083	–	5,142	91,650	9,1650
Over 335,000	34%	–	–		214,546	608,039
TOTAL TAX		**$ (53,449)**	**$ (4,008)**	**$ 33,980**	**$ 384,669**	**$ 845,520**

Officers' Compensation

	Mr. Smith	Mr. Skinner	Total
1995	$ 883,945	$ 351,100	$1,235,045
1994	426,955	190,604	617,559
1993	184,784	0[1]	184,784
1992	196,178	0[2]	196,178
1991	130,108	0[3]	130,108

[1] Prior year's financial statements included Mr. Skinner's compensation as a nonofficer.
[2] Ibid.
[3] Ibid.

We reviewed the following sources to estimate reasonable compensation:

- *1996 Executive Compensation Survey, Computers, Peripherals & Software Distributors*, Carey Associates, Inc.
- *1992–1996 Executive Compensation Survey*, National Institute of Business Management.
- *1992–1996 Annual Statement Studies*, Robert Morris Associates.
- *Business Profiler*, Integra Information.

The results of our research are as follows:

Officer Compensation Analysis

Year	1996 ECS[1,2]	Compensation[3]	NIBM[1,4]	Compensation[3]	RMA1[5]	Compensation	Integra[5]	Compensation
1991	$120,849	$120,849	N/A	N/A	5.00%	$250,441	N/A	N/A
1992	124,474	124,474	$145,000	$145,000	1.90%	110,449	N/A	N/A
1993	157,351	157,351	122,500	122,500	1.30%	153,727	1.60%	$189,203
1994	198,952	397,904	167,000	334,000	2.00%	445,716	1.70%	378,858
1995	251,390	502,781	144,000	288,000	1.10%	450,399	1.20%	491,345

[1] Median compensation.
[2] *1996 Executive Compensation Survey, Computers, Peripherals & Software Distributors*, Carey Associates, Inc.
[3] Multiplied by 2 in 1994 and 1995 to account for two officers.
[4] Historical National Institute of Business Management SIC 50 (Wholesale Trade) by Sales Volume.
[5] Percentage of sales by year and sales volume.

We performed a regression analysis of this data. The data produced by the National Institute of Business Management (NIBM), for all distributor types, does not fall in line with the other three sources. Since it did not focus on Quimby's specific industry and did not correlate with our industry-specific sources, we did not use it. We performed a linear regression of the remaining data, analyzing average and median compensation as a factor of sales volume. Regression of the median compensation to sales produced the strongest relationship. Therefore, we utilized the median officers' compensation of three sources to estimate reasonable officers' compensation, resulting in the following:

1991	1992	1993	1994	1995
$144,089	$152,409	$214,597	$322,800	$509,000

Quimby's Computer Solutions, Inc.
Schedule 15: Statements of Annual Net Free Equity Cash Flows
Calculated From Data as Adjusted
Fiscal Years Ended August 31,

	1991	1992	1993	1994	1995
Total Revenues	$5,008,819	$5,813,102	$11,825,174	$22,285,781	$40,945,386
Total Cost of Sales	4,405,459	5,064,854	9,775,873	18,276,690	33,588,165
Gross Profit	$603,360	$748,248	$ 2,049,301	$ 4,009,091	$ 7,357,221
Total Operating Expenses	725,906	669,264	1,885,838	2,854,244	4,946,935
Operating Income (Loss)	$(122,546)	$78,984	$163,463	$ 1,154,847	$ 2,410,286
Interest Expense	43,813	67,256	41,829	139,909	199,028
Total Other Income (Expenses)	620	(32,097)	(1,861)	7,303	35,672
Income (Loss) Before Taxes	$(165,739)	$ (20,369)	$ 119,773	$ 1,022,241	$ 2,246,930
Income Taxes	(53,449)	(4,008)	33,980	384,669	845,520
Net Income (Loss)	$(112,290)	$ (16,361)	$ 85,793	$ 637,572	$ 1,401,410
Depreciation and Amortization	8,150	5,996	4,212	23,758	77,199
Gross Cash Flow	$(104,140)	$ (10,365)	$ 90,005	$ 661,330	$ 1,478,609
Capital Expenditures	(23,756)	59,328	(10,429)	(24,973)	(273,763)
Change in Working Capital	(67,422)	(80,024)	(136,155)	(501,556)	(458,536)
Change in Other Assets/ Liabilities	11,455	12,668	(24,162)	(2,831)	(27,219)
NET CASH FLOW	$(183,863)	$ (18,393)	$ (80,741)	$ 131,970	$ 719,091

Quimby's Computer Solutions, Inc.
Schedule 16: Annual Adjusted Ratios Comparison
to Integra Data
August 31,

	1992	1993	1994	1995
LIQUIDITY / SOLVENCY				
Quick Ratio	0.63	0.72	0.75	0.66
Quick Ratio—Integra	0.76	0.76	0.73	0.73
Current Ratio	0.78	0.9	1.06	1.09
Current Ratio—Integra	1.6	1.61	1.53	1.53
Days Accounts Receivables Outstanding	34.88	27.3	40.41	38.12
Days Accounts Receivables Outstanding—Integra	55.56	54.4	50.98	50.98
Days Accounts Payable	43.67	35.84	27.53	16.56
Days Accounts Payable—Integra	27.11	53.57	51.81	57.18
Days Working Capital	−17.92	−4.61	5.77	7.23
Days Working Capital—Integra	–	50.76	45.74	45.74
Days Inventory Sales	8.62	8.58	20.81	29.92
Days Inventory Sales—Integra	82.39	81.29	76.04	76.04
TURNOVER				
Receivables Turnover	10.46	13.37	9.03	9.57
Receivables Turnover—Integra	6.57	6.71	7.16	7.16
Cash Turnover	908.65	331.17	72.62	49.24
Cash Turnover—Integra	41.77	41.27	41.99	41.99
Inventory Turnover	42.33	42.55	17.54	12.2
Inventory Turnover—Integra	4.43	4.49	4.8	4.8
Current Asset Turnover	8.29	10.04	5.78	5.19
Current Asset Turnover—Integra	2.66	2.63	2.69	2.69
Working Capital Turnover	−20.37	−79.22	63.26	50.5
Working Capital Turnover—Integra	–	7.19	7.98	7.98
Fixed Asset Turnover	155.92	921.43	729.86	227.6
Fixed Asset Turnover—Integra	33.45	34.65	34.89	34.89
Total Asset Turnover	7.72	9.76	5.69	5.05
Total Asset Turnover—Integra	2.32	2.31	2.35	2.35
Payables Turnover	8.36	10.18	13.26	22.04
Payables Turnover—Integra	13.46	6.81	7.04	6.38
SG&A Expense to Cash	104.61	52.81	9.3	5.95
SG&A Expense to Cash—Integra	14.36	7.39	7.76	7.22

Quimby's Computer Solutions, Inc.
Schedule 16: Annual Adjusted Ratios Comparison
to Integra Data
August 31, *(continued)*

	1992	1993	1994	1995
DEBT				
Times Interest Earned	1.17	3.91	8.25	12.11
Times Interest Earned—Integra	2.16	1.93	2.13	2.13
Total Liabilities to Total Assets	1.27	1.07	0.93	0.88
Total Liabilities to Total Assets—Integra	0.68	0.69	0.72	0.72
Total Liabilities to Equity	−4.74	−15.34	13.92	7.23
Total Liabilities to Equity—Integra	2.15	2.18	2.51	2.51
Short-Term Debt to Equity	–	–	–	–
Current Debt to Equity—Integra	0.58	0.59	0.66	0.66
Long-Term Debt to Equity	–	–	–	–
Long-Term Debt to Equity—Integra	0.38	0.4	0.45	0.45
Total Interest-Bearing Debt to Equity	–	–	–	–
Total Interest-Bearing Debt to Equity—Integra	0.97	0.98	1.11	1.11
Total Assets to Equity	−3.74	−14.34	14.92	8.23
Total Assets to Equity—Integra	3.15	3.18	3.51	3.51
Total Liabilities to Invested Capital	−4.74	−15.34	13.92	7.23
Total Liabilities to Invested Capital—Integra	1.1	1.1	1.19	1.19
Net Fixed Assets to Equity	−0.03	−0.18	0.1	0.27
Net Fixed Assets to Equity—Integra	0.22	0.21	0.24	0.24
PROFITABILITY				
EBITDA Return on Total Assets	8.43%	11.85%	18.34%	25.39%
EBITDA Return on Total Assets—Integra	6.73%	7.57%	7.34%	7.34%
EBIT Return on Assets	7.83%	11.56%	17.97%	24.60%
EBIT Return on Assets—Integra	6.26%	6.99%	6.72%	6.72%
Pretax Return on Assets	−2.02%	8.47%	15.91%	22.94%
Pretax Return on Assets—Integra	2.40%	2.40%	2.50%	2.50%
After-Tax Return on Assets	−1.62%	6.07%	9.92%	14.31%
After-Tax Return on Assets—Integra	12.10%	12.30%	14.10%	14.10%
EBITDA Return on Equity	−31.54%	−169.93%	273.66%	209.00%
EBITDA Return on Equity—Integra	21.22%	24.08%	25.77%	25.77%

EBIT Return on Equity	−29.32%	−165.66%	268.14%	202.51%
EBIT Return on Equity—Integra	19.75%	22.25%	23.62%	23.62%
Pretax Return on Equity	7.56%	−121.38%	237.35%	188.78%
Pretax Return on Equity—Integra	7.50%	7.60%	8.70%	8.70%
After-Tax Return on Equity	6.07%	−86.95%	148.04%	117.75%
After-Tax Return on Equity—Integra	1.60%	1.70%	1.70%	1.70%
EBITDA Return on Net Sales	1.46%	1.42%	5.29%	6.08%
EBITDA Return on Net Sales—Integra	2.90%	3.28%	3.13%	3.13%
EBIT Return on Net Sales	1.36%	1.38%	5.18%	5.89%
EBIT Return on Net Sales—Integra	2.70%	3.03%	2.87%	2.87%
Pretax Return on Net Sales	−0.35%	1.01%	4.59%	5.49%
Pretax Return on Net Sales—Integra	1.00%	1.00%	1.10%	1.10%
After-Tax Return on Net Sales	−0.28%	0.73%	2.86%	3.42%
After-Tax Return on Net Sales—Integra	1.00%	1.00%	1.10%	1.10%
EBITDA Return on Invested Capital	−31.54%	−169.93%	273.66%	209.00%
EBITDA Return on Invested Capital—Integra	10.80%	12.14%	12.19%	12.19%
EBIT Return on Invested Capital	−29.32%	−165.66%	268.14%	202.51%
EBIT Return on Invested Capital—Integra	10.05%	11.22%	11.18%	11.18%
Pretax Return on Invested Capital	7.56%	−121.38%	237.35%	188.78%
Pretax Return on Invested Capital—Integra	6.14%	6.22%	6.67%	6.67%
Return on Invested Capital	6.07%	−86.95%	148.04%	117.75%
Return on Invested Capital—Integra	3.79%	3.84%	4.14%	4.14%

WORKING CAPITAL

Working Capital ($000)	−28,542.80%	−14,927.30%	35,228.30%	81,081.90%
Working Capital—Integra	322.80%	343.90%	367.10%	367.10%
Short-Term Debt to Working Capital	0.00%	0.00%	0.00%	0.00%
Short-Term Debt to Working Capital—Integra	56.50%	55.80%	62.00%	62.00%
Long-Term Debt to Working Capital	0.00%	0.00%	0.00%	0.00%
Long-Term Debt to Working Capital—Integra	36.90%	37.60%	42.50%	42.50%

OPERATING EFFICIENCY

Operating Expense to Sales	11.51%	15.95%	12.81%	12.08%
Operating Expense to Sales—Integra	17.20%	17.40%	17.20%	17.20%

Quimby's Computer Solutions, Inc.
Schedule 16: Annual Adjusted Ratios Comparison
to Integra Data
August 31,

	1992	1993	1994	1995
Depreciation and Amortization to Sales	0.10%	0.04%	0.11%	0.19%
Depreciation and Amortization to Sales—Integra	0.60%	0.70%	0.70%	0.70%
Capital Expenditures to Sales	-1.02%	0.09%	0.11%	0.67%
Capital Expenditures to Sales—Integra	0.00%	0.70%	1.20%	1.20%
INDUSTRY GROWTH				
Revenue	16.06%	103.42%	88.46%	83.73%
Revenue—Integra	–	5.03%	18.27%	0.00%
Net Income	-85.43%	-624.36%	643.15%	119.80%
Net Income—Integra	–	6.87%	20.88%	0.00%
Officers' Compensation / Sales	0.03	0.02	0.01	0.01
Officers' Compensation / Sales—Integra	0.01	0.01	0.01	0.01
3-Year Compound Growth Rate—Earnings	–	–	–	303.62%
3-Year Compound Growth Rate—Revenues	–	53.65%	95.80%	86.08%
Size of Revenues ($000)	5,813	11,825	22,286	40,945
Size of Revenues ($000)—Integra	22,824	23,972	28,351	28,351
Earnings ($000)	-16	86	638	1,401
Earnings ($000)—Integra	233	249	301	301

Quimby's Computer Solutions, Inc.
Schedule 17: Extended Dupont Analysis Comparison
to Integra Data

	Profitability	×				Turnover	=		×	Solvency	=	ROE
	Taxes	Financing	Operations					Net		Total		Net
	Income/EBT	EBT/EBIT	EBIT/Sales	= Income/Sales	×	Sales/Total Assets	=	Income/Total Assets	×	Assets/Common Equity	=	Income/Common Equity
Quimby's												
1995	62.37%	93.22%	5.89%	3.42%		417.96%		14.31%		823.09%		117.75%
1994	62.37%	88.52%	5.18%	2.86%		346.87%		9.92%		1,491.77%		148.04%
1993	71.63%	73.27%	1.38%	0.73%		835.97%		6.07%		-1,433.59%		-86.95%
1992	80.33%	-25.79%	1.36%	-0.28%		576.64%		-1.62%		-374.18%		6.07%
Integra												
1995	62.06%	59.66%	2.87%	1.06%		234.50%		2.49%		351.25%		8.74%
1994	62.06%	59.66%	2.87%	1.06%		234.50%		2.49%		351.25%		8.74%
1993	61.79%	55.43%	3.03%	1.04%		230.54%		2.39%		318.18%		7.62%
1992	61.80%	61.10%	2.70%	1.02%		231.69%		2.37%		315.33%		7.46%

Note: Integra figures may not match Integra ratios due to rounding.

(EXERCISE 8) FINANCIAL ANALYSIS "AS ADJUSTED"

Observations   Impact on Value
                                                                           + / 0 / –

_____   _____

_____   _____

_____   _____

_____   _____

_____   _____

EXERCISE 9: FACTORS AFFECTING PREMIUMS AND DISCOUNTS

Exhibit 4 is material from Mergerstat *Review 1994* concerning control premiums, private versus public analysis and size differences. Exhibit 5 is material from *Control Premium Study 4th Quarter 1995*, also concerning control premiums.

Your assignment is to review this material as well as the lecture notes and the facts concerning Quimby's already presented, and then identify the most relevant factors that affect the application and magnitude of a control premium (or minority discount) and a discount for lack of marketability (DLOM). Also, if any other discounts should be applied, you should discuss those as well. Provide your answers on the exercise table.

Exhibit 4: Mergrstat Review 1994 (excerpted material)

(Permission for use granted by Mergerstat.)

Note: 1994 was used because 1995 had not yet been compiled. Do not let the year difference impact your analysis.

PREMIUM OFFERED OVER MARKET PRICE*

Both average and median premium offered over market price during 1994 increased from the prior year. The average premium was 41.9% for 1994 and the median was 35.0% based on 260 transactions in which price was disclosed and premiums were offered. However, due to the high number of announced divestitures and private sellers, few transactions have released sufficient data to calculate average premiums offered.

The level of premiums throughout the decade of the 1980s was relatively steady and very typical of a long term bull market despite the stock market crash of 1987 and subsequent volatility. The average premium in 1994 was consistent with those of the late 1980s.

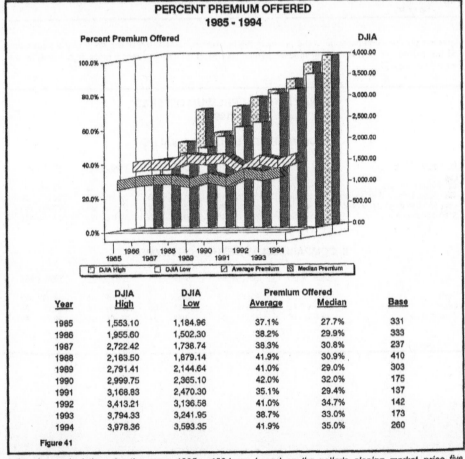

Year	DJIA High	DJIA Low	Premium Offered Average	Premium Offered Median	Base
1985	1,553.10	1,184.96	37.1%	27.7%	331
1986	1,955.60	1,502.30	38.2%	29.9%	333
1987	2,722.42	1,738.74	38.3%	30.8%	237
1988	2,183.50	1,879.14	41.9%	30.9%	410
1989	2,791.41	2,144.64	41.0%	29.0%	303
1990	2,999.75	2,365.10	42.0%	32.0%	175
1991	3,168.83	2,470.30	35.1%	29.4%	137
1992	3,413.21	3,136.58	41.0%	34.7%	142
1993	3,794.33	3,241.95	38.7%	33.0%	173
1994	3,978.36	3,593.35	41.9%	35.0%	260

Figure 41

* Premium calculations for the years 1985 - 1994 are based on the seller's closing market price five business days before the initial announcement.

Figure 43 compares the average percent premium offered for a controlling equity interest (acquisitions of 50.1% or more of a company's shares outstanding) with that for a minority equity interest (purchases of 10 - 50.0%). The average premium offered for a minority interest in 1994 was 54.5% and the average premium offered for a controlling interest increased to 40.7% from 38.7% in the prior year.

In 1994, in contrast to any prior year, buyers on average offered a lower premium for controlling equity interest purchases than minority equity interest purchases. The difference in premiums historically offered between controlling equity interests and minority equity interests reflects the difference in benefits between purchasing a minority investment and purchasing the right to control the future operations of a company. Caution should be used in drawing conclusions as statistics were often calculated using a small base.

AVERAGE PERCENT PREMIUM OFFERED
CONTROLLING VS. MINORITY
1990 - 1994

	1990	Base	1991	Base	1992	Base	1993	Base	1994	Base
Controlling Interest	42.3%	154	35.4%	125	41.3%	127	38.7%	151	40.7%	237
Minority Interest	39.6%	21	32.6%	12	38.3%	15	38.3%	22	54.5%	23

Figure 43

Figure 44 provides comparisons of the premium offered with respect to the dollar value of the transaction and the method of payment. The median percent premium offered increased most significantly in the lowest price category.

MEDIAN PERCENT PREMIUM OFFERED
1990 - 1994

I. COMPARISON BY DOLLAR VALUE

Purchase Price	1990	Base	1991	Base	1992	Base	1993	Base	1994	Base
$25.0 million or less	30.6%	76	27.7%	47	33.3%	35	32.3%	38	42.9%	45
Over $25.0 through $50.0 million	32.2%	29	37.1%	19	21.6%	30	36.7%	28	33.9%	36
Over $50.0 through $99.9 million	31.2%	16	21.9%	25	32.3%	22	31.5%	31	27.8%	53
$100 million or more	39.9%	54	31.9%	46	39.0%	55	32.0%	76	35.8%	126

II. COMPARISON BY METHOD OF PAYMENT

	1990	Base	1991	Base	1992	Base	1993	Base	1994	Base
Cash	34.0%	63	20.0%	24	29.6%	35	32.5%	46	36.8%	59
Stock	23.0%	42	28.9%	49	36.8%	58	32.1%	56	30.6%	95
Combination	45.6%	16	32.7%	24	41.9%	21	33.9%	36	39.7%	40

Figure 44

INDUSTRY CLASSIFICATIONS
PERCENT PREMIUM OFFERED (Base)
1990 - 1994

Industry Classification of Seller	1990 %		1991 %		1992 %		1993 %		1994 %	
Miscellaneous Services	39.6	(15)	16.5	(3)	7.9	(3)	68.9	(3)	68.8	(9)
Computer Software, Supplies & Services	51.3	(11)	44.6	(7)	60.8	(3)	43.5	(4)	59.1	(12)
Office Equipment & Computer Hardware	38.7	(8)	30.7	(3)	13.6	(2)	47.3	(7)	58.8	(11)
Electronics	52.1	(9)	40.0	(1)	26.7	(2)	0.0	(0)	56.5	(4)
Aerospace, Aircraft & Defense	2.6	(1)	0.0	(0)	0.0	(0)	0.0	(0)	55.5	(1)
Communications	52.8	(3)	26.5	(4)	64.2	(5)	52.7	(6)	54.6	(7)
Drugs, Medical Supplies & Equipment	44.1	(11)	33.0	(7)	16.7	(2)	34.8	(5)	51.2	(22)
Food Processing	88.5	(2)	51.5	(2)	0.0	(0)	40.5	(1)	49.1	(8)
Insurance	50.7	(3)	24.4	(4)	40.9	(8)	33.7	(5)	47.6	(12)
Health Services	33.4	(3)	18.4	(5)	37.0	(6)	41.9	(9)	46.5	(14)
Primary Metal Processing	37.4	(2)	32.4	(1)	0.0	(0)	34.7	(2)	46.4	(2)
Automotive Products & Accessories	8.9	(1)	0.0	(0)	0.0	(0)	25.0	(1)	45.2	(3)
Leisure & Entertainment	33.0	(8)	76.5	(1)	51.2	(2)	30.0	(8)	40.6	(9)
Broadcasting	28.4	(2)	16.4	(1)	49.3	(2)	66.5	(3)	40.4	(7)
Toys & Recreational Products	12.3	(2)	14.8	(1)	0.0	(0)	55.0	(2)	40.2	(2)
Electrical Equipment	11.6	(2)	38.9	(8)	10.5	(1)	27.2	(6)	39.7	(6)
Retail	58.6	(8)	29.3	(4)	38.2	(4)	38.4	(5)	38.6	(7)
Brokerage, Investment & Mgmt. Consulting	29.5	(4)	0.0	(0)	21.7	(3)	22.6	(10)	37.8	(7)
Oil & Gas	10.9	(2)	46.1	(10)	52.2	(4)	30.2	(4)	35.8	(8)
Toiletries & Cosmetics	0.0	(0)	0.0	(0)	89.9	(1)	29.5	(1)	35.7	(1)
Banking & Finance	41.8	(21)	32.6	(39)	42.9	(54)	39.4	(58)	34.6	(67)
Industrial & Farm Equipment & Machinery	19.7	(6)	39.2	(4)	0.0	(0)	0.0	(0)	34.6	(3)
Electrical, Gas, Water & Sanitary Services	36.0	(3)	13.8	(5)	23.1	(2)	21.4	(5)	33.8	(8)
Energy Services	90.6	(4)	27.7	(1)	0.0	(0)	0.0	(0)	31.9	(5)
Chemicals, Paints & Coatings	78.6	(2)	0.0	(0)	34.0	(2)	0.0	(0)	27.5	(2)
Construction, Mining & Oil Equip. & Mach.	22.5	(1)	45.4	(1)	0.0	(0)	20.7	(1)	26.7	(2)
Fabricated Metal Products	17.4	(4)	41.0	(2)	40.0	(1)	72.1	(1)	25.7	(4)
Wholesale & Distribution	37.0	(3)	20.0	(1)	61.9	(6)	67.5	(3)	21.2	(7)
Instruments & Photographic Equipment	21.7	(4)	99.2	(2)	33.3	(6)	76.1	(1)	19.1	(6)
Construction Contractors & Eng. Svcs.	26.1	(4)	27.8	(2)	20.6	(1)	19.8	(1)	18.6	(2)
Household Goods	0.0	(0)	0.0	(0)	118.7	(1)	4.0	(1)	11.7	(1)
Plastics & Rubber	0.0	(0)	0.0	(0)	24.6	(2)	77.2	(3)	7.7	(1)
Agricultural Production	0.0	(0)	0.0	(0)	28.6	(3)	0.0	(0)	0.0	(0)
Apparel	51.2	(4)	37.5	(1)	26.4	(2)	41.8	(3)	0.0	(0)
Autos & Trucks	48.2	(2)	0.0	(0)	0.0	(0)	27.3	(1)	0.0	(0)
Beverages	0.0	(0)	132.9	(1)	0.0	(0)	19.7	(1)	0.0	(0)
Building Products & Materials	106.0	(1)	0.0	(0)	0.0	(0)	0.0	(0)	0.0	(0)
Conglomerate	9.1	(1)	0.0	(0)	0.0	(0)	0.0	(0)	0.0	(0)
Furniture	15.0	(2)	30.4	(1)	16.7	(1)	16.8	(1)	0.0	(0)
Mining & Minerals	19.3	(1)	40.8	(5)	27.8	(1)	0.0	(0)	0.0	(0)
Miscellaneous Manufacturing	0.0	(0)	51.6	(1)	49.6	(1)	63.4	(2)	0.0	(0)
Packaging & Containers	0.0	(0)	0.0	(0)	9.7	(2)	0.0	(0)	0.0	(0)
Paper	65.0	(1)	0.0	(0)	115.4	(1)	21.9	(1)	0.0	(0)
Printing & Publishing	31.4	(2)	89.0	(1)	19.2	(1)	15.0	(3)	0.0	(0)
Real Estate	103.3	(2)	14.4	(1)	0.0	(0)	0.0	(0)	0.0	(0)
Stone, Clay & Glass	50.3	(5)	0.0	(0)	0.0	(0)	46.4	(2)	0.0	(0)
Textiles	0.0	(0)	0.0	(0)	31.0	(5)	2.8	(1)	0.0	(0)
Timber & Forest Products	0.0	(0)	9.8	(2)	0.0	(0)	0.0	(0)	0.0	(0)
Transportation	38.1	(3)	31.5	(5)	62.4	(2)	13.6	(2)	0.0	(0)
Valves, Pumps, & Hydraulics	43.6	(2)	0.0	(0)	0.0	(0)	0.0	(0)	0.0	(0)
All Industry Average	**42.0**	**(175)**	**35.1**	**(137)**	**41.0**	**(142)**	**38.7**	**(173)**	**41.9**	**(260)**

The all industry average is based on the price offered for each transaction disclosing a purchase price. The industry classified breakdowns are based on averages for each industry.

Exhibit 5: Control Premium Study 4th Quarter 1995 (adapted from Houlihan Lokey)

4th Quarter Summary Figures (1995)

Domestic Transactions

Number of transactions	80
Range	0.0%–242.0%
Median	30.4%
Mean	42.1%

International Transactions

Number of transactions	47
Range	2.4%–171.7%
Median	25.9%
Mean	38.7%

Total Domestic and International Transactions

Number of Transactions	127
Range	0.0%–242.0%
Median	26.9%
Mean	40.9%

12-Month Summary Figures (1995)

Number of Transactions	333
Range	0.0%–242.0%
Median	31.9%
Mean	40.1%

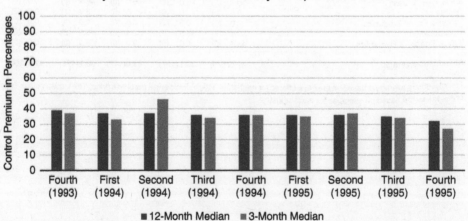

Industrywide Control Premium Study Comparative Results

	Fourth (1993)	First (1994)	Second (1994)	Third (1994)	Fourth (1994)	First (1995)	Second (1995)	Third (1995)	Fourth (1995)
Number of trans.	24	32	40	49	63	70	62	74	127

SIC Code	Target Category	Closing Date	Target Name	Control Premium
	4212	3/92	Courier Dispatch Group, Inc.	231.1%
	4215	10/91	Interlink Express Plc.	15.6%
	4225	11/91	Food Industries Plc.	8.1%

48 Communication

Range = 51.4%–51.4%   *Median = 51.4%*   *Mean = 51.4%*

	4812	9/91	Graphic Scanning Corp.	51.4%

49 Electrical, Gas, and Sanitary Services

Range = 26.0%–34.6%   *Median = 30.6%*   Mean = 30.4%

	4911	7/91	Iowa Southern, Inc.	26.0%
	4911	3/92	Kansas Gas and Electric Co.	30.6%
	4953	3/92	Environmental Systems Co.	34.6%

50–51 Wholesale Trade

Range 45.3%–152.1%   *Median = 89.4%*   *Mean = 95.7%*

50 Durable Goods

Range = 45.3%–92.2%   *Median = 66.7%*   *Mean = 67.7%*

	5045	4/91	Computer Factory, Inc.	46.7%
	5045	12/91	Businessland, Inc.	45.3%
	5046	11/91	XLS/Datacomp, Inc.	86.6%
	5065	2/91	Cityvision Plc.	92.2%

51 Nondurable Goods

Range = 151.3%–152.1%   *Median = 151.7%*   *Mean = 151.7%*

	5112	4/91	Office Club, Inc.	152.1%
	5122	10/91	Dow B. Hickam, Inc.	151.3%

52–59 Retail Trade

Range = 30.3%–106.3%   *Median = 57.1%*   *Mean = 63.6%*

50–51 Wholesale Trade

Range = 3.3%–33.3%   *Median = 23.0%*   *Mean = 20.7%*

SIC Code	Target Category	Closing Date	Target Name	Control Premium
50 Durable Goods				
	Range = 3.3%–33.3%		*Median = 13.9%*	*Mean = 16.9%*
5045		3/94	Corporate Software, Inc.	33.3%
5045		8/94	Gates/FA Distributing, Inc.	13.9%
5045		9/94	Kenfil, Inc.	-44.0%*
5049		9/94	Momentum Corp.	3.3%
51 Nondurable Goods				
5141		9/94	Independent Holdings Ltd.	32.2%
52–59 Retail Trade				
	Range = 20.7%–107.3%		*Median = 37.1%*	*Mean = 49.4%*
53 General Merchandise Stores				
5399		10/93	Price Co.	107.3%
54 Food Stores				
5499		9/94	Nature Food Centres, Inc.	37.1%
58 Eating and Drinking Places				
5812		5/94	On the Border Cafes, Inc.	20.7%
59 Miscellaneous Retail				
	Range = 31.1%–50.7%		*Median = 40.9%*	*Mean = 40.9%*
5912		7/94	Hook-SupeRx, Inc.	50.7%
5961		11/93	Medco Containment Service, Inc.	31.1%
5012		6/95	ADESA Corp.	19.3%
5065		11/94	Anthem Electronics, Inc.	40.8%
5045		8/94	Gates/FA Distributing, Inc.	13.9%
5045		9/94	Kenfil, Inc.	-44.0%*
5049		9/94	Momentum Corp.	3.3%
5031		10/94	Taiga Forest Products Ltd.	44.0%
51 Nondurable Goods				
	Range = 19.2%–44.0%		*Median = 32.2%*	*Mean = 31.5%*
5122		5/95	AAH Holdings Plc.	44.0%

SIC Code	Target Category	Closing Date	Target Name	Control Premium
5141		9/94	Independent Holdings Ltd.	32.2%
5169		1/95	Lambert Riviere SA	23.2%
5159		4/95	Monk-Austin, Inc.	39.1%
5112		4/95	United Stationers, Inc.	19.2%

52–59 Retail Trade

Range = 14.3%–50.7%   *Median = 37.1%*   *Mean = 35.7%*

54 Food Stores

5499		9/94	Nature Food Centres, Inc.	37.1%

59 Miscellaneous Retail

Range = 14.3%–50.7%   *Median = 38.2%*   *Mean = 35.4%*

5912		7/94	Hook-SupeRx, Inc.	50.7%
5995		6/95	NuVision, Inc.	32.2%
5912		2/95	Perry Drug Stores, Inc.	44.2%
5999		6/95	Petstuff, Inc.	14.3%

60–69 Finance, Insurance, and Real Estate

Range = 1.2%–132.2%   *Median = 33.3%*   *Mean = 36.5%*

49 Electric, Gas, and Sanitary Services

Range = 0.2%–86.3%   *Median = 37.4%*   *Mean = 36.0%*

4923		6/95	Allegheny & Western Energy	37.1%
4953		6/95	Chambers Development Co., Inc.	86.3%
4923		9/95	Eastex Energy, Inc.	27.5%
4911		11/95	Hameen Sahko Oy (Vattenfall Oy)	14.4%
4911		7/95	Iowa-Illinois Gas & Electric	0.2%
4911		2/95	Magma Power Co.	41.8%
4953		5/95	Resource Recycling Techs, Inc.	37.4%
4923		5/95	Transco Energy Co.	38.6%
4911		10/95	Wairarapa Electricity	40.2%

50–51 Wholesale Trade

Range = 19.2%–242.0%   *Median = 39.1%*   *Mean = 56.1%*

SIC Code	Target Category	Closing Date	Target Name	Control Premium
50 Durable Goods				
Range = 19.3%–242.0%			Median = 45.9%	Mean = 70.2%
5012		6/95	ADESA Corp.	19.3%
5047		11/95	Arjo AB	45.9%
5051		11/95	Atlas Steels Ltd.	20.7%
5031		9/95	Erith PLC	65.2%
5021		9/95	International Contour Tech, Inc.	-38.6%*
5045		11/95	Robec, Inc.	242.0%
5023		12/95	Salmond Smith Biolab Ltd.	31.8%
5049		12/95	Simmons Outdoor Corp.	66.4%
5045		11/95	Tiger Direct, Inc.	-39.5%*

*Not representative; not used in range, mean, or median calculations

(EXERCISE 9) FACTORS AFFECTING PREMIUMS AND DISCOUNTS

Observations	Impact on Value +/ 0 / –
Control Premium	
Marketability Discount	
Other Considerations	

EXERCISE 10: SELECTION OF PUBLICLY TRADED GUIDELINE COMPANIES

In Appendix 3 (to be downloaded) you will find brief descriptions of possible guideline companies. Select the ones you believe are appropriate for use with Quimby's. There is a worksheet for your list. Also, give your selection criteria.

(EXERCISE 10) SELECTION OF GUIDELINE COMPANIES

Selections

_____

_____

_____

_____

_____

Selection Criteria

_____

_____

_____

_____

_____

EXERCISE 11: FURTHER REFINEMENT OF POSSIBLE GUIDELINE COMPANIES

Using the trading volume and pricing information included in Appendix 4 (to be downloaded), calculate the trading volume as a percentage of the shares outstanding for the possible guideline companies. Which companies should be used as guideline companies after considering this information?

(EXERCISE 11) REFINEMENT OF GUIDELINE COMPANIES

Guideline Company Trading Activity Analysis

Company	Ticker	Stock Price 12/29/95	Outstanding ($000s)	Average Volume	Volume as a % of Shares Outstanding

EXERCISE 12: COMPARATIVE ANALYSIS OF QUIMBY'S VERSUS PUBLICLY TRADED GUIDELINE COMPANIES

Exhibit 6 is a ranking of certain key financial performance and pricing ratios of one group of selected guideline companies. The performance ratios are compared to those of Quimby's. Also, Appendix 5 (to be downloaded) contains more detailed information on the selected guideline companies from several published sources. Using this information, prepare an analysis of the relative strengths and weaknesses of Quimby's compared to the guideline companies. There is a worksheet for your use dividing your analysis into quantitative and qualitative factors.

Exhibit 6: Guideline Companies Ranking of Financial Performance and Pricing Ratios

Exhibit 6
Guideline Company Comparative Analysis
Financial Ratios 1995

	MTMC	PMRY	SECX	Quimby's Computer	
				Unadjusted	Adjusted
LIQUIDITY/SOLVENCY					
Quick Ratio	2.53	0.73	0.57	0.66	0.66
Current Ratio	2.86	1.19	1.61	1.09	1.09
Days Accounts Receivables Outstanding	68.63	60.6	23.9	38.12	38.12
Days Accounts Payable	43.53	56.24	40.31	16.56	16.56
Days Working Capital	57.31	14.97	31.73	5.18	7.23
Days Inventory Sales	11.51	42.66	49.24	29.92	29.92
TURNOVER					
Receivables Turnover	5.32	6.02	15.27	9.57	9.57
Cash Turnover	23.63	1,111.13	537.76	49.24	49.24
Inventory Turnover	31.7	8.56	7.41	12.2	12.2
Current Asset Turnover	3.8	3.72	5.06	5.19	5.19
Working Capital Turnover	6.37	24.38	11.5	70.41	50.5
Fixed Asset Turnover	179.74	62.35	100.58	227.6	227.6
Total Asset Turnover	3.71	3.32	4.61	4.94	5.05
Payables Turnover	8.39	6.49	9.05	22.04	22.04
SG&A Expense to Cash	2.42	120.58	23.54	6.81	5.95
DEBT					
Times Interest Earned	172.5	4.67	10.52	9.07	12.11
Total Liabilities to Total Assets	0.34	0.76	0.59	0.85	0.88
Total Liabilities to Equity	0.52	3.15	1.46	5.68	7.23
Short-Term Debt to Equity	–	0.96	–	–	–
Long-Term Debt to Equity	–	–	0.12	–	–
Total Interest-Bearing Debt to Equity	–	0.96	0.12	–	–
Total Assets to Equity	1.52	4.15	2.46	6.68	8.23
Total Liabilities to Invested Capital	0.52	1.61	1.31	5.68	7.23
Net Fixed Assets/Equity	0.03	0.21	0.1	0.21	0.27
PROFITABILITY					
EBITDA Return on Total Assets	13.84%	12.73%	10.23%	17.47%	25.39%
EBIT Return on Assets	13.12%	11.82%	9.42%	16.71%	24.60%
Pretax Return on Assets	13.05%	9.29%	8.53%	15.87%	22.94%
After-Tax Return on Assets	7.66%	5.49%	5.28%	15.87%	14.31%
EBITDA Return on Equity	21.03%	52.88%	25.20%	116.63%	209.00%

EBIT Return on Equity	19.95%	49.08%	23.21%	111.54%	202.51%
Pretax Return on Equity	19.83%	38.58%	21.00%	105.95%	188.78%
After-Tax Return on Equity	11.65%	22.81%	13.01%	105.95%	117.75%
EBITDA Return on Net Sales	4.67%	4.31%	2.31%	4.32%	6.08%
EBIT Return on Net Sales	4.43%	4.00%	2.13%	4.13%	5.89%
Pretax Return on Net Sales	4.40%	3.14%	1.92%	3.92%	5.49%
After-Tax Return on Net Sales	2.59%	1.86%	1.19%	3.92%	3.42%
EBITDA Return on Invested Capital	21.02%	27.01%	27.34%	116.63%	209.00%
EBIT Return on Invested Capital	19.94%	25.07%	25.18%	111.54%	202.51%
Pretax Return on Invested Capital	19.82%	19.70%	22.78%	105.95%	188.78%
Return on Invested Capital	11.64%	11.65%	14.11%	105.95%	117.75%
WORKING CAPITAL					
Working Capital ($000)	10,026	10,233	31,524	811	811
Short-Term Debt to Working Capital	–	1.64	–	–	–
Long-Term Debt to Working Capital	–	–	0.15	–	–
OPERATING EFFICIENCY					
Operating Expense to Sales	10.25%	10.85%	4.38%	13.84%	12.08%
Depreciation and Amortization to Sales	0.24%	0.31%	0.18%	0.19%	0.19%
Capital Expenditures to Sales	0.61%	0.47%	0.33%	0.67%	0.67%
OTHER					
Size of Revenues ($000)	46,732	215,559	419,186	40,945	3
Earnings ($000)	1,209	4,003	4,997	1,606	40,945
Three-Year Compound Growth Rate—Earnings	70.28%	53.08%	-10.93%	227.21%	303.62%
Three-Year Compound Growth Rate—Revenues	31.33%	45.24%	26.06%	86.08%	86.08%

Exhibit 6
Financial Ratio Ranking Analysis

Quick Ratio		Current Ratio		Days Accounts Receivables	
MTMC	2.53	MTMC	2.86	MTMC	68.63
PMRY	0.73	SECX	1.61	PMRY	60.6
Quimby's	0.66	PMRY	1.19	Quimby's	38.12
Quimby's—Adj.	0.66	Quimby's	1.09	Quimby's—Adj.	38.12
SECX	0.57	Quimby's—Adj.	1.09	SECX	23.9

Days Accounts Payable		Days Working Capital		Days Inventory Sales	
PMRY	56.24	MTMC	57.31	SECX	49.24
MTMC	43.53	SECX	31.73	PMRY	42.66
SECX	40.31	PMRY	14.97	Quimby's	29.92
Quimby's	16.56	Quimby's—Adj.	7.23	Quimby's—Adj.	29.92
Quimby's—Adj.	16.56	Quimby's	5.18	MTMC	11.51

Receivables Turnover		Cash Turnover		Inventory Turnover	
SECX	15.27	PMRY	1,111.13	MTMC	31.7
Quimby's	9.57	SECX	537.76	Quimby's	12.2
Quimby's—Adj.	9.57	Quimby's	49.24	Quimby's—Adj.	12.2
PMRY	6.02	Quimby's—Adj.	49.24	PMRY	8.56
MTMC	5.32	MTMC	23.63	SECX	7.41

Current Asset Turnover		Working Capital Turnover		Fixed Asset Turnover	
Quimby's	5.19	Quimby's	70.41	Quimby's	227.6
Quimby's—Adj.	5.19	Quimby's—Adj.	50.5	Quimby's—Adj.	227.6
SECX	5.06	PMRY	24.38	MTMC	179.74
MTMC	3.8	SECX	11.5	SECX	100.58
PMRY	3.72	MTMC	6.37	PMRY	62.35

Total Asset Turnover		Payables Turnover		SG&A Expense to Cash	
Quimby's—Adj.	5.05	Quimby's	22.04	PMRY	120.58
Quimby's	4.94	Quimby's—Adj.	22.04	SECX	23.54
SECX	4.61	SECX	9.05	Quimby's	6.81
MTMC	3.71	MTMC	8.39	Quimby's—Adj.	5.95
PMRY	3.32	PMRY	6.49	MTMC	2.42

Times Interest Earned		Total Liabilities to Total Assets		Total Liabilities to Equity	
MTMC	172.5	Quimby's—Adj.	0.88	Quimby's—Adj.	7.23
Quimby's—Adj.	12.11	Quimby's	0.85	Quimby's	5.68
SECX	10.52	PMRY	0.76	PMRY	3.15
Quimby's	9.07	SECX	0.59	SECX	1.46
PMRY	4.67	MTMC	0.34	MTMC	0.52

Short-Term Debt to Equity		Long-Term Debt to Equity		Interest-Bearing Debt to Equity	
PMRY	0.96	SECX	0.12	PMRY	0.96
MTMC	–	PMRY	–	SECX	0.12
SECX	–	MTMC	–	MTMC	0
Quimby's	–	Quimby's	–	Quimby's	–
Quimby's—Adj.	–	Quimby's—Adj.	–	Quimby's—Adj.	–

Total Assets to Equity		Total Liabilities to Invested Capital		Net Fixed Assets/Equity	
Quimby's—Adj.	8.23	Quimby's—Adj.	7.23	Quimby's—Adj.	0.27
Quimby's	6.68	Quimby's	5.68	Quimby's	0.21
PMRY	4.15	PMRY	1.61	PMRY	0.21
SECX	2.46	SECX	1.31	SECX	0.1
MTMC	1.52	MTMC	0.52	MTMC	0.03

Pretax Return on Equity		After-Tax Return on Equity		EBITDA Return on Net Sales	
Quimby's—Adj.	188.78%	SECX	13.01%	Quimby's—Adj.	6.08%
Quimby's	105.95%	PMRY	22.81%	MTMC	4.67%
PMRY	38.58%	MTMC	11.65%	Quimby's	4.32%
SECX	21.00%	Quimby's—Adj.	117.75%	PMRY	4.31%
MTMC	19.83%	Quimby's	105.95%	SECX	2.31%

EBIT Return on Net Sales		Pretax Return on Net Sales		After-Tax Return on Net Sales	
Quimby's—Adj.	5.89%	Quimby's—Adj.	5.49%	Quimby's	3.92%
MTMC	4.43%	MTMC	4.40%	Quimby's—Adj.	3.42%
Quimby's	4.13%	Quimby's	3.92%	MTMC	2.59%
PMRY	4.00%	PMRY	3.14%	PMRY	1.86%
SECX	2.13%	SECX	1.92%	SECX	1.19%

Exhibit 6
Financial Ratio Ranking Analysis (continued)

EBITDA Return on Invested Capital		EBIT Return on Invested Capital		Pretax Return on Invested Capital	
Quimby's—Adj.	209.00%	Quimby's—Adj.	202.51%	Quimby's—Adj.	188.78%
Quimby's	116.63%	Quimby's	111.54%	Quimby's	105.95%
SECX	27.34%	SECX	25.18%	SECX	22.78%
PMRY	27.01%	PMRY	25.07%	MTMC	19.82%
MTMC	21.02%	MTMC	19.94%	PMRY	19.70%

Return on Invested Capital		Working Capital (000)		Short-Term Debt to Working Capital	
Quimby's—Adj.	117.75%	SECX	31,524	PMRY	1.64
Quimby's	105.95%	PMRY	10,233	MTMC	0
SECX	14.11%	MTMC	10,026	SECX	–
PMRY	11.65%	Quimby's	811	Quimby's	–
MTMC	11.64%	Quimby's—Adj.	811	Quimby's—Adj.	–

Long-Term Debt to Working Capital		Operating Expense to Sales		Depreciation and Amortization to Sales	
SECX	0.15	Quimby's	13.84%	PMRY	0.31%
PMRY	–	Quimby's—Adj.	12.08%	MTMC	0.24%
MTMC	–	PMRY	10.85%	Quimby's	0.19%
Quimby's	–	MTMC	10.25%	Quimby's—Adj.	0.19%
Quimby's—Adj.	–	SECX	4.38%	SECX	0.18%

Capital Expenditures to Sales		Size of Revenues ($000)	
Quimby's	0.67%	SECX	419,186
Quimby's—Adj.	0.67%	PMRY	215,559
MTMC	0.61%	MTMC	46,732
PMRY	0.47%	Quimby's	40,945
SECX	0.33%	Quimby's—Adj.	40,945

(EXERCISE 12) COMPARATIVE ANALYSIS OF GUIDELINE COMPANIES

Quantitative Comparisons	Comparison	Impact on P/E
Size	_____	_____
Growth	_____	_____
Liquidity	_____	_____
Profitability	_____	_____
Turnover	_____	_____
Leverage	_____	_____

Qualitative Comparisons		Impact on P/E
_____	_____	_____
_____	_____	_____
_____	_____	_____
_____	_____	_____
_____	_____	_____

EXERCISE 13: VALUATION USING PUBLICLY TRADED GUIDELINE COMPANIES

Using all information provided, determine the fair market value of the subject blocks of stock in Quimby's. During your work, note why you chose the type of multiples and the time period of earnings you used. Also, note which comparative factors you believed most important and the degree to which your multiples were adjusted from their starting place. Provide your answer in aggregate form, not value per share and not the value of the specific block. A worksheet is provided.

(EXERCISE 13) VALUATION WORKSHEET—MARKET APPROACH

Guideline Companies from the Public Market

	Multiple	Multiple	Multiple
MTMC			
PMRY			
SECX			
Mean			
Median			
Selected Multiple			
Quimby's Earnings Stream			
Estimate of Value			
Control Premium/ Minority Discount			
Indication of Value			
Less: DLOM			
Indication of Value			

EXERCISE 14: VALUATION USING ACQUISITION DATA

In Appendix 6 (to be downloaded), you will find some information on certain transactions that occurred in the industry. Would you use this data to determine a value for the subject block of common stock of Quimby's?

EXERCISE 15: EQUITY NET CASH FLOW FORECAST FACTORS

Based on all information provided, prepare a list of factors to reflect in a net cash flow forecast on an equity basis used in valuing the common stock in Quimby's. Include assumptions regarding growth in sales, net profit margin, capital expenditures, working capital needs, depreciation assumptions, and borrowings. Provide answers on the worksheet.

(EXERCISE 15) INCOME APPROACH: MULTIPERIOD DISCOUNTED NCF TO EQUITY

	1996	1997	1998	1999	2000
Income Statement Assumptions					
Sales Growth					
Gross Profit					
Operating Expenses					
Depreciation					
Interest Expense					
Interest Income					
Taxes					
Balance Sheet Assumptions					
Cash					
Accounts Receivable					
Inventory					
Other Current Assets					
Capital Expenditures					
Other Assets					
Accounts Payable					
Income Taxes Payable					
Other Current Liabilities					
IBM Credit Line					

CASE STUDY EXERCISE 16: DETERMINE DISCOUNT RATE

Using Exhibit 7 (*Federal Reserve Bulletin*) and Exhibit 8 (return data from Ibbotson's *Stocks, Bonds, Bills, and Inflation Yearbook* and *Cost of Capital Quarterly*), determine an appropriate discount rate to apply to the equity net cash flow of Quimby's using the buildup method.

Exhibit 7: *Federal Reserve Bulletin*

A26 Domestic Financial Statistics □ March 1996

1.35 INTEREST RATES Money and Capital Markets

Percent per year; figures are averages of business day data unless otherwise noted

Item	1993	1994	1995	1995 Sept.	1995 Oct.	1995 Nov.	1995 Dec.	1995, week ending Dec. 1	Dec. 8	Dec. 15	Dec. 22	Dec. 29
MONEY MARKET INSTRUMENTS												
1 Federal funds[1,2,3]	3.02	4.21	5.83	5.80	5.76	5.80	5.60	5.91	5.75	5.73	5.90	5.48
2 Discount window borrowing[2,4]	3.00	3.60	5.21	5.25	5.25	5.25	5.25	5.25	5.25	5.25	5.25	5.25
Commercial paper[3,5,6]												
3 1-month	3.17	4.43	5.93	5.82	5.81	5.80	5.84	5.80	5.83	5.87	5.83	5.83
4 3-month	3.22	4.66	5.93	5.74	5.82	5.74	5.64	5.72	5.67	5.65	5.61	5.61
5 6-month	3.30	4.93	5.93	5.66	5.71	5.59	5.43	5.53	5.46	5.44	5.42	5.39
Finance paper, directly placed[3,5,7]												
6 1-month	3.12	4.33	5.81	5.71	5.71	5.69	5.70	5.67	5.74	5.77	5.69	5.60
7 3-month	3.16	4.53	5.78	5.58	5.66	5.59	5.47	5.58	5.51	5.47	5.46	5.39
8 6-month	3.15	4.56	5.68	5.45	5.51	5.35	5.20	5.29	5.23	5.22	5.19	5.12
Bankers acceptances[3,5,8]												
9 3-month	3.13	4.56	5.81	5.66	5.71	5.64	5.52	5.62	5.56	5.57	5.49	5.46
10 6-month	3.21	4.83	5.80	5.58	5.61	5.47	5.34	5.43	5.39	5.38	5.31	5.28
Certificates of deposit, secondary market[3,9]												
11 1-month	3.11	4.38	5.87	5.74	5.75	5.75	5.75	5.81	5.81	5.81	5.71	5.64
12 3-month	3.17	4.63	5.92	5.73	5.79	5.74	5.62	5.73	5.67	5.67	5.60	5.53
13 6-month	3.28	4.96	5.98	5.73	5.76	5.64	5.49	5.59	5.51	5.52	5.47	5.42
14 Eurodollar deposits, 3-month[3,10]	3.18	4.63	5.93	5.74	5.81	5.75	5.64	5.75	5.69	5.69	5.59	5.56
U.S. Treasury bills Secondary market[3,5]												
15 3-month	3.00	4.25	5.49	5.28	5.28	5.36	5.14	5.33	5.32	5.26	5.02	4.89
16 6-month	3.12	4.64	5.56	5.30	5.32	5.27	5.13	5.25	5.20	5.19	5.09	4.98
17 1-year	3.29	5.02	5.60	5.31	5.28	5.14	5.03	5.11	5.08	5.06	5.01	4.94
Auction average[3,5,11]												
18 3-month	3.02	4.29	5.51	5.26	5.30	5.35	5.16	5.32	5.29	5.30	5.15	4.91
19 6-month	3.14	4.66	5.59	5.28	5.34	5.29	5.15	5.25	5.19	5.20	5.15	5.04
20 1-year	3.33	5.02	5.69	5.21	5.30	5.15	5.06	n.a.	n.a.	5.06	n.a.	n.a.
U.S. TREASURY NOTES AND BONDS												
Constant maturities[12]												
21 1-year	3.43	5.32	5.94	5.62	5.59	5.43	5.31	5.39	5.35	5.35	5.30	5.21
22 2-year	4.05	5.94	6.15	5.81	5.70	5.48	5.32	5.40	5.33	5.38	5.35	5.22
23 3-year	4.44	6.27	6.25	5.89	5.77	5.57	5.39	5.47	5.38	5.42	5.43	5.29
24 5-year	5.14	6.69	6.38	6.00	5.86	5.69	5.51	5.59	5.49	5.55	5.56	5.44
25 7-year	5.54	6.91	6.50	6.13	5.97	5.83	5.63	5.74	5.60	5.66	5.69	5.56
26 10-year	5.87	7.09	6.57	6.20	6.04	5.93	5.71	5.82	5.68	5.73	5.78	5.64
27 20-year	6.29	7.49	6.95	6.65	6.45	6.33	6.12	6.25	6.10	6.13	6.19	6.06
28 30-year	6.59	7.37	6.88	6.55	6.37	6.26	6.06	6.19	6.04	6.07	6.12	6.00
Composite												
29 More than 10 years (long-term)	6.45	7.41	6.93	6.63	6.43	6.31	6.11	6.24	6.09	6.12	6.17	6.04
STATE AND LOCAL NOTES AND BONDS												
Moody's series[13]												
30 Aaa	5.38	5.77	5.80	5.71	5.74	5.63	5.40	5.55	5.60	5.40	5.29	5.29
31 Baa	5.83	6.17	6.10	5.90	5.95	5.79	5.66	5.72	5.74	5.68	5.61	5.00
32 Bond Buyer series[14]	5.60	6.18	5.95	5.91	5.80	5.64	5.45	5.54	5.35	5.51	5.51	5.44
CORPORATE BONDS												
33 Seasoned issues, all industries[15]	7.54	8.26	7.83	7.56	7.39	7.30	7.11	7.22	7.10	7.12	7.16	7.05
Rating group												
34 Aaa	7.22	7.97	7.59	7.32	7.12	7.02	6.82	6.94	6.81	6.83	6.87	6.76
35 Aa	7.40	8.15	7.72	7.45	7.27	7.18	6.99	7.10	6.99	7.01	7.04	6.93
36 A	7.58	8.28	7.83	7.56	7.39	7.32	7.13	7.24	7.12	7.14	7.19	7.07
37 Baa	7.93	8.63	8.20	7.93	7.75	7.68	7.49	7.61	7.48	7.50	7.54	7.43
38 A-rated, recently offered utility bonds[16]	7.46	8.29	7.86	7.55	7.36	7.30	7.10	7.14	7.10	7.13	7.10	6.98
MEMO												
Dividend-price ratio[17]												
39 Common stocks	2.78	2.82	2.56	2.42	2.41	2.37	2.30	2.33	2.28	2.28	2.34	2.31

1. The daily effective federal funds rate is a weighted average of rates on trades through New York brokers.
2. Weekly figures are averages of seven calendar days ending on Wednesday of the current week; monthly figures include each calendar day in the month.
3. Annualized using a 360-day year for bank interest.
4. Rate for the Federal Reserve Bank of New York.
5. Quoted on a discount basis.
6. An average of offering rates on commercial paper placed by several leading dealers for firms whose bond rating is AA or the equivalent.
7. An average of offering rates on commercial paper directly placed by finance companies.
8. Representative closing yields for acceptances of the highest-rated money center banks.
9. An average of dealer offering rates on nationally traded certificates of deposit.
10. Bid rates for Eurodollar deposits at 11:00 a.m. London time. Data are for indication purposes only.
11. Auction date for daily data; weekly and monthly averages computed on an issue-date basis.

12. Yields on actively traded issues adjusted to constant maturities. Source: U.S. Department of the Treasury.
13. General obligation bonds based on Thursday figures; Moody's Investors Service.
14. State and local government general obligation bonds maturing in twenty years are used in compiling this index. The twenty-bond index has a rating roughly equivalent to Moody's A1 rating. Based on Thursday figures.
15. Daily figures from Moody's Investors Service. Based on yields to maturity on selected long-term bonds.
16. Compilation of the Federal Reserve. This series is an estimate of the yield on recently offered, A-rated utility bonds with a thirty-year maturity and five years of call protection. Weekly data are based on Friday quotations.
17. Standard & Poor's corporate series. Common stock ratio is based on the 500 stocks in the price index.
NOTE. Some of the data in this table also appear in the Board's H.15 (519) weekly and G.13 (415) monthly statistical releases. For ordering address, see inside front cover.

Exhibit 8: Ibbotson's *Stocks, Bonds, Bills, and Inflation Yearbook and Cost of Capital Quarterly*

(Permission for use granted by Morningstar.)

Table 8-1   Key Variables in Estimating
the Cost of Capital

	Value
Yields (Riskless Rates)*	
Long-term (20-year) U.S. Treasury Coupon Bond Yield	6.0%
Intermediate-term (5-year) U.S. Treasury Coupon Note Yield	5.4
Short-term (30-day) U.S. Treasury Bill Yield	4.6
Risk Premia**	
Long-horizon expected equity risk premium: large company stock total returns minus long-term government bond income returns	7.4
Intermediate-horizon expected equity risk premium: large company stock total returns minus intermediate-term government bond income returns	7.8
Short-horizon expected equity risk premium: large company stock total returns minus U.S. Treasury bill total returns[†]	8.8
Expected default premium: long-term corporate bond total returns minus long-term government bond total returns	0.5
Expected long-term horizon premium: long-term government bond income returns minus U.S. Treasury bill total returns[†]	1.4
Expected intermediate-term horizon premium: intermediate-term government bond income returns minus U.S. Treasury bill total returns[†]	1.0
Size Premia***	
Expected mid-capitalization equity size premium: capitalization between $696 and $3,015 million	1.1
Expected low-capitalization equity size premium: capitalization between $171 and $696 million	1.8
Expected micro-capitalization equity size premium: capitalization below $171 million	3.6

* As of December 31, 1995. Maturities are approximate.
** Expected risk premia are based on the simple differences of historical arithmetic mean returns from 1926 to 1995.
***See Chapter 7 for complete methodology.
† For U.S. Treasury bills, the income return and total return are the same.

Note: An example of how these variables can be used is found with equation (35).

STATISTICS FOR SIC CODE 5045
Computers and Computer Peripheral Equipment and Software
This Industry Comprises 20 Companies

Industry Description

Establishments primarily engaged in the wholesale distribution of computers, computer peripheral equipment, and computer software. These establishments frequently also may sell related supplies, but establishments primarily engaged in wholesaling supplies are classified according to individual product.

Sales (in $Millions)

Total	13,970
Average	698

5 Largest Companies

MERISEL INC	3,086
INTELLIGENT ELECTRONICS IN	2,646
MICROAGE INC	2,221
TECH DATA CORP	1,532
SAFEGUARD SCIENTIFICS INC	1,166

Distribution

	Latest	5 Year Average
90th Percentile	2,263.30	1,281.20
75th Percentile	1,053.70	646.03
Median	202.08	132.12
25th Percentile	80.65	51.31
10th Percentile	23.93	15.24

Total Capital (in $Millions)

Total	2,941
Average	147

5 Largest Companies

TECH DATA CORP	550
SAFEGUARD SCIENTIFICS INC	439
MERISEL INC	397
INTELLIGENT ELECTRONICS IN	319
COMPUCOM SYSTEMS INC	228

Distribution

	Latest	5 Year Average
90th Percentile	400.89	420.63
75th Percentile	197.79	216.95
Median	88.31	66.16
25th Percentile	24.03	22.14
10th Percentile	8.75	8.11

Growth Over Last Five Years (in %)

	Net Sales	Operating Income	Net Income
90th Percentile	39.64	39.20	49.96
75th Percentile	33.69	33.45	38.69
Median	24.80	18.58	18.89
25th Percentile	2.79	0.96	-14.81
10th Percentile	0.29	-24.60	-53.19
Ind. Composite	27.58	14.71	34.78
Lg. Composite	30.32	26.04	27.61
Sm. Composite	22.97	-12.41	-23.00

Compound Annual Equity Returns (in %)

	5-Years	10-Years
90th Percentile	23.64	20.36
75th Percentile	11.55	9.85
Median	0.98	-6.22
25th Percentile	-7.74	-16.97
10th Percentile	-24.42	-26.11
Ind. Composite	39.07	25.92
Lg. Composite	23.12	16.69
Sm. Composite	110.00	49.35

Ending Value of $1 Invested Over: (in $)

	5-Years	10-Years
S&P 500	1.72	3.85
Ind. Composite	5.19	10.02
Lg. Composite	2.82	4.66
Sm. Composite	40.61	55.23

Annualized Statistics For Last 10 Years (in %)

	Average Return	Standard Deviation
S&P 500	15.78	17.52
Ind. Composite	34.70	51.19
Lg. Composite	30.68	63.33
Sm. Composite	793.87	NMF

Sales, Operating Income, and Net Income (in $ Billions)

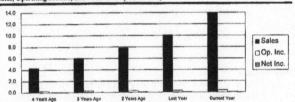

Market Capitalization - Equity and Debt (in $Billions)

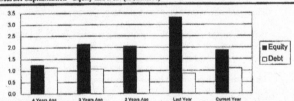

Number of Companies and Total Capital by S&P Ratings and Capitalization (Capital in $Millions)

S&P Ratings	Large Cap	Mid Cap	Low Cap	Micro Cap	Totals
AAA,AA,A	0	0	0	0	0
	0	0	0	0	0
BBB	0	0	0	0	0
	0	0	0	0	0
BB,B,CCC, CC,D	0	0	0	1	1
	0	0	0	397	397
Not Rated	0	0	3	16	19
	0	0	1,307	1,237	2,545
Totals	0	0	3	17	20
	0	0	1,307	1,634	2,941

Margins (in %)

| | Operating Margin | | Net Margin | | Return On Assets | | Return On Equity | | | Capital Structure Ratios (in %) | | | |
| | | | | | | | | | | Debt/Total Capital | | Debt/MV Equity | |
	Latest	5 Yr Avg	Latest	5 Yr Avg	Latest	5 Yr Avg	Latest	5 Yr Avg		Latest	5 Yr Avg	Latest	5 Yr Avg
90th Percentile	6.71	7.68	1.94	1.90	6.85	6.65	9.93	9.00		66.08	58.25	196.00	140.00
75th Percentile	3.97	4.36	1.03	1.44	3.83	3.94	8.35	6.18		49.99	42.55	101.00	74.51
Median	2.63	3.21	0.57	0.75	1.39	2.73	2.60	1.95		29.08	25.75	41.01	34.68
25th Percentile	0.91	0.73	-2.76	-3.00	-4.59	-2.93	-10.08	-13.49		0.41	6.59	0.41	7.06
10th Percentile	-8.69	-7.82	-11.78	-8.98	-22.47	-14.79	-43.69	-29.71		0.00	1.48	0.00	1.50
Ind. Composite	2.87	3.61	0.84	0.87	2.91	2.43	4.67	3.88		37.62	35.37	58.61	54.73
Lg. Composite	2.42	2.62	1.11	1.08	4.82	4.32	8.93	6.03		32.31	21.09	47.16	26.73
Sm. Composite	-6.33	0.79	-20.01	-11.33	-30.65	-17.30	-33.84	-14.52		34.25	28.62	60.53	40.09

Equity Valuation Ratios (in Decimal)

| | Price/Earnings | | Market/Book | | Price/Sales | | Yields (in % of Price) | | | | Betas (in Decimal) | |
| | | | | | | | Dividends | | Cash Flow | | Unlevered | Levered |
	Latest	5 Yr Avg	Latest	5 Yr Avg	Latest	5 Yr Avg	Latest	5 Yr Avg	Latest	5 Yr Avg	Asset Beta	Equity Beta
90th Percentile	NMF	NMF	2.25	3.33	0.59	0.97	0.00	0.04	12.38	8.76	1.35	2.12
75th Percentile	NMF	NMF	1.78	2.37	0.27	0.36	0.00	0.00	9.48	6.58	1.18	1.65
Median	33.96	51.28	1.21	1.69	0.19	0.24	0.00	0.00	3.28	1.45	0.52	1.14
25th Percentile	10.29	16.19	0.77	0.98	0.11	0.15	0.00	0.00	-8.40	-4.16	0.09	0.28
10th Percentile	7.67	11.12	0.39	0.36	0.05	0.09	0.00	0.00	-34.14	-20.93	-0.29	-0.37
Ind. Composite	16.08	25.77	1.38	1.95	0.14	0.22	0.72	1.03	4.46	4.55	1.14	1.72
Lg. Composite	6.82	16.58	0.98	2.03	0.08	0.18	2.24	2.27	10.14	5.06	1.89	2.29
Sm. Composite	NMF	NMF	4.05	5.60	0.47	0.78	0.00	0.00	-38.62	-13.28	-4.75	-6.54

Costs Of Equity Capital (in %)

| | CAPM | | | | 3-Factor | Discounted Cash Flow | | | | DCF Growth Rates (in %) | |
| | | | | | | | | | | | Sustainable |
	S-L Form	S-L Sm Cap	Empirical	Emp Sm Cap		Analysts	Sustainable	3-Stage		Analysts	Growth
90th Percentile	22.42	26.25	19.43	22.90	35.37	20.62	22.15	36.05		20.59	22.15
75th Percentile	19.06	21.91	17.35	20.64	30.00	20.59	12.93	30.68		20.59	12.73
Median	15.51	18.71	15.14	18.52	25.36	20.59	NMF	22.91		20.59	6.90
25th Percentile	9.51	13.53	11.42	15.44	16.64	20.53	NMF	18.24		20.25	-8.43
10th Percentile	NMF	8.96	8.59	12.61	8.59	18.95	NMF	16.15		18.45	-29.60
Ind. Composite	19.62	22.56	17.69	20.74	29.28	21.38	9.71	22.61		20.59	9.00
Lg. Composite	23.55	26.55	20.13	23.13	24.33	19.78	12.54	32.57		17.41	10.31
Sm. Composite	NMF	NMF	NMF	NMF	NMF	20.59	NMF	NMF		20.59	5.50

Weighted Average Costs Of Capital (in %)

| | CAPM | | | | 3-Factor | Discounted Cash Flow | | |
	S-L Form	S-L Sm Cap	Empirical	Emp Sm Cap		Analysts	Sustainable	3-Stage
90th Percentile	16.49	20.44	15.70	19.64	26.35	20.59	18.80	36.05
75th Percentile	14.49	16.61	13.69	16.61	24.58	20.56	10.70	21.62
Median	10.34	12.57	10.65	12.77	14.14	16.49	NMF	16.11
25th Percentile	8.13	10.05	8.69	10.02	10.10	12.73	NMF	14.81
10th Percentile	NMF	NMF	NMF	8.81	7.86	10.76	NMF	13.93
Ind. Composite	14.55	16.47	13.33	15.25	20.64	15.66	8.30	16.44
Lg. Composite	18.08	20.12	15.75	17.79	18.61	15.52	10.60	24.21
Sm. Composite	NMF	NMF	NMF	NMF	NMF	15.52	NMF	NMF

(EXERCISE 16) EQUITY NET CASH FLOW DISCOUNT RATE

EXERCISE 17: VALUATION USING MULTIPERIOD MODEL

Using the forecasted income statements and balance sheets from Appendix 7 (to be downloaded), calculate the net cash flow and then discount it to determine the fair market value of the subject stock using the multiperiod discounting model income method. Do the work directly on the following sheet.

(EXERCISE 17) INCOME APPROACH DISCOUNTED CASH FLOW CALCULATION

	1996	1997	1998	1999	2000	Terminal Value
Net Income						
Plus: Depreciation/ Amortization						
Less: Capital Expenditures						
Less: Increase in Working Capital						
Plus/Less: Debt						
Net Cash Flow						
Discount Periods						
Present Value Factor						
Terminal Value						
Present Values						
Sum of Present Values						
Control Premium						
Control Marketable Value						
DLOM						
Control Nonmarketable Value						
Rounded						

EXERCISE 18: VALUATION USING SINGLE-PERIOD NET INCOME METHOD

Based on the information that you have learned about The Company, do you think that it is appropriate to use a single-period capitalization model in this assignment?

EXERCISE 19: RECONCILIATION TO SINGLE-VALUE ESTIMATES

Summarize your value estimates on the worksheets provided. Using all information given, determine a value estimate for the subject block of shares of Quimby's. Note your rationale.

(EXERCISE 19) RECONCILIATION

Method	Indication	Weight	Rationale
_____	_____	_____	_____
_____	_____	_____	_____
_____	_____	_____	_____
_____	_____	_____	_____

Fair Market Value   _____

Solutions

CHAPTER 1: OVERVIEW OF BUSINESS VALUATION

1. c
2. b
3. c
4. b
5. c
6. c
7. a
8. d
9. c
10. a
11. d
12. c

CHAPTER 2: BUSINESS VALUATION STANDARDS

1. c
2. a
3. c
4. b
5. d
6. a
7. b
8. a
9. c
10. a
11. b
12. b
13. c
14. a
15. d
16. b
17. c
18. d
19. a
20. b
21. d
22. a
23. d
24. b

CHAPTER 3: GETTING STARTED

1. a
2. b
3. c
4. c
5. a
6. b
7. d
8. b
9. c
10. a
11. d
12. d
13. a
14. c
15. a
16. a
17. c
18. c
19. b
20. d
21. d

CHAPTER 4: VALUATION PRINCIPLES AND THEORY

1. d
2. b
3. a
4. c
5. c
6. b
7. a
8. b
9. d
10. d
11. c
12. c
13. b
14. b
15. b
16. b
17. a
18. d
19. d
20. b
21. c
22. a
23. b

24. c
25. a
26. c
27. a
28. c
29. d
30. d

CHAPTER 5: DATA GATHERING

1. c
2. b
3. b
4. c
5. c
6. b
7. a
8. b
9. d
10. a
11. c
12. b
13. a
14. c
15. c
16. a
17. b
18. d
19. d
20. b
21. a
22. c
23. b
24. b
25. a
26. c
27. a
28. a
29. d

CHAPTER 6: DATA ANALYSIS

1. a
2. d
3. c
4. d

5. c The current assets include cash, accounts receivable, and inventory, and the current liabilities include accounts payable. Therefore, the current ratio is calculated as $(250,000 + 400,000 + 200,000)/(200,000) = 4.25$.

6. c The debt-to-equity ratio is calculated as total debt/total equity. Therefore, the ratio is $(200,000 + 750,000)/(800,000) = 1.19\times$

7. b The average collection period is calculated as accounts receivable/(revenue/365). Therefore, the collection period is $400,000/(1,400,000/365) = 104$ days.

8. d The average holding period is calculated as inventory/(cost of goods sold/365). Therefore, the holding period is $(200,000)/(500,000/365) = 146$ days.

9. b

10. b

11. d

12. b

13. c

14. b

15. b

16. a

17. d

18. d

19. b

20. b

21. d

22. b

23. b

24. a

25. d

26. d

27. d

28. d

29. c

30. d

31. d

32. c

33. b There are many suppliers of lumber, as it is a commodity. There is no credible substitute for wood for doors and trim. Lumber is generally undifferentiated. Lumber suppliers (e.g., Georgia-Pacific) do not pose a credible threat to get into the custom door fabrication business.

34. b There are no viable substitutes for doors and trim packages in homes.

35. d Answers a, b, and c are all generic strategies published in Porter's works.

36. d The industry is highly fragmented, indicating large numbers of competitors and competitive pricing. Industry growth is not slow, as the number of housing starts is numerous. There is no mention in the memo about fixed costs, and common knowledge about the subject company's products (fabrication of prehung doors and trim) suggests that it is not capital intensive requiring significant investment in capital assets. The memo does not mention high barriers to exit, and common knowledge of the company's products suggests that there are no particular barriers to exit (e.g., environmental issues).

37. d

38. a

39. d

40. d

41. b
42. c
43. c
44. d
45. d
46. b
47. d
48. c
49. a
50. c
51. c
52. b
53. a
54. a
55. d
56. b
57. b
58. b
59. c
60. d
61. d
62. d
63. c
64. a
65. b
66. d
67. c
68. a
69. b
70. b
71. c
72. c
73. d
74. d
75. c
76. c
77. d
78. c
79. c
80. b
81. d
82. d
83. b
84. a
85. d
86. b
87. c
88. d

CHAPTER 7: STATISTICS FOR VALUATION AND ECONOMIC DAMAGES

1. d
2. d
3. b
4. d
5. a
6. c
7. b
8. c
9. b
10. c
11. b
12. b
13. a
14. c
15. a
16. c
17. c
18. a
19. c

CHAPTER 8: DEVELOPING FORECASTS FOR BUSINESS VALUATIONS AND ECONOMIC DAMAGES

1. c
2. d
3. b
4. d
5. c
6. c
7. b
8. a

CHAPTER 9: THE MARKET APPROACH—PART I

1. d
2. b
3. a
4. b
5. c
6. b
7. c
8. c
9. b

10. b

11. d

12. c

13. b PDF's total liabilities/total asset ratio of 0.73 is the closest to Electech's of 0.75.

14. a ABC's growth rate of 8% is closest to Electech's growth rate of 7%. ABC's EBIT margin of 18% is similar to Electech's EBIT margin of 17.5%.

15. c Working capital turnover is calculated as revenue/(current assets – current liabilities). Therefore, the answer is 5.9 × [10,000,000/(4,300,000 – 2,600,000)].

16. d Earnings before interest, tax, and amortization of $2,500,000 divided by $10,000,000 in revenue.

17. b Net income of $910,000 × 10.0 P/E = 9,100,000.

18. c Electech's EBITDA of $2,500,000 × 6.0 = $15,000,000 – $2,500,000 (interest-bearing debt) = 12,500,000.

19. c

20. b

21. d

22. c

23. d

24. c

25. d

26. a

27. a

28. b

29. a

30. b

31. d

32. b

33. b

34. d

35. c 67,034,000 shares @ $32.79 = $2,198,044,860 or $2.2 billion rounded.

36. c Operating income = $113,922 + depreciation and amortization $13,091 = $127,013. MVIC 31,157 shares @ $41.10 = $1,280,553 + debt $182,884 = $1,463,437. $1,463,437/$127,013 = 11.52.

37. b Operating Cash Flow

Operating Income	$9,163,221
Depreciation and Amortization	1,591,268
Operating Cash Flow	$10,754,489
Multiple	6.6
Minority, Marketable Value	$70,979,627
DLOM (30%)	$21,293,888
Minority, Nonmarketable Value	$49,685,739
Rounded	$49,700,000

38. b Since the other indications of value (transactions and DCF) give similar indications of value, the GPCM would get less weight, if any, in light of the fact that there were only three guideline companies. There may be too little data for this method to be considered strong even if the guideline companies are considered good. The transaction method is directly on point with other closely held businesses and may be better indicator in light of the DCF.

CHAPTER 10: THE MARKET APPROACH—PART II

1. b
2. b
3. b
4. b
5. a
6. d
7. c
8. c
9. c
10. a
11. b
12. d
13. b
14. c
15. a
16. c
17. d
18. c
19. d

CHAPTER 11: THE ASSET-BASED APPROACH

1. a
2. b
3. c
4. c
5. a
6. c
7. b
8. c
9. c
10. a
11. a
12. c
13. b
14. d
15. b
16. c
17. a
18. b
19. c
20. c
21. d
22. a
23. c

24. c
25. a
26. b
27. b
28. c

CHAPTER 12: THE INCOME APPROACH

1. a
2. b
3. c
4. b
5. a
6. d
7. b
8. c

Minority Cash Flow		1,000,000
Excess Comp.	500,000	
Taxes	200,000	300,000
Control Cash Flow		1,300,000
Growth	5%	65,000
Next Year Cash Flow		1,365,000
Cap Rate	15% – 5%	10%
MVIC		13,650,000

9. a
10. c
11. a
12. a
13. d
14. d
15. c
16. b
17. a
18. c
19. d
20. a
21. c
22. b
23. a
24. b
25. a
26. d
27. b
28. d
29. b
30. d
31. b
32. d

33. c
34. d

Future Income Stream		1,200,000
Tangible Assets		1,000,000
Rate of Return	12%	120,000
Excess Earnings		1,080,000
Cap Rate		30%
Intangible Value		3,600,000
Tangible Value		1,000,000
Total Value		4,600,000

35. d
36. c
37. d
38. a $85,000 + 94,000 - 110,000 + 50,000 - 40,000 - 20,000 = \$59,000$
39. b $85,000 + 94,000 + [30,000 \times (1 - 0.40)] - 110,000 - 20,000 = \$67,000$
40. c
41. a
42. c $5.5\% + 7.0\% + 3.5\% + 2.0\% + 3.0\% = 21.0\%$
43. b $167,866 + 166,525 = \$334,391/2 = \$167,196 \times 1.04 = \$173,883/21\% - 4\%$
$= \$1,022,841$ or $\$1,023,000$ rounded
44. d $166,525 + 90,911 + 25,279 = 282,815$
45. c
46. c

CHAPTER 13: DISCOUNT AND CAPITALIZATION RATES

1. d
2. a
3. a
4. a
5. c
6. d
7. b
8. c
9. a
10. d
11. b
12. c $\{[4\% + (7\% \times 1.2) + 6\%] \times 70/80\} + [7.5\% \times (1 - 0.4) \times 10/80] = 16.7\%$
13. d
14. a
15. b $6.0\% + 8.0 \times 0.9 + 2.0\% = 15.2$. Therefore, 16% without the beta $- 15.2\% = 0.8\%$.
16. c $\$0.75 \times 4 = \$3.00/\$75 = 4\%$
17. c
18. c
19. c $12\% - 4\% = 8\%$
20. b $4\% + (12\% - 4\%) + 5\% + 2\% = 19\%$
21. b
22. c Unlevered beta is calculated as levered beta/$[1 + (debt/equity) \times (1 - tax rate)]$
$= 1.2/[1 + (0.6 \times 0.6)]$

23. c Levered beta is calculated as unlevered beta × [1 + (debt/equity) × (1 – tax rate)]
= $0.95 \times [1 + (.67)(0.6)]$

24. b

25. b

26. d Net cash flow × (1 + growth rate)/(capitalization rate) = $175,000 \times 1.04/0.18$
= \$1,011,111

27. b 125,000/175,000 × 22%

28. b

29. d

30. b $5\% + (13\% - 5\%) \times 1.3 + 5\% + 3\% = 23.4\%$

31. c

32. c

33. c

34. b 20% × 10/15 (MVE/MVIC) + 10% × (1 – 0.35) × 5/15 = 15.50 – 4% growth
= 11.50%

35. d 25% × 10/15 (MVE/MVIC) + 10% × (1 – 0.35) × 5/15 = 18.84%

36. c

37. c

CHAPTER 14: PREMIUMS AND DISCOUNTS (VALUATION ADJUSTMENTS)—PART I

1. c
2. b
3. d
4. a
5. b
6. c
7. a
8. b
9. d
10. c
11. c
12. c
13. b

CHAPTER 15: PREMIUMS AND DISCOUNTS (VALUATION ADJUSTMENTS)—PART II

1. b
2. c
3. a
4. a
5. a
6. c
7. a
8. c
9. a

10. c
11. d
12. d
13. d
14. b
15. a
16. c
17. d
18. a
19. c
20. d

CHAPTER 16: REVENUE RULING 59-60

1. c
2. a
3. a
4. b
5. d
6. a
7. c

CHAPTER 17: THE VALUATION REPORT

1. c
2. d
3. a
4. b
5. b
6. a
7. a
8. c
9. a
10. c
11. d
12. b
13. a
14. b
15. b
16. c
17. c
18. c

CHAPTER 18: VALUATION OF PASS-THROUGH ENTITIES

1. a
2. b

3. c
4. c
5. a
6. a
7. d
8. c

CHAPTER 19: VALUATION IN FINANCIAL REPORTING

1. d
2. b
3. c
4. a
5. b
6. b
7. a

CHAPTER 20: VALUING INTANGIBLE ASSETS: AN OVERVIEW

1. c
2. c
3. d

Purchase Price	5,000,000
Assumed Liabilities	389,000
	5,389,000
Less: Current Assets	800,000
Less: Net Fixed Assets	400,000
Gap	4,189,000

4. b

Purchase Price	5,000,000
Plus: Assumed Liabilities	389,000
	5,389,000
Less: Current Assets	800,000
Less: Net Fixed Assets	400,000
Less: Developed Technology	782,000
Less: Customer Relationships	350,000
Equals: Goodwill	3,057,000

5. a
6. b
7. a
8. a
9. c The answer is calculated as after-tax income with an agreement in place less after tax income with no agreement in place. Therefore, the answer is $1,000,000 less $750,000, or $250,000.
10. a
11. c
12. b
13. d

14. c
15. c
16. d $(425,000 + 350,000 + 300,000) \times 0.8 \times (1 - 0.4) = 516,000$
17. c $425,000/210 \times 0.8 \times (1 - 0.4) = 971$
18. c $[(425,000 + 350,000 + 300,000) \times 0.8]/(210 + 152 + 140) \times (1 - 0.4)$
    $\times 2,500 = 2,569,721$
19. d $[(200,00/10) \times 100] \times (1 - 0.15) \times (1 - 0.4) = 102,000$
20. a
21. b
22. a

CHAPTER 21: ESTATE AND GIFT VALUATIONS

1. b
2. a
3. b
4. c
5. d
6. c
7. a
8. b
9. d
10. a
11. b
12. c
13. c
14. a
15. a

CHAPTER 22: DIVORCE VALUATIONS

1. c
2. d
3. c
4. d
5. d
6. a
7. b
8. b

CHAPTER 23: PROFESSIONAL PRACTICE VALUATIONS

1. b
2. a
3. a
4. d

5. d
6. b

CHAPTER 24: OWNERSHIP DISPUTES

1. d
2. b
3. a
4. c
5. d
6. a
7. c
8. c
9. b
10. a
11. d
12. a

CHAPTER 25: OTHER VALUATION ASSIGNMENTS

1. a
2. c
3. d
4. d
5. a
6. c
7. c
8. a
9. b
10. d
11. b
12. b
13. c
14. a
15. b
16. a
17. b
18. c
19. c
20. b
21. a
22. c $= PV(8\%, 10.5\% \times 1,000, 1,000)$
23. a
24. a
25. d
26. b

27. c
28. b
29. c

CHAPTER 26: ECONOMIC DAMAGES

1. b
2. d
3. a

CHAPTER 28: INTERACTIVE CASE STUDY

The following materials contain my suggested solutions for the various exercises that are contained in Chapter 28. Each exercise must follow in order for the students to properly get to the next step. There is room for an instructor to have discussion points about many of these topics, but the direction must take the students back to the suggested solutions in order for this to make sense. Certain sections may be best done for homework, considering the amount of reading material or to allow the students to set up an Excel spreadsheet to perform some of these calculations.

(EXERCISE 1) DEFINING THE APPRAISAL ASSIGNMENT

What Is Being Appraised?

90$ percent of common stock C corporation

One class, Delaware corporation

When Is the Appraisal as-of Date?

December 29, 1995.

Why Is the Appraisal Being Performed (the Function)?

The valuation will be used as part of a litigation. It really does not matter what type of litigation as long as the standard of value is fair market value. It can be used to challenge a prenuptial agreement if the students ask.

How Is the Value to Be Defined?

Fair market value per Revenue Ruling 59-60.

How Will the Appraisal Be Performed (the Scope)?

Valuation engagement.

Who Is the Client?

1. Attorney   2. Mr. Smith   3. Corporation

Theoretically, it can be any of these. Many attorneys prefer to be the client to maintain privilege in the courts between the expert and the attorney until the expert is named as an expert.

(EXERCISE 1) PRACTICAL ASSIGNMENT CONSIDERATIONS

General Practical Considerations

1. Size of report(s) _____

2. Timing _____

3. Has the company's financial condition changed since the last fiscal year statement?

_____

4. Lapse of time between valuation date and now _____

5. Number of locations to visit _____

6. Recent transactions in stock to look into _____

7. Number of potential guideline companies in the computer field _____

In this valuation, one of the areas of controversy was the correct Standard Industrial Classification (SIC) code for the company. A review of the company's website made it seem that it should be 7373 (Systems integration) but it was not until the management interview that the appraiser found out that it should be 5045 (Computer hardware). There was a large difference in the number of potential guideline companies and very different multiples between these two SIC codes.

Tangible asset appraisal? Probably will not be needed. There will be intangible value, and the highest and best use will most likely be achieved using the income and market approaches.

(EXERCISE 2) PROBLEMS WITH THE ENGAGEMENT LETTER

1. No limiting conditions are included.
2. Define type and scope clearly.
3. Risky terminology—delete "comprehensive level of due diligence."
4. Only copy(ies) to you and you alone.
5. Get representation letters; in engagement letter.
6. "Cash-in-fist" payment terms.

(EXERCISE 3) GENERAL ECONOMIC ANALYSIS CONCLUSIONS

Observations	Impact on Value +/ 0 / −
GDP up	+
Unemployment steady but low	+
Consumer prices steady but low	+
Interest rates up and down	0
Credit conditions favorable	+
Business investment growing	+
Business profits up	+
Technology investment up	+
Economic expansion—57 months	+
Overall forecast—strong	+
Corporate mergers and acquisitions strong	+
Equity markets very strong	++
NASDAQ strength due to tech stocks	+
_____	_____
_____	_____

(EXERCISE 4) SPECIFIC INDUSTRY ANALYSIS CONCLUSIONS

Observations	Impact on Value +/ 0 / −
Growth industry	+
Systems integration strong	+
National Information Infrastructure project	+
U.S. government high priority to remove barriers to trade	+
Information availability in electronic format	+
Value-added resellers' growth in service areas	+
Price cutting	−
Technical standardization enhanced growth	+
Industrial consolidation but still many independents	0
Desktop publishing systems growth	+
Global information markets growth	+
Mainframe conversions to PCs	+
Local area networks (LANs) growth	+
Competition stiff	−
Strong orders	+

(EXERCISE 5) COMPARATIVE FINANCIAL ANALYSIS
"AS REPORTED"

Observations	Impact on Value +/0/−
Size: Within Integra range but larger	+
Growth: Large sales growth	+
Substantial growth in earnings	+
Leverage: No long-term debt	+
Profitability: High profitability	+
Turnover: Stronger	+
Liquidity: Not great, but access to IBM credit line	0
Other: IBM credit line	+

(EXERCISE 5) COMPARATIVE FINANCIAL ANALYSIS
"AS REPORTED" *(CONTINUED)*

Strength of Integra Comparison

Much stronger than peer group

_____

_____

Possible Adjustments

Stockholder loans

Employee advances

Officers' compensation

Other income

Income taxes

_____

_____

_____

_____

(EXERCISE 6) PREPARATION FOR MANAGEMENT INTERVIEW

Specific Inquiries

Succession

Industry trends

Company plans

Business model

Competitive advantage

Competition

IBM relationship

Customer concentration

Suppliers

Contracts

Lawsuits

SIC code

_____

_____

_____

(EXERCISE 7) ASSESSMENT OF THE MANAGEMENT INTERVIEW

Observations	Impact on Value +/0/−
1993 acquisition of 10% stock by Skinner—value?	0
Not customer dependent	+
IBM dependent	−
IBM brand strength	+
Price competition	−
Dependent on corporate spending	+/−
Organization structure	−
No long-term debt	+

Recommended Adjustments for Control

Possibly officers' compensation (the question that must be asked is whether this truly represents a control adjustment or if it is an adjustment needed to make the company more comparable to the guideline companies).

For this group of exercises, we are going to assume that this is not a control adjustment.

(EXERCISE 8) FINANCIAL ANALYSIS "AS ADJUSTED"

	Impact on Value
Observations	+/ 0 / –
Growth in income substantially increased during the five-year period	+

(EXERCISE 9) FACTORS AFFECTING PREMIUMS AND DISCOUNTS

Observations

Control Premium

SIC	Date	Target Name	Premium
5045	April 1991	Computer Factory, Inc.	47%
5045	Dec. 1991	Businessland, Inc.	45%
5045	March 1994	Corporate Software, Inc.	33%
5045	Aug. 1994	Gates	14%
5045	Sept. 1994	Kenfil, Inc.	−44%
5045	Nov. 1995	Robec	242%
		Average	56%
		Deviation	97%
		Median	39%

Used 35% based on median in the overall data.

Marketability Discount

Used 10% based on an estimated brokerage cost to gain liquidity.

Other Considerations

None.

(EXERCISE 10) SELECTION OF GUIDELINE COMPANIES

Selections

Amplicon, Inc.

CHS Electronics, Inc.

Dataflex Corporation

EMarketplace, Inc.

Liuski International, Inc.

Micros to Mainframes, Inc.

Pomeroy Computer Resources, Inc.

SED International Holdings, Inc.

Selection Criteria

Size: 10 times smaller and 10 times larger

Profitability: positive

Product line: similar

EXERCISE 11: WORKSHEET

Guideline Company Trading Activity Analysis

Company	Ticker	Stock Price 12/29/1995	Outstanding ($000)	Average Volume	Volume as a Percentage of Shares Outstanding
Amplicon, Inc.	AMPI	$8.00	11,567	92,317	0.8%
Chs Electronics, Inc.: Com New	CHSE	$6.00	58,099	134,592	0.2%
Emarketplace, Inc.	MKPL	$1.87	5,846	115,695	2.0%
Dataflex Corporation	DFLX	$3.38	15,212	819,883	5.4%
Liuski International, Inc.: Com New	LSKI	$8.28	4,610	103,987	2.3%
Micros to Mainframes, Inc.	MTMC	$5.13	4,878	913,242	18.7%
Pomeroy Computer Resources, Inc.	PMRY	$6.00	12,092	1,085,441	9.0%
Sed International Holdings, Inc.	SECX	$4.75	7,378	446,125	6.0%

All guideline companies with volume below 5% were eliminated. Dataflex was also eliminated based on the slowdown in its trading activity during the latest six months.

(EXERCISE 12) COMPARATIVE ANALYSIS OF GUIDELINE COMPANIES

Quantitative Comparisons	Comparison	Impact on P/E
Size	Smaller	–
Growth	Better	+
Liquidity	Worse	–
Profitability	Much better	+
Turnover	Better	+
Leverage	Comparable	0

Qualitative Comparisons	Impact on P/E
Depth of management	–
Less diversified product line	–
Market share—small	–/0
Global diversification limited	–
Access to capital markets	–/0
Reliance on supplier	–

(EXERCISE 13) VALUATION WORKSHEET— MARKET APPROACH

Guideline Companies from the Public Market

Company		MVE to EBTDA	MVE to EBT	MVE to Net Income
MTMC		7.20	7.60	12.93
PMRY		4.63	5.08	8.60
SECX		3.92	4.29	6.93
Mean		5.25	5.66	9.49
Median		4.63	5.08	8.60
Selected Multiple		5.40	5.60	9.00
Quimby's Earnings Stream		$2,324,129	$2,246,930	$1,401,410
Indication of Value, Minority, Marketable		$12,550,297	$12,582,808	$12,612,692
Plus: Control Premium*	35.00%	4,392,604	4,403,983	4,414,442
Indication of Value—Control, Marketable		$16,942,900	$16,986,791	$17,027,134
Less: Discount for Lack of Marketability	10.00%	(1,694,290)	(1,698,679)	(1,702,713)
Indication of Value—Control, Nonmarketable		$15,248,610	$15,288,112	$15,324,421

*The control premium would not be added if the officers' compensation adjustment was considered to be a control adjustment. Otherwise, a double counting would take place. As indicated in the textbook, the benefit stream is the determining factor if it is on control or minority.

(EXERCISE 14) VALUATION WORKSHEET—
TRANSACTION METHOD

There is not enough data to apply this method with any confidence.

(EXERCISE 15) INCOME APPROACH MULTIPERIOD
DISCOUNTED NET CASH FLOW TO EQUITY

Income Statement Assumptions	1996	1997	1998	1999	2000
Sales Growth	50%	33%	25%	10%	5%
Gross Profit	82%	82%	82%	82%	82%
Operating Expenses	11%	11%	11%	11%	11%
Depreciation	Straight-line 7 years based on existing assets and expected capital expenditures				
Interest Expense	0.4%	0.4%	0.4%	0.4%	0.4%
Interest Income (Based on Forecasted Cash)	5%	5%	5%	5%	5%
Taxes	40%	40%	40%	40%	40%
Balance Sheet Assumptions					
Cash (% of Sales)	2.4%	2.4%	2.4%	2.4%	2.4%
Accounts Receivable (sales)	39 days	39 days	39 days	39 days	39 days
Inventory	30 days	30 days	30 days	30 days	30 days
Other Current Assets (% of Sales)	0.04%	0.04%	0.04%	0.04%	0.04%
Capital Expenditures	500,000	500,000	500,000	500,000	500,000
Other Assets			Kept Constant		
Accounts Payable (Sales)	12 days	12 days	12 days	12 days	12 days
Income Taxes Payable (% of Income Tax Expense	10%	10%	10%	10%	10%
Other Current Liabilities (% of Sales)	1.75%	1.75%	1.75%	1.75%	1.75%
IBM Credit Line (Based on a regression analysis)	$0.5483 \times$ (inventory + accounts receivable) + $1,144,100				

These assumptions are applied in the forecast. The forecast should now be downloaded from Appendix 7. It has the suggested solution necessary for completing Exercise 17.

(EXERCISE 15) NET INCOME FORECAST

	Adjusted 1995	1996	1997	1998	1999	2000
Sales	$40,945,386	$61,418,079	$81,686,045	$102,107,556	$112,318,312	$117,934,228
Cost of Goods Sold	33,588,165	50,362,825	66,982,557	83,728,196	92,101,016	96,706,067
Gross Profit	$ 7,357,221	$11,055,254	$14,703,488	$ 18,379,360	$20,217,296	$ 21,228,161
Operating Expenses	4,869,736	6,755,989	8,985,465	11,231,831	12,355,014	12,972,765
Earnings Before Depreciation, Interest and Taxes	$ 2,487,485	$ 4,299,265	$ 5,718,023	$ 7,147,529	$7,862,282	$ 8,255,396
Depreciation and Amortization	77,199	88,512	159,940	231,369	302,797	374,226
Earnings Before Interest and Taxes	$2,410,286	$4,210,753	$5,558,083	$6,916,160	$7,559,485	$7,881,170
Interest Expense	199,028	245,672	326,744	408,430	449,273	471,737
Interest Income	35,672	64,818	82,914	99,037	111,243	120,620
Earnings Before Taxes	$2,246,930	$4,029,899	$5,314,253	$6,606,767	$7,221,455	$7,530,053
Taxes	845,520	1,611,960	2,125,701	2,642,707	2,888,582	3,012,021
NET INCOME	$1,401,410	$2,417,939	$3,188,552	$3,964,060	$4,332,873	$4,518,032

(EXERCISE 15) *(CONTINUED)*

Sales growth forecasts were made considering the state of the economy and Quimby's Computer Solutions, Inc.'s industry, the historical growth of The Company, and opportunities to add products to The Company's product line. The economic outlook of The Company is strong, fueled by high expectation of a continuing economic expansion. One of the drivers of the expansion, as indicated by Alan Greenspan, is advances in information technology (IT). Both IT companies and IT infrastructure companies have been enjoying strong growth, with the IT equipment and services industry projected to grow at a compound annual growth rate of 9% through 2000. IBM, The Company's main supplier, boasted 11 percent growth in hardware sales in the third quarter of 1995 over 1994, and continues to develop relationships with distribution channel partners. As indicated by IBM chairman Louis Gerstner, "Our job is to help them succeed to make money."

As indicated in the "Financial Analysis" section, Quimby's has had a compound annual growth rate of about 92% over the previous four years. The growth rate has been decreasing over this period, down from 103% in 1993 to 67% in 1995. The opportunity of adding storage products is promising, and is a vehicle for continued growth of The Company. For these reasons, we have selected the following growth rates:

Actual			Forecasted				
1993	1994	1995	1996	1997	1998	1999	2000
103%	89%	67%	50%	33%	25%	10%	5%

Cost of sales has been approximately 82% of sales since Quimby's signed its agreement with IBM. One of the underlying assumptions of this forecast is that relations with IBM will continue. Therefore, we have selected 82% of sales as indicative of cost of sales.

Operating expenses have ranged from 18.72% to 12.04% of sales over the past five years, with an average of approximately 13%. Operating costs have been decreasing with increasing sales, and we believe this trend will continue. We have forecasted operating expenses at 11% of sales.

The fixed assets of The Company are largely comprised of office furniture and equipment, with depreciable lives of 5 to 10 years. Considering the forecasted sales growth of The Company, it will have to make additional capital expenditures in order to upgrade its office space. We have forecasted $500,000 in capital expenditures over the next five years based on historical acquisitions, and we have depreciated the fixed assets of The Company using the straight-line method with a useful life of seven years. The fixed assets listed on the books as of the valuation date have been purchased over the previous two years. As such, the remaining $316,784 of net fixed assets have been depreciated over six years. It looks like this:

(EXERCISE 15) CAPITAL EXPENDITURE AND DEPRECIATION EXPENSE FORECAST

Fiscal Year	Economic Life		Depreciation—Forecast Year				
	(Years)	Expenditure	1996	1997	1998	1999	2000
1996	7	$500,000	$35,714	$71,429	$71,429	$71,429	$71,429
1997	7	500,000		35,714	71,429	71,429	71,429
1998	7	500,000			35,714	71,429	71,429
1999	7	500,000				35,714	71,429
2000	7	500,000					35,714
Total Depreciation of Future Capital Expenditures			35,714	107,143	178,571	250,000	321,429
Historical Assets	6	316,784	52,797	52,797	52,797	52,797	52,797
Total Depreciation			88,512	159,940	231,369	302,797	374,226

Interest expense relates to the interest paid to IBM's financing affiliate based on advances used in funding inventory and working capital. Since these are short-term loans and directly attributable to sales, we forecast interest expense as a percentage of sales. In 1994 and 1995, interest expense was 0.33% and 0.49% of sales, respectively. Therefore, we have estimated future interest expense at 0.4% of sales.

Interest income is forecasted at 5% of the average forecasted cash balances, representing an estimated return at money market rates.

The forecast assumes that The Company is taxed as a C corporation. Therefore, income taxes for The Company have been calculated at a rate of 40%. This has been done knowing that The Company is an S corporation, but understanding that the most probable willing buyer would be a C corporation.

(EXERCISE 15) BALANCE SHEET FORECAST AS OF DECEMBER 31

	Adjusted 1995	1996	1997	1998	1999	2000
Current Assets						
Cash	$1,118,697	$1,491,516	$1,983,716	$2,479,644	$2,727,608	$2,863,989
Accounts Receivable	4,589,646	6,562,480	8,728,098	10,910,122	12,001,135	12,601,191
Inventory	3,693,293	4,139,410	5,505,416	6,881,770	7,569,947	7,948,444
Other Current Assets	15,484	24,567	32,674	40,843	44,927	47,174
Total Current Assets	$9,417,120	$12,217,973	$16,249,904	$20,312,379	$22,343,617	$23,460,798
Fixed Assets						
Gross Fixed Assets	$316,784	$316,784	$816,784	$1,316,784	$1,816,784	$2,316,784
Capital Expenditures	-	500,000	500,000	500,000	500,000	500,000
Accumulated Depreciation	-	(88,512)	(248,452)	(479,821)	(782,618)	(1,156,844)
Net Fixed Assets	$316,784	$728,272	$1,068,332	$1,336,963	$1,534,166	$1,659,940
Total Other Assets	$62,603	$62,603	$62,603	$62,603	$62,603	$62,603
Total Assets	$9,796,507	$13,008,848	$17,380,839	$21,711,945	$23,940,386	$25,183,341
Current Liabilities						
Accounts Payable	$1,361,785	$2,207,685	$2,752,708	$3,211,492	$3,280,310	$3,179,378
Income Taxes Payable	-	161,196	212,570	264,271	288,858	301,202
Other Current Liabilities	7,244,516	8,086,763	10,377,842	12,686,277	13,840,495	14,475,314
Total Liabilities	$8,606,301	$10,455,644	$13,343,120	$16,162,040	$17,409,663	$17,955,894
Total Equity	1,190,206	2,553,204	4,037,719	5,549,905	6,530,723	7,227,447
Total Liabilities and Equity	$9,796,507	$13,008,848	$17,380,839	$21,711,945	$23,940,386	$25,183,341

(EXERCISE 15)

The forecasted balance sheet was developed using the following assumptions.

Cash was calculated based on sales. Quimby's cash turnover has been decreasing over time, as The Company has acquired cash. In the absence of a recognizable trend in cash turnover, we have used historical industry cash turnover ratios as indicative of future cash requirements, which have been consistent at 42 times. Based on industry cash requirements, we have estimated levels at 2.4% of sales.

Accounts receivable was also calculated based on sales. Over the previous five years, days accounts receivable has ranged from 11.82 to 40.33. Over the previous two years (1994 and 1995), it has been 40.33 and 38.12, respectively. *Business Profiler* statistics indicate its industry peer group is not as adept at handling its accounts receivable, with days outstanding over 50 during the same period. We forecasted The Company's accounts receivable outstanding at 39 days.

Inventory is forecasted to increase with sales. Days inventory sales have been increasing for The Company over the previous five years, ranging from two to 30 days, which is still significantly lower than the 76 days averaged by its industry peer group. We forecasted inventory at 30 days of sales, which is the high end of Quimby's historical inventory requirements.

Other current assets are comprised of prepaid assets. This amount was $24,397 in 1994 and $15,484 in 1995, and was as high as $91,934 in 1993. This item is expected to grow with sales. We have forecasted other current assets at 0.04% of sales, which reflects the 1995 percentage of sales.

We forecasted capital expenditures at $500,000 per year. The Company is forecasted to grow substantially and will need to invest in fixed assets to keep up with its growth.

Other assets totaled $62,603 in 1995, which is immaterial in this forecast. This line item has been projected as a constant, so that it will not affect the forecasted cash flows.

Accounts payable has varied from a low of 15 days of sales in 1991 to a high of 44 days of sales in 1992, with an average of 28 days. In 1995, The Company's results indicate 17 days. The Company's payables have been decreasing over the previous four years. We forecasted accounts payable to continue decreasing with sales, and to level off at 12 days in 2000.

Income taxes payable was forecast assuming that The Company would have 10% of their annual income tax expense as a payable at the end of each period.

Other current liabilities is comprised of accrued expenses and Quimby's revolving credit line financed by IBM. Accrued expenses accounted for 1.79% of sales and 1.72% of sales, in 1994 and 1995, respectively. Therefore, we have forecasted these items at an average of 1.75% of sales.

In order to estimate The Company's credit line, we performed a regression analysis and found that it correlated with the sum of inventory and accounts receivable. We used the linear relationship to forecast credit line levels based on the forecasted levels of accounts receivable and inventory. The linear relationship is as follows:

(EXERCISE 15)

Credit line = 0.5483 (inventory and accounts receivable) + 1,144,100

Analysis of IBM Working Capital Financing

Actual	1994	1995	1996	1997	1998	1999
Sales	22,285,781	40,945,386	61,446,471	94,963,680	107,113,495	109,546,500
A/R	3,963,550	4,589,646	9,828,785	17,030,113	16,957,697	23,910,373
Inventory	1,814,009	3,693,293	15,512,739	6,172,760	3,364,249	6,063,122
A/R + Inventory	5,777,559	8,282,939	25,341,524	23,202,873	20,321,946	29,973,495
Credit Line	3,603,175	6,540,143	18,220,075	13,611,522	10,795,435	15,997,924
% Sales	16%	16%	30%	14%	10%	15%
% A/R + Inventory	62%	79%	72%	59%	53%	53%

A/R = accounts receivable

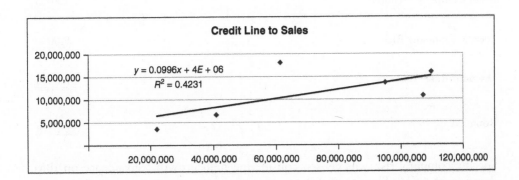

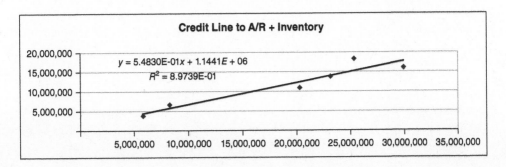

As a sanity check, we compared this relationship with The Company's actual operating results from 1996 to 1999. The relationship holds true for subsequent years.

Retained earnings were adjusted to account for other changes in the balance sheet.

(EXERCISE 16) DEVELOPMENT OF DISCOUNT RATE

Development of Discount Rate

Risk-Free Rate (composite long-term rate from Federal Reserve Bulletin)	6.06%
Equity Risk Premium	7.40%
Small Company Premium	3.60%
Specific Company Risk	9.00%
Discount Rate	26.06%
Rounded	26.00%

Specific company risk was chosen considering high growth, dependence on IBM, dependence on Mr. Skinner, and changes in the industry.

EXERCISE 17 INCOME APPROACH

Discounted Cash Flow Calculation

	1996	1997	1998	1999	2000	Terminal Value
Net Income	$2,417,939	$3,188,552	$3,964,059	$4,332,873	$4,518,032	$4,518,032
Plus: Depreciation/Amortization	88,512	159,940	231,369	302,797	374,226	374,226
Less: Capital Expenditures	(500,000)	(500,000)	(500,000)	(500,000)	(500,000)	(500,000)
Less: Increase in Working Capital	(951,510)	(1,161,937)	(1,266,806)	(812,678)	(602,919)	(602,919)
Plus/Less: Debt						
Net Cash Flow	$1,054,941	$1,686,555	$2,428,622	$3,322,992	$3,789,339	$3,978,806
Discount Periods	0.5	1.5	2.5	3.5	4.5	4.5
Present Value Factor	0.9091	0.7513	0.6209	0.5132	0.4241	0.4241
Terminal Value						$24,867,537
Present Values	959,047	1,267,109	1,507,932	1,705,359	1,607,059	10,546,322
Sum of Present Values	$17,592,828					
Control Premium (30%)	5,277,848		Note: A control premium was added here for the same reason as in the market approach.			
Control—Marketable Value	22,870,676					
DLOM (10%)	(2,287,068)					
Control—Nonmarketable Value	$20,583,608					
Rounded	$20,600,000					

(EXERCISE 18) SINGLE-PERIOD NET INCOME METHOD

The forecasted growth is too great to use a single-period model in this valuation. Therefore, a multiperiod model is appropriate.

(EXERCISE 19) RECONCILIATION

Method	Indication	Weight	Rationale
Guideline Company			
MVE to EBTDA	$15,200,000	30%	
MVE to EBT	$15,300,000	30%	
MVE to Net Income	$15,300,000	30%	
Income Approach			
DCF	$20,600,000	10%	

The rationale for the weights is that while the market approach had only a few guideline companies, each multiple seemed to give a reasonable indication of value. The income approach was weighted the lowest because the valuation analyst had less confidence in this methodology.

Fair Market Value	$15,800,000
+ Nonoperating Assets	325,933
Total	$16,125,933
Ownership Interest	90%
Value	$14,513,340
Rounded	$14,500,000